Victorian Negatives

SUNY series, Studies in the Long Nineteenth Century

Pamela K. Gilbert, editor

Victorian Negatives

Literary Culture and the Dark Side of Photography in the Nineteenth Century

Susan E. Cook

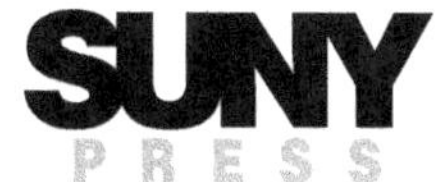

Published by State University of New York Press, Albany

Printed in the United States of America

For information, contact State University of New York Press, Albany, NY
www.sunypress.edu

Library of Congress Cataloging-in-Publication Data

Names: Cook, Susan E., 1980– author.
Title: Victorian negatives : literary culture and the dark side of photography in the nineteenth century / Susan E. Cook.
Description: Albany : State University of New York Press, [2019] | Series: SUNY series, studies in the long nineteenth century | Includes bibliographical references and index.
Identifiers: LCCN 2018040333 | ISBN 9781438475370 (hardcover : alk. paper) | ISBN 9781438475387 (ebook) | ISBN 9781438475363 (pbk : alk. paper)
Subjects: LCSH: English literature—19th century—History and criticism. | Literature and photography—Great Britain—History—19th century. | Literature and technology—Great Britain—History—19th century. | Literature and society—Great Britain—History—19th century. | Photography—Great Britain—History—19th century. | Realism in literature.
Classification: LCC PR468.P46 C67 2019 | DDC 820.9/356—dc23
LC record available at https://lccn.loc.gov/2018040333

10 9 8 7 6 5 4 3 2 1

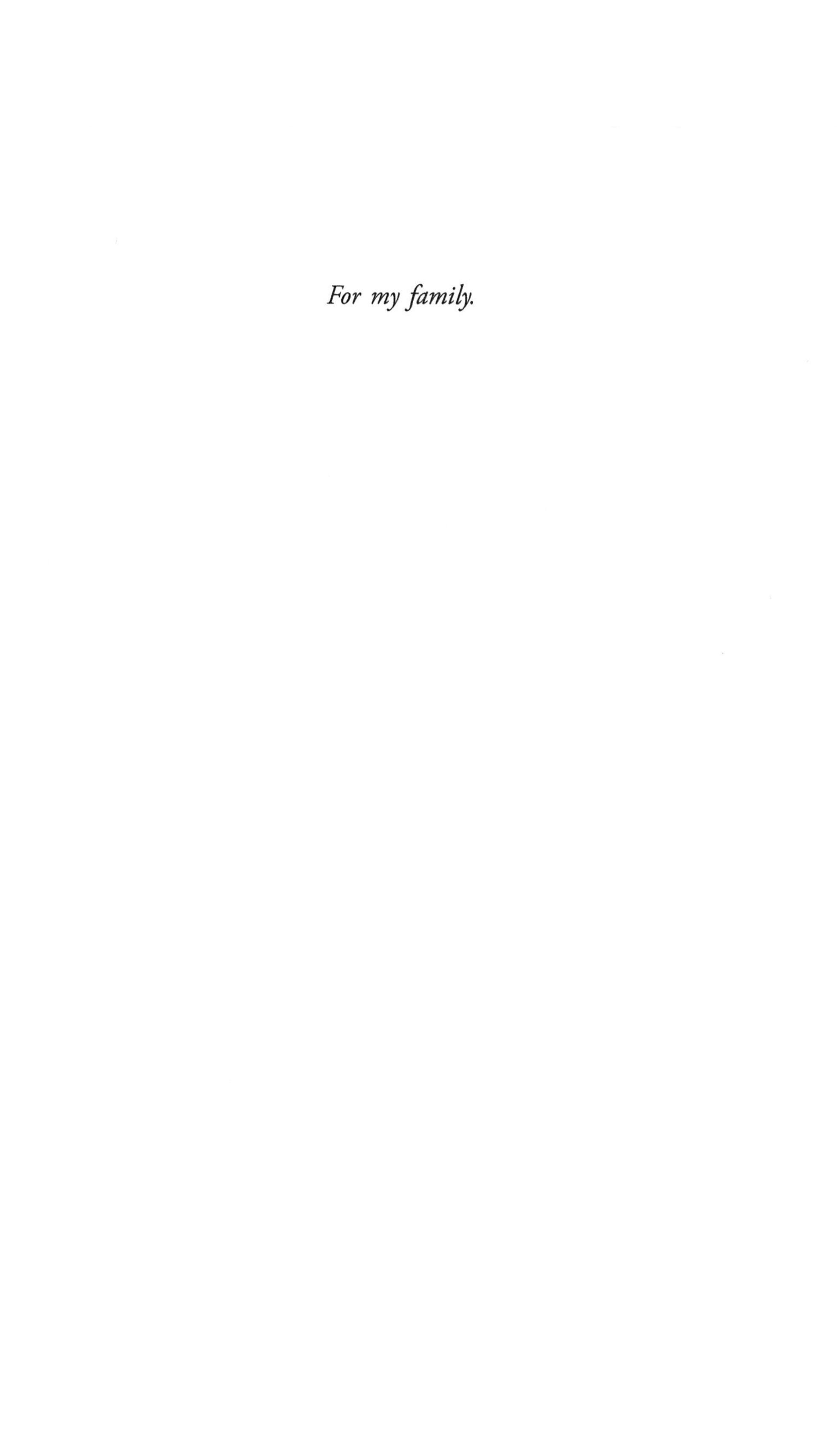

For my family.

"The true mystery of the world is the visible, not the invisible."

—Henry Wotton in Oscar Wilde,
The Picture of Dorian Gray (62)

The negative is the all-important element; for by it we seek to record some effect of nature, and according to our success in the light-action we get on our plate, so is our print from it valuable or the reverse. Photography is one of the finest of methods for rendering atmosphere and light and shade in all the subtleties of nature's gradations, and for this we need an approximately perfect negative and that perfectly printed from.

—Frederick H. Evans, "On Pure Photography" (181)

Contents

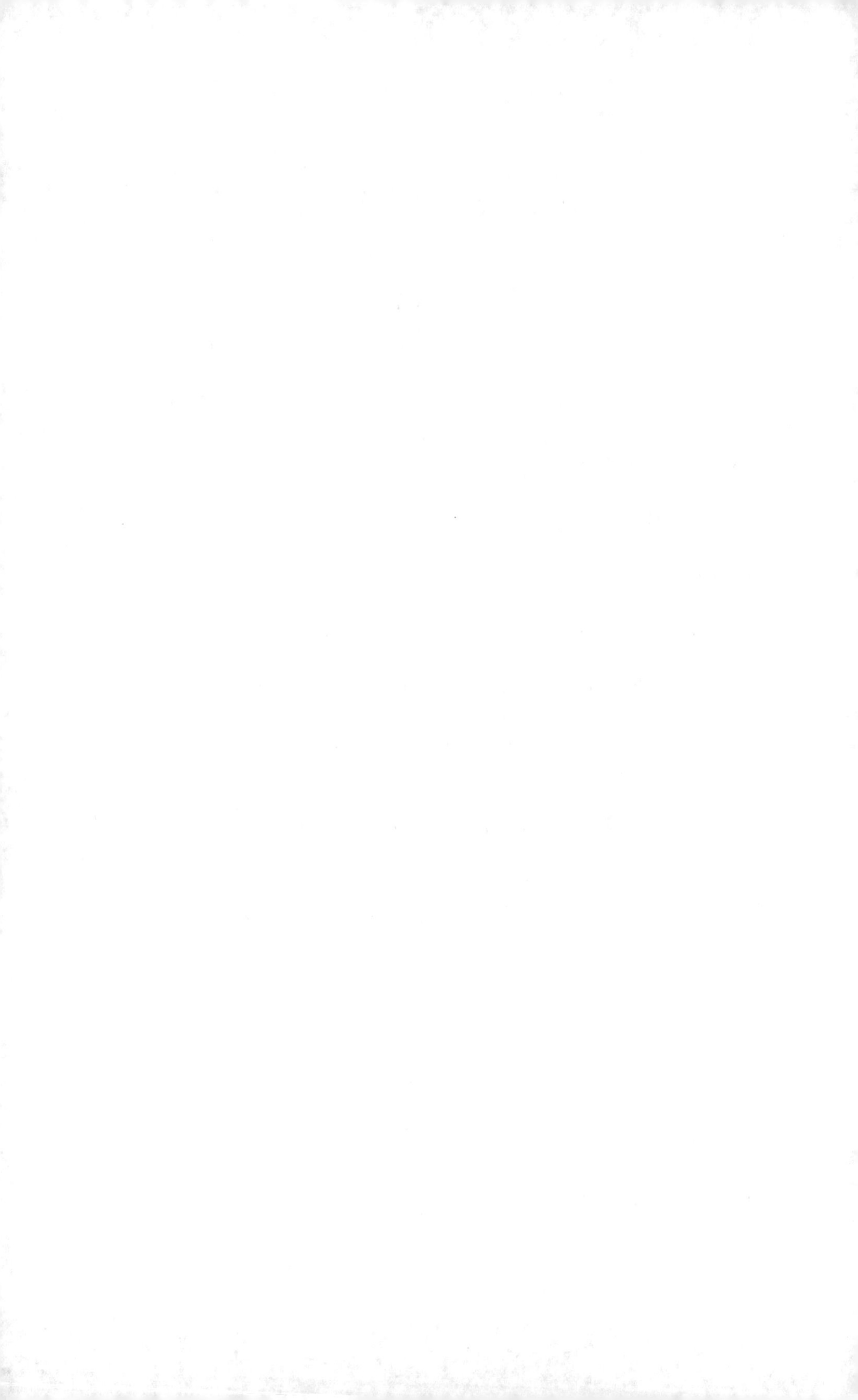

List of Illustrations

Acknowledgments

This project developed over time, and I am grateful to have had the support of so many colleagues, friends, and family members throughout the process.

Diana Polley, Victoria Ford Smith, and Ryan Fong all deserve special thanks. Each read the entire manuscript multiple times over the span of several years and gave me invaluable feedback along the way. I am absolutely indebted to their careful readings and advice. Laura Miller and Beth Womack read portions of the project at critical junctures and offered much-appreciated guidance.

My college photography professors Roy W. Traver, Charles Meyer, and Karl Baden helped inspire this project and taught me how to navigate a darkroom. Years later, Pat Stanbro showed me how to use software to create a negative effect digitally. When I was a graduate student, my faculty mentors, Maurizia Boscagli, Janis Caldwell, Julie Carlson, and Erika Rappaport, all taught me the meaning of research. My graduate school community, including Ben Shockey, Rachel Mann, Yanoula Athanasakis, Summer Star, Mike Frangos, Curtis Asplund, and Susie Keller, helped me think through early versions of some of this material. John Jordan and the Dickens Universe helped me tremendously as a young scholar learning the ropes of academia. Communities created through the Dickens Universe, such as the Dickens Project Winter Conference and the 19th-Century Sciences Group—and Dickens Camp people including but by no means limited to Sarah Allison, Karen Bourrier, Rae Greiner, Deanna Kreisel, Rebecca Stern, and Maria Bachman—were in various ways pivotal to my development as a writer and an academic. Colleagues such as Lucy Morrison, Maura Coughlin, Meg Cronin, Natalie McKnight, and Elif Armbruster—and organizations like the Nineteenth Century Studies Association, the Dickens Society, the North American Victorian Studies Association, and the Victorians Institute—have been instrumental to me in the years I have worked on this project. I appreciate Lucinda Matthews-Jones and the *Journal of Victorian Culture Online* for giving me a forum to test some of this material in its early stages. Special thanks to Margaret Mitchell for inviting me to guest edit the special issue of *LIT: Literature, Interpretation, Theory* on literature and photography. That project helped me realize that this book was a possibility.

Southern New Hampshire University (SNHU) generously supported this project with four summer research grants and a yearlong sabbatical. My colleagues at SNHU, past and present, have enriched my life as a scholar. I am lucky I am able to bring my passion into the classroom: students from three seminars over the span of eight years challenged me to think differently about some of the material in this book. I am thankful to have had the opportunity to travel to and work with a number of outstanding collections and curators. Mark Osterman, Joe Struble, and Ross Knapper at the George Eastman Gannett Foundation Photographic Study Center were particularly generous with their time during my visits. I am also fortunate to have been able to work with archives and collections at the J. Paul Getty Research Institute, the Victoria and Albert Museum, the Bayerisches Nationalmuseum, the British Library, and the Charles Dickens Museum. I am grateful to the Charles Dickens Museum, the British Library, Image Works, and Universal Pictures for their permission to reproduce images in this book. At SNHU, Chris Cooper and Jeremy Moore helped me scan additional images from my own collection, and my dean's office and Jackie Hickox helped make my research travel possible.

Material from chapter 1 was published as "Season of Light and Darkness: *A Tale of Two Cities* and the Daguerrean Imagination" in *Dickens Studies Annual* 42 (Summer 2011), and an earlier version of chapter 2 was published as "Sun and Shadow: Solarization and *Little Dorrit*" in *Nineteenth Century Studies* 27 (2013). Thanks to the editors of *Dickens Studies Annual* and *Nineteenth Century Studies* for allowing me to reprint this material here. I am extremely grateful to Pamela K. Gilbert, Amanda Lanne-Camilli, and the Editorial Board of SUNY Press for their support of this project and to the wonderful production team at SUNY Press for making this such a good experience. I cannot thank my anonymous peer reviewers enough for their thoughtful readings of my work.

I am lucky to have also had the support of friends and family outside academia. Amanda Moceri, Sarah Fisher, Sara Scott, Ivy Irvine, Hayde Castillo, Erika Chen, Julie Ciollo, Sarah Cote, Melissa Harris, Lara Hubner, Michelle Feeney, and my running and roller derby communities have helped keep me centered. My family taught me the meaning of intellectual curiosity, and they are at the core of this project. My godmother, Thea Hoeth, challenged me from an early age to be precise with my syntax. My father, Jim Cook, gave me my first camera, a Pentax. My mother, Vicky Cook, kept a dictionary in our kitchen when I was growing up and made me look up words I didn't know as we sat at the dinner table—and she read the full manuscript of this book and offered helpful advice. My brilliant husband, Randy Brown, also read the full manuscript. He should be granted an honorary degree and more for his unwavering support over the years. Randy's incisive and careful editing is the reason this project does not contain more paradoxes.

Introduction

> When you are in Paris you will no doubt have an opportunity of seeing Daguerre's pictures. I shall be glad to hear from you, what you think of them. Whatever their merit, which no doubt is very great, I think that in one respect our English method must have the advantage. To obtain a second copy of the same view, Daguerre must return to the same locality & set up his instrument a second time; for he cannot copy from his metallic plate, being opaque. But in our method, having first obtained one picture by means of the Camera, the rest are obtainable from this one, by the method of re-transferring which, by a fortunate & beautiful circumstance rectifies both of the errors in the first picture *at once.* viz. the inversion of right for left; & that of light for shade.
>
> —William Henry Fox Talbot to John Frederick William Herschel, April 27, 1839 (Herschel, emphasis in original)

> I have so much to do and such a disinclination to multiply my "counterfeit presentments."
>
> —Charles Dickens to John J. E. Mayall, 1856 (*Letters* 8:199)

In 1856, Charles Dickens declined John J. E. Mayall's request to sit for a daguerreotype, explaining he had "a disinclination to multiply" his "counterfeit presentments" (*Letters* 8:199). The author, a celebrity at that point in his career, had been the subject of numerous daguerreotypes before—many by Mayall—and would sit for daguerreotypists and other photographers again. In this letter, however, he articulates what became a hallmark not only of his celebrity but also the broader challenge to photography this book interrogates. Dickens's complaint is threefold: he is busy, he does not want his image to be multiplied, and he feels such images are counterfeit.

Although he writes here about daguerreotypy—a nonreproducible form of photography—and not a reproducible form such as calotypy or the collodion process, the salient features of his critique are also distinctive qualities of negatives. Specifically, the multiplication of the image and distortion of reality that troubles Dickens about posing for a daguerreotype are even more pronounced in photographs with negatives. Indeed, these multiplication and distortion issues are absolutely central features of the negative process.

In *Victorian Negatives*, I argue that both technical and figurative appreciations of the photographic negative are fundamental to understanding how nineteenth-century photography came to be culturally embedded and expressed through literary works of the period. Furthermore, the negative gives us a new and useful means of historicizing Victorian debates surrounding origins and copies, particularly as these debates played out in the literary arena. The negative is a technology that facilitates image inversion and reproduction. These qualities are essential to the photographic imagination as it developed throughout the nineteenth century, and they played a role in how that imagination in turn shaped literary genres such as the historical novel, detective fiction, Gothic narratives, and—perhaps most significant—the realist novel. In the chapters that follow, I examine several experimental photographic forms and techniques that rely on or are in conversation with negative technology, and I trace how these negative-based techniques were understood and articulated in literary culture—a culture likewise invested in the art of representation. Notions of photographic reproducibility and verisimilitude may appear in sync with the aims of Victorian literary realism, but writers such as Charles Dickens, Arthur Conan Doyle, E. W. Hornung, Cyril Bennett, Robert Louis Stevenson, Oscar Wilde, Thomas Hardy, and Bram Stoker complicate these qualities in their lives and works, at times expressing concern about and at other times interest in how negative technologies erode older ideals of representational truth as well as ideas of singularity and artistic control. They do this by featuring failed or troubled photographic reproduction within their works and challenging visual objectivity obliquely and metaphorically across their oeuvres. Several also resist photographic reproduction directly in their lives as celebrity authors. Rather than focusing on literary texts or literary lives in isolation, I see the two as entwined: literary texts and the role of literary celebrity within and beyond those texts reveal a negotiation with the negative, and a reading of one without the other misses the extent to which the negative troubles the barrier between art and life.

The negative is an essential part of photography's nineteenth-century history. In May 1844, Scottish photographer and politician George Smith Cundell published "On the Practice of the Calotype Process of Photography" in the *London, Edinburgh and Dublin Philosophical Magazine and Journal of Science*. Cundell champions calotypy, a paper-negative photographic process that had, up to that point, somewhat languished in the shadows of daguerreotypy. As Cundell notes, "If the comparative merits of the Daguerreotype and of the Calotype were to be judged by the interest which each has excited, or by the progress which has been made in the practice of either, the English invention [the calotype] would justly be classed in a very subordinate rank" (321). This, he goes on to claim, is because "while the Daguerreotype was at once understood, and successfully practised, over the whole civilized world, most of the few persons who have attempted the sister art, after failing of success, have given it up in disappointment" (321). The calotype process disappointed so many, according to Cundell, because its inventor, William Henry Fox Talbot, had maintained a patent and tight control over the details of the process since 1841.[1] In publishing his paper, Cundell hoped to bring these details of calotypy to light: "there is reason to believe," he writes, "that it only requires to be better known to be appreciated as an art not less beautiful than that of Daguerre, and that it is well deserving of a much greater share than it has yet received of the public attention" (321). Its virtues, he claims, are numerous, and among them is that the process "requires but little apparatus; its materials are comparatively inexpensive; and it is possessed besides of the striking advantage, of yielding a great number of perfect copies from every original picture" (321).

The calotype process differs from the daguerreotype process in several key ways, but as Cundell notes, its primary difference is in its use of a negative, from which it is possible to make many "perfect" copies of the image.[2] Whereas daguerreotypes are unique photographic objects for which there is no negative, calotypes are produced or "retransferred" using a paper negative or "reverse," as photographers such as Talbot, John Frederick William Herschel, and others called it.[3] This process has a distinct advantage, writes Talbot in his letter to Herschel on April 27, 1839. Indeed, in 1851 Frederick Scott Archer developed the negative further with the glass-negative wet collodion process. This process produced a sharper final image that was easier and faster to reproduce than the calotype process and also ultimately contributed to the decline of the daguerreotype. Collodion-based processes went on to dominate the photographic scene from the 1850s through the 1880s, the notion of "a great number of perfect copies" becoming ever more part of the definition of the photograph. According to Beaumont Newhall's *History of Photography*, "The daguerreotype was doomed" from this point on, its "disadvantage" the fact that "each picture was unique" and the process relatively expensive (28, 19).

Cundell's preference for the negative process over daguerreotypy is typical of many photographers in the era. Amateur photographer George Shadbolt notes in an 1864 *British Journal of Photography* essay that whereas he suffered "disappointment on finding the expensive nature of the materials requisite for pursing" the daguerreotype, he felt "gratification at being able to repeat the experiments" of the calotype (199). Writing in 1859, photographic entrepreneur Francis Frith likewise admits that while the daguerreotype is "very beautiful," "the fact of its being a *non-reproductive* process excluded the idea of its application to the various commercial and valuable purposes for which the great principle of photographic representation was seen to be so strikingly available . . . they are no more available for the popular uses of Art than are the costly illuminated manuscripts in the British Museum" (119, emphasis in original).[4] This preference for the reproducible was encoded into popular instruction books, such as the 1857 manual *The A B C of Photography*, which notes that the value of a negative is "in its power of producing an unlimited number of positives on paper" (ii).[5] As this range of texts indicates, the negative's value as a means of offering multiple reproductions became a common motif throughout the century, noted in philosophical essays, utilitarian instruction manuals for beginners, and specialist articles in the periodical press.

Yet photographic reproduction was not unvaryingly praised. Photography "must make a revolution in art," acknowledged Nathaniel Parker Willis and Timothy O. Porter in their 1839 essay, "The Pencil of Nature: A New Discovery" (46). However, they express concern over this revolution when it comes to the imitative quality of photographic reproduction:

> People prefer a poor representation of an object made by a human hand to the beauty of the thing itself. They will throw away a leaf, a flower, of exquisite beauty, and treasure up the veriest daub, that shall have the slightest resemblance to it. . . . We are afraid something of this indifference will arise from the new invention [of photography]. . . . If this view be correct, it may be presumed that the number of artists will be greatly lessened. (46–47)

In other words, the "slightest resemblance" offered by photography risks making people indifferent to natural beauty, and art in turn will suffer. It is notably photography's imitative quality that poses the threat here—a quality that is exacerbated by reproducing the image, even if that image is but a "poor representation." Photographic reproduction through the negative, notes Sir William J. Newton in 1853, is imprecise: "I lose something by this means in sharpness, and perhaps in softness" (qtd. in Zillman 147). Indeed, writes William John Hubbard in 1872, "every portrait photographer" will attest that "in almost every negative he takes . . . there is some part in it that does not come out truthfully" (144–45). The photographer must therefore retouch the negative to produce the desired print. Thus, although some lauded the negative's promise, others observed that the negative introduced complications by making reproduction too easy, producing an inferior image, or suggesting that the photograph itself is not "truthful" unless it is manipulated.

These complications are richly developed in the literary arena. Two years after Dickens demurred having his daguerreotype taken, writer John Hollingshead exploited the same Shakespearean reference to "counterfeit presentments" in the context of photography in the July 3, 1858 issue of Dickens's own journal, *Household Words*. Hollingshead's story, "A Counterfeit Presentment," features Sweetwort, a famous author reluctant to have his photograph taken because his "face and head are of that peculiar character, that, under no possible combination of lights and attitude could they be agreeable in a photographic portrait, or give any correct idea of the original" (71). Sweetwort is hounded by photographers until the day a particularly determined one shows him an image of another famous individual, prize-fighter Bill Tippets. The photographer then blackmails Sweetwort: "knowing your objection to sit for a photograph," he says,

> I have been compelled to look amongst my stock for something like you, and I can find nothing so near the mark as Bill Tippets. . . . This order for two thousand copies of your likeness for home consumption, and fifteen hundred for exportation . . . must be executed within ten days, and I can only give you till ten o'clock to-morrow morning to decide. At that hour I must know whether it is to be Bill Tippets, or Mr. Edgar Sweetwort. (72)

Sweetwort "helplessly" ends up having his photograph taken rather than suffering the substitution of Tippets's image for his own.[6] In the age of the negative, Sweetwort is not in control over his own photographic likeness.

This story illustrates the undesirable possibilities of the photographic image—possibilities of reproducibility that are negative because of their reliance on the negative. The story banks on the eeriness of interchangeable photographic subjects and amplifies this eeriness through the risk of photographic reproduction, the promised "two thousand copies of your likeness for home consumption, and fifteen hundred for exportation" wielded as a threat. Sweetwort cannot bear the idea that another individual should represent himself in such abundance. Of course, the irony is that his initial objection to being photographed is his concern that photographs do not correctly capture the way he actually looks. In short, there is no possibility of an accurate photographic image—and we must imagine that either Sweetwort fails to understand the irony of giving in to the photographer's demands, or that his acquiescence is the only way he can claim some small measure of agency in the process of his celebrity. This "agency" is a farce: in the story's final paragraph, Sweetwort finds himself forced to sit "helplessly, under a broiling sun, in a glass cage upon the tiles of an elevated house near the Haymarket," much like an animal and asked to compose his "countenance according to the imperious instructions of the relentless photographer" (Hollingshead 72). In Dickens's personal experiences with photographers and in this story written for his magazine, negative-based photography provides a great number of perfect—or, perhaps more troublingly, imperfect—copies. This process of photographic duplication threatens the subjectivity of the individual. The person no longer has control over his own image, his own celebrity, and by proxy his own identity.

"A Counterfeit Presentment" participated in a growing trend of literary treatments of photography. From the mid-nineteenth century on, British literary culture—the world inside and surrounding the production of texts—increasingly featured, referenced, and encoded photography. As Jane M. Rabb notes in her anthology of literature and photography,

> Literature greeted photography warmly when the daguerreotype and the calotype were announced in 1839. Less threatened than painters by the new child of science, writers like Edgar Allan Poe and Walt Whitman in America and John Ruskin in England and others throughout the world heralded the daguerreotype process. . . . Photography became a metaphor for the veracity and even creativity of many nineteenth-century writers, and the supposedly objective camera became a model for ways of seeing and representing the world. ("Introduction: Notes" xxxv–xxxviii)

Beginning in the 1990s, many scholars have focused their attention on intersections between Victorian literature and visual culture.[7] Building on this tradition, my work shifts focus and argues that the development of the photographic negative—the calotype initially and then the collodion wet plate and fast gelatin halide dry plate negatives—played an instrumental role in the representation of Victorian photography in literary culture.

Scholars most frequently discuss photography as a monolithic whole,[8] but I argue that as a specific technology used to produce specific types of photographs, the negative concurrently enabled distinct literary and cultural responses. Methodologically, my approach shares much with that of Owen Clayton's in *Literature and Photography in Transition, 1850–1915*. Clayton suggests it is "problematic . . . for scholars to offer a single cultural reading of photography across the nineteenth century, because of the wide range of photographic technologies, and the variety of attitudes towards these technologies, which appeared during that time" (6). Specifically, he investigates "how authorial engagements with photography were affected when technologies altered" (6). His approach highlights the fact that rather than a singular product, photography is a set of distinct processes.[9] Similarly, I consider multiple photographic forms and techniques—some mainstream, others experimental and less prominent—that had a substantial cultural impact on the Victorians. As Clayton notes, photography was not monolithic, but I also argue that the negative may be simultaneously and productively understood as a broader and more figurative category. The history of photography is also the history of the negative, and it is a history that is multifaceted and complex.

The negative, furthermore, provides us with a lens through which we might re-view the relationship between photography and Victorian culture. In this regard, my project is in sympathy with Nicoletta Leonardi and Simone Natale's edited collection, *Photography and Other Media in the Nineteenth Century*, which "moves away from the notion of an autonomous history of photography" by considering photography in relation to other media (2). By centering my project on the role of the negative in the terrain of a diverse photographic landscape, I propose to revise how we understand the history of photography and how we understand its role in nineteenth-century literature and literary culture. In addition to considering the negative materially, as multiple forms emerging out of distinct technologies and accompanied by discourses that evolve over time, I read its impact figuratively through metaphors of visual inversion and reproduction that persist in nineteenth-century fiction. Through this dual material and figurative focus, I develop a multidimensional theory of the negative based on the meanings it produces and how these meanings are articulated both directly and indirectly through literary culture. In other words, this project proposes to destabilize previous readings of the relationship between photography and literature by insisting on the centrality of what is often thought of as marginal: specific experimental photographic techniques and the ever-present specter of the negative. In addition to literary texts, this project examines the letters and more public writings of photographers, photo historians, and the nineteenth-century popular press, as well as debates surrounding Victorian celebrity authorship. I examine discussions of daguerreotypy, calotypy, the collodion process, and the dry plate process; experimental developments such as print solarizations; the rise of the cabinet card; forensic photography; spirit photography and other double exposures; and the popularization of postmortem photography. This list is not exhaustive but rather, to borrow from Elizabeth Edwards's methodology in *The Camera as Historian: Amateur Photographers and the Historical Imagination, 1885–1918*, representative of particular photographic types. Edwards notes that instead of specific images she is interested in " 'the photography complex'—the process through which the photographs could emerge" (27). I am also interested in the photographic process—more specifically, negative photographic processes. My focus on the negative illuminates an often-marginalized part of the history of photography and demonstrates how this marginalized history is in fact central to Victorian literary culture.

Photography is frequently lauded for its verisimilitude. As Talbot writes, describing one of his early experiments in 1839, "I found out a way of fixing a picture on silver plate, which gives *normal* lights, i.e. lights for lights & shades for shades. . . . The image of a piece of lace done so, is so perfect that when examined by a lens, it still remains doubtful to the eye weather [*sic*] it is not the real object" (Herschel, November 15, 1839). This view of photography was shared by photographers and the general public alike. Edgar Allan Poe, for example, lauded photography early on as "perhaps the most extraordinary triumph of modern science," a technology with the ability to produce a "perfect identity of aspect with the thing represented" (4–5). Not only was photography seen by many as a means of perfectly capturing reality, it was considered superior to the human eye in this regard. As Corey Keller notes, "Photography's potential contributions were seen as twofold: as a mechanical replacement for the draftsman's arduous task of manually transcribing visual observations, and as a corrective for the human tendency toward subjective interpretation" (21). Indeed, Keller continues,

"Within a scientific culture that placed great weight on empirical observation, this idea of the camera-eye served not only as a physical model, but also as a metaphor that underscored the relationship between visibility and knowability" (30).[10] In its early decades, photography was repeatedly classified according to its use value in this way. Despite a protracted debate as to photography's proper designation as art or science, it was categorized along with "Philosophical Instruments and Processes" at the 1851 Crystal Palace exhibition and cataloged under "The Science of the Exhibition" in the *Art Journal*'s Great Exhibition catalog.[11]

Reminding us that "photography was not one but several inventions," Lorraine Daston and Peter Galison note that many of photography's earliest uses were in the service of art, for "scientific photography was only one species of nineteenth-century photography, and objective photography was in turn only one variety of scientific photography" (125–26).[12] Photography was notoriously difficult to categorize in relation to art and science. Robert Hunt defends the *Art Journal*'s inclusion of photography in various articles in 1851 with the note that "we have, from time to time, kept our readers acquainted with the progress of photography, both at home and abroad. We have done so because we felt certain that it must, sooner or later, become highly useful to the artist in the study of the natural" ("On the Application of Science" 106). In other words, the value of photography is what it might contribute to art—not necessarily its status *as* art.[13] In the 1860s, some were willing to argue that "photography belonged among the fine arts," while others maintained that it should "properly be understood as an objective scientific practice untouched by human hands" (S. Edwards 11).[14] The protracted art/science debate gives us another way of considering the extent to which the issue of representation in photography was vexed throughout the period.[15] Photography's proximity to scientific objectivity indicates a type of mimesis that becomes a source of anxiety when we consider that images of ourselves might be endlessly reproduced. This is the anxiety of the doppelgänger or uncanny double; it is the anxiety Dickens articulates when he writes about his disinclination to see his likeness multiplied. Conversely, photography's proximity to art suggests a distance from mimesis—a sense that despite appearing to be mimetic, such mimesis is "counterfeit." Victorian photography did not belong wholly to the art world or the world of scientific objectivity, and its position in between vexed a public that would have preferred to see it more clearly defined.

From its inception, then, photography did not enjoy uniform acceptance as a medium of scientific, objective truth—in fact, writes Jordan Bear, "the milieu into which this supposedly revolutionary medium was inserted was primed *not* to receive photography as unquestionably objective" (5).[16] Instead, photography participated in a "vast mosaic of visual discernment," whereby "The capacity for the visual discrimination of photographic representations emerges as both a criterion for political agency and a skill to be commodified, developments that depended precisely upon an ambivalence of photography's representational role" (5). This ambivalence is precisely what I identify and analyze here. The mixed cultural reception of the photographic negative, the uses to which that negative was put, and the ways these uses emerge in Victorian literary culture support Bear's thesis. We may then push the implications of that thesis further by considering how photographic debates were encoded into literary culture. Bear describes the "intense ambiguity of the photograph's verisimilitude," and developments in literary realism particularly echo this ambiguity of photographic verisimilitude (8). We may read these echoes as figurative evocations of not just photography but negative-based photography more specifically.

This project thus situates itself alongside interdisciplinary studies of photography and literary realism.[17] As numerous critics have argued, literary realism is more complex than its name suggests.[18] If we understand realism strictly as a product of mimesis, we understand it to be an attention to the "everyday real" (Brooks 7). Yet counterintuitively, writes Alexander Bove, mimesis "depends for its success on a suppression of the relation of the sign to its referent" (655). As James Eli Adams notes, from George Eliot on, realism has provided a "suggestion of psychic depth," and "our illusion of vicarious participation" (Adams 189). The reality of realism is in many ways a misnomer, a term that seems forever subject to qualifications and exclusions, and the problem of defining realism is not simply a modern interpretative concern. Daniel Brown claims that in the nineteenth century, "those who entered into debates about realism questioned the extent to which artistic representation might—or even should—achieve the same sort of objective proof expected of scientific or technical projects" (10). Yet the notion that all "technical projects" were objective is also a misnomer, writes Daniel A. Novak: "What photography and realism shared was not necessarily their fidelity to detail but rather their inability to present those details in any coherent form" (63). In other words, photography and literary realism share an uneasy relationship with the real.

Several studies of visual culture and literature have attended to poetry or romance,[19] but realism has received the most sustained critical attention. Brown observes that "a large volume of scholarship shows connections between nineteenth-century representational practices, particularly realism in literature and painting, and an increasingly visually oriented society" (5–6). Relatedly, writers such as Novak, Clayton, Jonathan Crary, Jennifer Green-Lewis, Nancy Armstrong, Ronald R. Thomas, Regina B. Oost, Helen Groth, and Michael North have pioneered a critical tradition of reading nineteenth-century realism alongside photography. As Crary has influentially argued, "some of the most pervasive means of producing 'realistic' effects in mass visual culture, such as the stereoscope, were in fact based on a radical abstraction and reconstruction of optical experience, thus demanding a reconsideration of what 'realism' means in the nineteenth century" (9). Crary's watershed study in turn led others to consider the relationship between photography and literary realism. For example, Armstrong argues that nineteenth-century literary realism shares common ground with photography, for both evolved in response to an increasing cultural interest in visual information.[20] This visual information, according to North, was often "iconic"—photography had a "disorienting hyperreality," a hyperreality that produced a "distancing and aestheticizing effect" (*Camera Works* 25).[21] Novak's sustained critique of photographic realism goes a step further and "redefines what 'photographic realism' meant for the Victorians and changes our definition of and expectations for literary realism" (6). Proposing that photography and realism share an aesthetics of fiction or abstraction,[22] Novak challenges the critical perception that Victorians trusted photographic objectivity.[23] In other words, photography demonstrates the Victorians didn't necessarily regard visual or literary realism as mimetically real. Photography allows us to see that realism is an illusive/elusive whole constructed of the very things it purports not to be: contingency, interpretation, the subjective, and the fragmentary.

My study participates in this critical tradition, and by focusing on the role of the negative in particular, it highlights tensions surrounding origins and copies as well as reality and representation. I begin by analyzing primarily Victorian realist fiction, because my claim is that many Victorian authors grappled with and rewrote the narrative of photography in relation to realism, and I trace that rewritten narrative through their works. At times this writing and rewriting is expressed as an articulation of a realism seemingly rooted in its inverse: fidelity less to "reality" than to what is "true," as Elaine Freedgood describes it (402).[24] At other points, it is expressed in literary works that go beyond the limits of realism. For this reason, I also analyze nonrealist works in this project. Robert Louis Stevenson's *Strange Case of Dr. Jekyll and Mr. Hyde*, Oscar Wilde's *The Picture of Dorian Gray*, and Bram Stoker's *Dracula* are all examples of texts that veer into the supernatural, their challenge to realism concurrent with their critique of the image.

While literary realism ostensibly promises us a copy of an original, the "great number of perfect copies" made possible by the negative process became the subject of critique in literary culture for their abundance and their purported perfection. Many lauded the negative's capacity to reproduce images over and over again, but this potential reproducibility is often treated with ambivalence and concern by the authors I consider here. As Robin Kelsey notes in *Photography and the Art of Chance*, "Uniformity was a watchword of the modern economy, which aimed to produce precise and interchangeable parts and commodities. Because many Victorians feared a loss of humanity in this pursuit of exact equivalence, accident and error took on connotations of human vitality and uniqueness" (10). This fear is registered by celebrity authors, such as Dickens, who was himself photographed, and it is encoded into works of fiction, such as the Sherlock Holmes stories "A Scandal in Bohemia" and "The Adventure of Charles Augustus Milverton." In these cases, the circulation of the image exceeds any one person's control, indicating an anxiety around photographic reproduction at large. The idea of reproduction—the negative processes' primary "advantage," to use Talbot's phrase—produces what I suggest to be a kind of existential anxiety. As Walter Benjamin puts it in "The Work of Art in the Age of Mechanical Reproduction," whereas art has always been reproducible "in principle," the technological reproduction of works of art heralds a new relationship between viewer and reproduction: technological reproduction "is more independent of the original than manual reproduction" and "can put the copy of the original into situations which would be out of reach for the original itself" (218, 220). Here Benjamin is describing the massification of art: "By making many reproductions it substitutes a plurality of copies for a unique existence. And in permitting the reproduction to meet the beholder or listener in his own particular situation, it reactivates the object reproduced" (221). This process erodes the notion of singular authenticity and the aura, which is good from a Benjaminian perspective if we are talking about mobilizing the masses through technological representation to fight fascism in the early twentieth century. However, the erosion of singular authenticity is potentially troubling from the perspective of an author like Dickens, whose own photographic reproduction exceeded his control, much like the unauthorized reproduction of his novels in the United States exceeded his control. If Dickens's image were "reactivated" or re-created by a viewer without his knowledge, what power might this image have?

The anxiety of an image reproduced to the point where the reproduction is severed from the original referent foreshadows the anxiety of simulation. As Jean Baudrillard writes,

> Representation stems from the principle of the equivalence of the sign and of the real (even if this equivalence is utopian, it is a fundamental axiom). Simulation, on the contrary, stems from the utopia of the principle of equivalence, *from the radical negation of the sign as value,* from the sign as the reversion and death sentence of every reference. Whereas representation attempts to absorb simulation by interpreting it as a false representation, simulation envelops the whole edifice of representation itself as a simulacrum. (*Simulacra and Simulation* 6, emphasis in original)

Like Benjamin, Baudrillard writes about an era beyond the confines of the present study, yet his observations about the dissociation between representation and referent within late twentieth-century mass media is prefigured in Victorian photography, and his response is presaged in the uneasiness with which Victorian writers considered photographic reproducibility in their lives and works.[25] Indeed, notes Roland Barthes, "the age of Photography corresponds precisely to the explosion of the private into the public, or rather into the creation of a new social value, which is the publicity of the private: the private is consumed as such, publicly" (98). Thus an author like Dickens, who expresses concern about the loss of control over his image, in fact speaks to a larger awareness and anxiety over the "new social value" of "the publicity of the private." One manifestation of this photograph-enabled publicity is the development of celebrity culture.

Literary celebrity, write James English and John Frow, "is thoroughly, if problematically, intertwined with the construction of the British literary canon" from the eighteenth century forward (40). Celebrity is that extratextual interest in an author, a notoriety that becomes all the more pronounced in the age of photography, for "to be photographically famous was to be more *familiar*," as Joss Marsh puts it ("Rise of Celebrity Culture" 106, emphasis in original). The fiction of the celebrity photograph is that it promises to "put one in the presence of fame" (106). The celebrity photograph gives its owner a false sense of being close to the celebrity—of owning a piece of that individual by way of the image. At the heart of the celebrity photograph's logic lies its failure to live up to that promise, for the owner of the celebrity photograph does not own a piece of the celebrity and is not in the presence of fame. This is particularly true because the celebrity image is not singular but multiple, existentially tied to the negative that makes its reproduction possible. There is nothing special about the celebrity photograph; there are numerous copies. Far from bringing the celebrity closer to the viewer, the multiplied celebrity image instead holds the celebrity at a greater remove.

The negative's role in reinforcing the logic of celebrity is a more pronounced iteration of its role in literary culture more broadly. The negative promises presence but then negates that presence.

The negative's most obvious contribution to photography is image reproduction, while somewhat less attention has been paid to how the negative facilitates this reproduction by inverting light and dark. Although it is a translation of the word "photography," the expression "light writing" is a curious way to describe the photographic process. Photographic images are, of course, dependent on light for their very existence. They are created by the controlled harnessing of directed light through a box and onto a piece of chemically treated metal, glass, paper, or plastic. In this way, the true subject of every photograph is light, more so than any other visual representation.[26] The expression "light writing" is curious, however, because it suggests but never states its reliance on darkness, that opposite quality so necessary to the success of the light writing. Traditionally, film must be developed in absolute darkness, and photographs are printed in a room with only red-tinged safelights. Beyond this, the portions of a photograph that appear the lightest in the final print are those parts that have received the least, rather than the most, light: the photographic representation of light relies on the obstruction of light in the development process. A negative-based photograph relies on its own inverse.

The omission of darkness in the word "photography" can be interpreted historically and culturally. "Light writing" borrows from Enlightenment rhetoric, reflecting a Victorian critique of religious faith in favor of a more scientific epistemology. Photography promises to shed light on the world truthfully and honestly. Yet darkness remains embedded in the fabric of the photographic image. Discussions of photography typically reference light as part of a dialectic: light *and* dark. This dialectic, moreover, is often expressed figuratively, replete with metaphoric associations. As Oliver Wendell Holmes writes in describing the negative-based photographic process in 1859,

> This *negative* is now to give birth to a *positive*,—this mass of contradictions to assert its hidden truth in a perfect harmonious affirmation of the realities of Nature. . . . Out of the perverse and totally depraved negative,—where it might almost seem as if some magic and diabolic power had wrenched all things from their properties, where the light of the eye was darkness, and the deepest blackness was gilded with the brightest glare,—is to come the true end of all this series of operations, a copy of

> Nature in all her sweet graduations and harmonies and contrasts. (55, emphasis in original)

Holmes waxes poetic in this passage about the philosophical significance of the negative, which appears so "perverse" and "totally depraved" before it is used to create copies of Nature. Thus behind every positive print lies a "diabolic" negative. Photography was not alone in accruing such metaphoric weight: Rolf Reichardt examines the way light and dark imagery more generally was mobilized during the Enlightenment and into the nineteenth century, coopting older religious metaphoric associations between light as true and good and dark as false and evil.[27] As I discuss in chapter 1, the metaphoric resonance of good and evil in particular attaches itself to photography in this period, as writers struggled for ways to describe negative technologies.

These evocations of light/good and dark/evil at times proliferated other, historically significant metaphoric associations. Thus Henry Morley and William Henry Wills write in their 1854 article "Photography" that the inversion of light and dark in a portrait may be thought of in racial terms as rendering a white face black:

> The image was then made perfect; but, as the light parts were all depicted by the blackest shades, and the black parts were left white, the courteous assistant was there represented as a negro. . . . That negro stage was not of course the finished portrait, it was "the negative"—or stereotype plate, as it were—from which, after it had been fixed with a solution of the sulphate of the peroxide of iron, any number of impressions could be taken. . . . The black face will obstruct the passage of the light and leave a white face underneath, the white hair will allow the light to pass, making black hair below, and so on. (61)

In this description, the negative face is a "negro stage" only, not the finished image of the final photograph. Far from innocuous, metaphoric associations between light and dark may wield enormous cultural weight as in this racialized description, reinforcing associations that are not limited to abstraction but concretized in social life.

The negative illuminates the dark side of photography and a literary culture increasingly engrossed by that technology. In this project, I identify three types of literary references that evoke the negative: direct references to photography in relation to the celebrity author, direct references to photography in Victorian narratives, and metaphoric and/or formal references to daguerreotypy and negative-based processes in works of largely realist fiction. The chapters that follow illustrate the extent to which the reproduction of the image is not merely a modern concern but a preoccupation very much present in the works and lives of major Victorian fiction writers, such as Dickens, Conan Doyle, Hornung, Bennett, Stevenson, Wilde, Hardy, and Stoker. Most of these authors are canonical, for canons, as Kelsey puts it, "are conversations around which a culture can define itself, and without them collective aspiration and social value threaten to dissipate into the blunt and banal exchanges of commerce" (4). In each chapter, I focus on a particular form of Victorian photography with a distinct relationship to the negative and read each photographic technique in relation to Victorian fiction and literary culture to demonstrate how this technique affects or is in conversation with the literary sphere. The impact is often implicit rather than explicit. I contend that the photographic negative has shaped the way we see in ways we no longer see. The negative is thus an absent presence in photography as well as culture.

The book is organized chronologically only in the broadest sense. I begin with two chapters on Dickens's fiction from the 1850s, when the collodion process made photography more accessible to a general, amateur public. The remainder of the book focuses on the diversification of photographic techniques and literary representations of photographic sensibilities in the 1870s through the 1890s. The technological development of the negative necessarily grounds this project in particular technologies and precise historical moments, yet despite this specificity, the more figurative implications of the negative stretch across the era. This project pairs historical specificity with a broader, theoretical analysis. I treat the negative as a distinct material process and read the figurative implications for this process in relation to literature and literary culture. This method allows me to treat the negative as at once a set of particular practices and techniques and as an overarching quality embedded in most photography and literary works that address photography. Specific negative-based techniques and the overarching figure of the negative are often treated as marginal to histories of the photographic image. When it is seen at all, the negative is often disregarded as peripheral, but here I insist that it is absolutely central to how we understand the photographic image and that image's relationship to other forms of representation.

❧

Chapter 1 examines Charles Dickens's ambivalent relationship to photography. Dickens was photographed many times, and his image was central to the establishment of his literary celebrity. At the same time, photography made him uncomfortable in physical and philosophical terms: he found sitting for his photographic portrait awkward, and he was wary of the uncontrolled multiplication and circulation of his image. Critics have noted a photographic subtext in Dickens's realist fiction. I argue that in *A Tale of Two Cities*, Dickens manages this photographic subtext by rendering it nonreproducible: in short, it follows a Daguerrean logic. By the time Dickens wrote *Tale* in 1859, the wet-plate collodion process had somewhat eclipsed the daguerreotype in popularity in England. Yet the novel—which is set in a period before the invention of either collodion or daguerreotype photography—is formally invested, I argue, in the photographic imagination of the daguerreotype. Through the doppelgängers Darnay and Carton, Dickens introduces the idea of reproducible photographic technology but then stifles its spread. His critique of the past in the service of the present, his fixation on and disruption of dark and light imagery, and his concluding meditation on Sydney Carton's individual "I see" are part of a unified figurative system: a photographic imagination.

Little Dorrit also reveals a photographic subtext, and in chapter 2 I read this subtext as solarized rather than Daguerrean. Solarization is an nonreproducible photographic technique in which a negative or print is exposed to flashes of unfiltered light during development. This partially inverts dark and light in the finished image, such that the image appears part positive and part negative. Reading contemporaneous discourses about and examples of solarization alongside Dickens's famous novel of light and dark, I suggest that *Little Dorrit*'s shadows are important because of the irregular way dark and light interact in the novel. Experimental photography illuminates a reading of *Little Dorrit*'s shadows and its light. By extension, experimental photography is more central to the history of photography and Victorian realism than we presently acknowledge. A fringe photographic experiment, one that is not explicitly referenced in *Little Dorrit*, solarization nevertheless shares with this novel a critique of an established metaphoric connection between light and truth, plus a challenge to a nineteenth-century conception of realism understood as photographic objectivity. Chapters 1 and 2 read metaphoric treatments of photography in Dickens's fiction and suggest that both texts are photographic even as they limit a key component of the negative process: multiplication. At the same time, these treatments repurpose inversion, the other primary component of the process, in the interest of undermining photography's truth claims. These literary treatments, carried out largely at the level of metaphor, are in sync with Dickens's distaste for and need to cultivate a photographic celebrity persona.

While the Dickensian use of a photographic sensibility undermines reproducibility and objectivity, Arthur Conan Doyle's Sherlock Holmes stories would appear, at first glance, to reassert photography's ostensible truth claims and value as a reproducible form of documentation. The development of forensic photography in the 1870s and its increasing use to document crime scenes and compile visual catalogs of known criminals speak to a broader cultural reliance on photography's documentary effects, particularly in the field of law enforcement. This use of photography was also negative-based, relying on reproduction to spread information in the service of law enforcement. It is noteworthy, therefore, that the nineteenth century's most famous literary detective does not make use of a camera in his own investigations. Chapter 3 analyzes photography's role in the Holmes canon and the incongruity between this role and the public perception of the technology. In the first Holmes short story, "A Scandal in Bohemia," a photographic portrait is proof of the king of Bohemia's indiscretion with an actress named Irene Adler, and thereby also serves as a means of blackmail. Although this type of photograph would have been reproducible, the king and Holmes pursue the portrait as though this visual representation is a unique object. Holmes is a scientist, but his scientific method begins to fray when vision comes into the picture. He fails to truly observe Adler, which—ironically—matters very little in the final analysis, for she gives the king "her word" that she will never use the photograph against him. The word bests the image in the final analysis, and the story comes to an abrupt conclusion. Caught up in his own way of seeing, Holmes fails to notice the solution to the case. This is the negation of perception—a breakdown between the machine-like functioning of the eye and the work of interpretation.

Chapter 4 builds on the idea of photographic exposure, developed in this book's treatment of Dickens's life and the works of Conan Doyle, by considering the motif of the double exposure: a single image produced from two negatives or two images combined in one negative. Moving from fin-de-siècle short fiction about photography and double exposures to works by Robert Louis Stevenson and Oscar Wilde, the chapter argues that the technique/mistake of the double exposure operates as a salient metaphor for the complications of narrative and social reputation at the end of the century. The double exposure is then duplicated in the rhetorical figuration of the double negative. Whereas the photographic negative connects with themes and concerns about the reproduction of representation in works by Dickens and Conan Doyle, reproduction happens at the level of the negative itself in E. W. Hornung's "A Spoilt Negative," Cyril Bennett's "The Spirit Photograph," Robert Louis Stevenson's *Strange Case of Dr. Jekyll and Mr. Hyde*, and Oscar Wilde's *The Picture of Dorian Gray*. Instead of a single image capable of being reproduced over and over again, the image in a double exposure is at its core already multiple, calling into question the idea of originality and authenticity even more dramatically than in traditional negative processes. While the short stories depict an optimistic view of the implications underlying photographic reproduction at the level of the negative, Stevenson's and Wilde's Gothic tales are implicitly much more skeptical, illustrating figuratively and grammatically the negative impact double exposures can play on representation, the individual, and reality itself. This plays out most dramatically in the instance of Wilde's celebrity persona and infamous trials.

Chapter 5 analyzes how photography exposes absence rather than presence in Thomas Hardy's *Jude the Obscure*. Photographs appear throughout the novel, consistently signifying affective attachment. Yet Sue and Jude have no portraits of their children. Why, in an era when postmortem images were so prevalent and in a text that features photography repeatedly in conjunction with affective attachment, don't Jude and Sue reproduce images of their dead children through photography? I read the novel's missing postmortem photographs as part of a broader failure to see and record. In other words, if "A Scandal in Bohemia" is a story about the problems inherent in trusting the visual record, *Jude* depicts the results of denying that visual record altogether. Such a negotiation between the photographic record and its absence may be seen in the development of Hardy's Wessex more generally. Wessex is a historic/fictional palimpsest of southwestern England and serves as the famed location of most of Hardy's major novels. Hardy created maps of the region, commissioned etchings of Wessex locales for the collected Wessex Novels edition of 1895–96, and contracted a photograph for each of the collected Wessex edition novels of 1912. Like postmortem images, these "Wessex" photographs reproduce nostalgia and even bereavement for a rural England that no longer is and paradoxically—given the photographic record—never was.

By way of conclusion, the book turns to Bram Stoker's *Dracula* to address the connection between photography and memory via the first literary example of a vampire whose image cannot be reflected and (implicitly) duplicated photographically. Dracula abounds with technology: shorthand, the phonograph, and the telegraph all help the characters tell their stories. Yet the novel is notably missing the most prevalent photographic technologies of the day and is thus a photographic negative of a different sort. Dracula cannot be visually contained or reproduced, and the conclusion addresses this characteristic alongside late Victorian fan culture. I suggest Dracula's absent reflection mirrors for us the experience of the fan: no matter how many photographs one might have of a given celebrity, the logic of celebrity dictates that something is always at a remove, unreproducible, and unseen. The logic of fandom is one that relies on the literal and the metaphoric negative in that it requires the reproduction of the celebrity's image and the negation of the celebrity's presence. The idea of containing the image and its reproductions is one we can trace through early twentieth-century film adaptations of *Dracula*; in a broader sense, this idea of containment and loss of control is very much still with us as we consider the implications of a digital photographic process. We no longer need negatives, but the implication of the negative persists residually, influencing photographic culture through new forms.

Photography, writes Jennifer Green-Lewis, "has an unusual relationship with the idea of truthfulness. . . . Built into the idea of photography is the fantasy of perfect re-presentation, a mirroring of the object which surpasses mimesis. A photograph, in theory, can more than replicate appearance. It can duplicate it" (*Framing the Victorians* 25). I argue that it is precisely this "more than" replication that so preoccupied Victorian novelists and that the negative illuminates a specific and sustained concern with reproducibility and inversion embedded in Victorian literary culture's preoccupations with celebrity, representation, and realism. These are preoccupations we share with the Victorians, and by better understanding the logic by which photography and literature intersected in the nineteenth century, perhaps we might illuminate and better understand our own uses of photographic images and literary texts alike.

Chapter 1

The Daguerreotype

Dickens's Counterfeit Presentment

Charles Dickens was, as Joss Marsh puts it, "the most photographically famous person in Britain outside the royal family" in the nineteenth century ("Rise of Celebrity Culture" 104). He was photographed at least 120 times—an impressive number in an era when sitting for a photographic likeness was an expensive and arduous experience (Wilkins and Matz). Dickens's photographic excess took on a notoriety of its own: for instance, an editorial in the *New York Herald* hyperbolically claims that by 1867 the author had posed for 500 distinct images (Kappel 170). Just as famously, Dickens was ambivalent about having his photograph taken. He first sat for a photographer in 1841, a scant two years after the public announcement of the daguerreotype and calotype processes. Sitting for a daguerreotype in Richard Beard's studio, the first of its kind in England, Dickens found the lengthy process unpleasant and advised Miss Burdett Coutts in 1841, "If anybody should entreat you to go to the Polytechnic Institution and have a Photographic likeness done—don't be prevailed upon, on any terms. The Sun is a great fellow in his way, but portrait painting is not his line. I speak from experience, having suffered dreadfully" (*Letters* 2:284). Some years later, he was asked by Herbert Fry to sit for the series *Photographic Portraits of Living Celebrities*, but he declined: "Nor can I have the pleasure of complying with your request. I have but just now finished sitting to a distinguished French painter, and have thoroughly made up my mind to sit no more" (*Letters* 8:72–73).[1] Nevertheless, he did sit again—and again (see figure 1.1). Perhaps the next one would be more accurate, less of a counterfeit presence.

Dickens's response to the photographer Mayall, discussed in the introduction, illuminates several reasons for the author's distaste of photographic

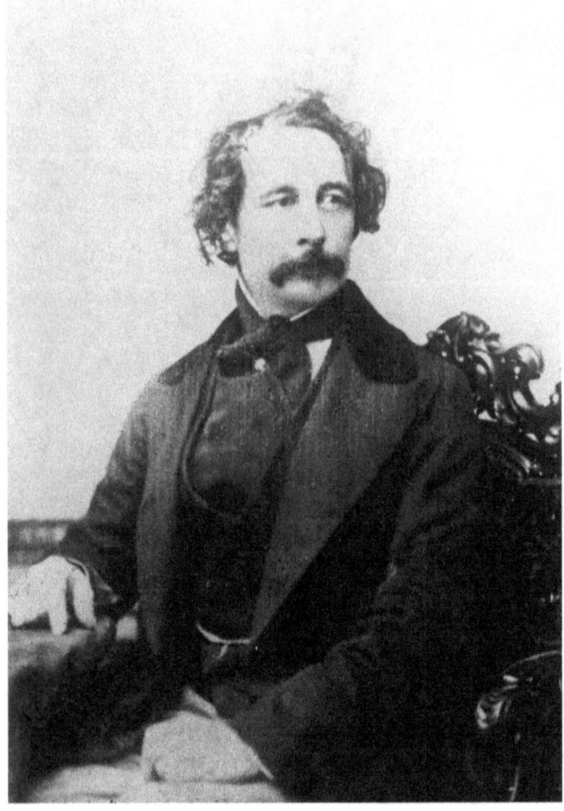

Figure 1.1. John Edwin Mayall, "Charles Dickens," daguerreotype (c. 1855). Reproduced by permission of The Charles Dickens Museum, London.

portraiture: the Inimitable was concerned that these images were giving viewers a "counterfeit presentment," or false sense of his presence, and he expressed anxiety over the idea of multiplication—the idea that his image could be reproduced again and again beyond his control.[2] Yet he goes on to write in his letter to Mayall in October 1856, "I am not the less sensible of your valuable offer" (*Letters* 8:199). Indeed, photographic portraiture was quite valuable as a means of "shaping the authorial persona," as Leon Litvack notes in his essay on the relationship between Dickens and photographer Herbert Watkins (97). Litvack describes this positive relationship with Watkins, for whom Dickens sat on several occasions and who "took the first mass-produced photographs of the novelist, thus facilitating the ownership and consumption of 'authentic' Dickens images by a multitude of readers and admirers, and in the process enhancing his reputation" (100). Thus Dickens's reaction to his own portrait was complex: while on some occasions he expressed his discomfort with sitting for multiple reproducible portraits, on others he acknowledged the value of those portraits due to the increasing power of the celebrity photographic market in the mid-nineteenth century.

It is part of the coy logic of celebrity that Dickens was at times famously recalcitrant about his photographic image, while at others invested in the creation of his own celebrity. A celebrity is someone you know about but about whom you want to know more—a person in some respects available to you, yet withheld.[3] Dickens's resistance to his numerous photographic images cultivates just such a sense of mystery. Yet celebrity's logic of exposure and withholding, of the abundance of the celebrity image and the elusiveness of the celebrity, does not account for the entirety of his reaction to his photographic image. As this chapter shows, Dickens's anxiety about and interest in photography is made manifest not only in his reaction to his celebrity but in his fiction. Moreover, the figure of the negative illuminates Dickens's particular concerns. The material photographic negative, that inverse image used to multiply photographic prints beyond the celebrity author's control, challenges the stability of light and dark: to create a positive print using negative-based photographic technology, one must first create a negative image. An image's inverse is thus an essential element in the reproduction of an image. This purely technical observation can be destabilizing to the idea of photographic verisimilitude. The idea that a photographic reproduction requires an inversion of light and dark challenges a centuries-old metaphoric system and calls the very nature of realistic representation into question by showing things not as they appear but as their tonal opposites.

Dickens's desired elusiveness and the abundance of his images is mirrored through the style of realism he adopts: the profusion of detail and the concurrent elusiveness of complete verisimilitude within that detail. Developing his realist style during the time when photography began to dominate the discursive landscape, he encodes a photographic sensibility into his fictions. In this way, his fictions participate in what Christopher Rovee has described as "a different kind of photographic history from the ones we are used to reading"—a history of photography that is less about chemistry or industry, and more "a *desire* spelled out in words and lines that summon into presence a dead man's touch" (388, emphasis in original).[4] Dickens's fictions, in other words, express a more abstract, more affective engagement with photography. Yet just as the author was uneasy with the role of photography in the construction of his celebrity image, so did the photographic qualities of his fiction demonstrate an unease with reproducibility.

Dickens's 1859 novel, *A Tale of Two Cities*, is a historical novel set before the advent of photography, and as such does not directly reference any photographic technique. The novel does, however, reflect a figurative investment in photography as a means of meditating on individuality, duplication, and the past versus the present—ideas invoked through Dickens's discussions of his celebrity photographs. In this chapter I read *Tale* through the lens of the daguerreotype specifically, to illustrate how this novel not only expresses a photographic sensibility but also demonstrates a working through of concerns around image multiplication made possible with negative-based photographic technologies. As discussed in the introduction, daguerreotypes have no negatives and are thus generally permanent, singular, and not reproduced.[5] While the novel also features motifs of duplication that would align it with a more negative-based photographic logic, the logic of the daguerreotype ultimately dominates. The typical daguerreotype portrait was, as Peppino Ortoleva writes, "perceived as a portrait and at the same time as a direct projection of the person," thought of "in terms of a presence more than a representation" (156). Daguerreotypes are also highly reflective and rely on specific lighting conditions to be viewed. Thus, the experience of viewing a daguerreotype is the experience of seeing light in two temporalities: the light of the past represented in the image and the light of the present of its viewing. This temporal duality is particularly evocative when read metaphorically alongside Dickens's novel. The author's critique of the past, his use of dark and light imagery, and Sydney Carton's concluding "I see" contribute to a unified figurative system—what I read here as a photographic imagination.[6] Yet light and dark remain unsettled and the figuration of duplication featured through Darnay and Carton is short-circuited by Carton's death. Read in this way, the novel is photographic, but its photographic sensibility is distinctly Daguerrean.

Reading Dickens's responses to his own celebrity image alongside *Tale* reinforces this logic of daguerreotypy. Both demonstrate a preference for control over the image, a resistance to the multiplication of that image, and an interest in the duality of past and present. Every daguerreotype is at once highly original, but linked to each moment it is viewed—a way out of the endless proliferation of the image made possible through negative-based technologies and yet itself a technology that emphasizes temporal duality. Dickens's critique of the French Revolution, as we see from the novel's opening page with its list of oppositions—best and worst, light and darkness, past and present—suggests that just as this novel will be about the past, it will also be about the present of its composition. Coupling dark and light inversion together with time, in his pithy figuration "it was the season of Light, it was the season of Darkness," Dickens establishes a connection between the Enlightenment past and his own era. As Roland Barthes notes, photography can be "reality in a past state: at once the past and the real" (82). Dickens likewise thematizes the reality of the past in his historical novel, his fiction obliquely reenacting his own preoccupation with self-image and originality in the present.

Photography and the Celebrity Author

Whereas Dickens's thematic evocation of photography in *A Tale of Two Cities* is anachronistic, photography was very much a present reality for him, affecting his celebrity image and thus contributing to the success of his literary works. Moreover, his concern over the circulation and control of his celebrity images parallels his more infamous preoccupation with the circulation of his literary works. Dickens was outspoken about the absence of international copyright laws and made this cause a focus of his first visit to the United States in 1842, publishing the following upon his return: "You may perhaps be aware that during my stay in America I lost no opportunity of endeavouring to awaken the public mind to a sense of the unjust and iniquitous state of the law in that country, in reference to the wholesale piracy of British works" ("International Copyright" 97). Copyright concerned Dickens, for his works were often pirated in the US press. Playing up the piracy metaphor, Dickens announced in a letter in 1842, "As to the Pirates, let them wave their black flag, and rob under it, and stab into the bargain, until the crack of doom. I should hardly be comfortable if they *bought* the right of blackguarding me in the Model Republic; but while they steal it, I am happy" (*Letters* 3:256–59, emphasis in original). In his comments about copyright, Dickens characterizes himself as a victim of relentless, unlawful trade. Aside from financial loss, the copyright issue troubles him because it means a loss of control over his work. As Tara Moore writes, "Dickens grieved over his loss of control of the physical quality of his books" in their pirated forms: "American reprints appeared with tiny type and narrow margins. For an author who carefully planned the paper quality, illustrations, and covers of his books whenever possible, as with the Christmas books, such cheap, uncontrollable printing caused pain" (280).[7]

This well-known instance of Dickens's response to copyright contextualizes his reaction to the circulation of his celebrity image, a circulation that, like US editions of his fiction, quickly exceeded his control. John Plunkett notes the celebrity photograph was "one of the most notable consequences of the commercialisation of photography," with celebrity images abounding and proliferating at staggering rates. From 1860 to 1862, Plunkett writes, between three and four million copies of Queen Victoria's cartes de visite were claimed to have been sold. In 1862 the London wholesale house Marion & Co. sold 50,000 cartes of various celebrities each month (280–81).[8] This proliferation of images soon exceeded the control of photographers or photographic subjects, and "forgeries of the celebrity photographs became commonplace and large profits were made out of an immense number of quasi-illegal pictures" (281). A revised Copyright Bill in 1862 helped control the proliferation, but only to a certain extent.

As we have seen, Dickens was often vocal about his distaste for sitting for photographic portraits, claiming such sittings were uncomfortable, that the resulting image failed to capture his true image, and that his image was thereafter multiplied and implicitly out of his control. Paul Fox and Gil Pasternak have argued that photo portraiture "in general is instrumental in identity work," but this does not account for how celebrity portraits were reproduced and circulated (140). Dickens was increasingly photographed, particularly after the development of the wet-plate process in 1851 reduced exposure times and made the experience less of an ordeal, and Litvack documents several instances when Dickens adopts a more favorable attitude toward the technology. On one hand, "Dickens's dislike of the various workings of his face is well documented" (Xavier 88). Baillargeon comments that this more negative attitude "may have been intended by Dickens to reiterate his dislike for the sitting process, but it may also reflect the uneasiness with which he viewed himself in a daguerreotype, the so-called 'mirror with a memory' " (4). However, in declining Mayall's invitation Dickens uses the term "multiplication," not just "duplication"—his concern, it seems, is not with a single daguerreotype but the idea that by this point his image was reproduced beyond his control.

This concern with a personal portrait out of control is echoed in *Bleak House*, which Dickens had finished three years before declining to sit for Mayall. In *Bleak House*, Lady Dedlock's dignified oil portrait, part of the family gallery at Chesney Wold, is juxtaposed against the mass-produced Galaxy Gallery of British Beauty copy of this image. Regina B. Oost and Ronald R. Thomas both read Lady Dedlock's Galaxy portrait as a sign of Dickens's increasing awareness—and uneasiness—with the potential reproduction of one's image, as well as a sign of the rising middle class. As Thomas puts it, "it is fitting that the plot of *Bleak House* should come to focus upon a pair of portraits—one a distinguished oil, the other a mass-produced copy—in recounting the scandalous fall of an old aristocratic family and the solution of a murder mystery" (*Detective Fiction* 133). Although daguerreotypes are one-of-a-kind photographic images, engraving and increasingly photographic technologies were making image reproduction more ubiquitous by the 1850s. In *Bleak House*, this reproduction is Lady Dedlock's potential undoing, for through the circulation of her image, the likes of Guppy and Weevle may ponder her likeness at length. While Guppy may have recognized the similarity between Lady Dedlock and Esther when looking at the Chesney Wold portrait, the circulation of Lady Dedlock's Galaxy portrait—a kind of celebrity portrait presaging the cartomania of the 1860s[9]—opens this connection to anyone and everyone. Although the mass-produced image reveals a secret in *Bleak House*, it does not expose all of the novel's mysteries—it does not explain who shot Tulkinghorn, for instance, or what happened to Krook. It does not resolve *Jarndyce v. Jarndyce*. It exposes but also misdirects, suggesting revelations that nevertheless do not resolve all of the novel's major plot points.

Dickens was aware that his photographic celebrity image was in some respects a lie, and his discomfort is specifically with the multiplication of that lie.[10] This may be read as symptomatic of his well-documented oscillation between private person and public persona—a professional writer who, as Grahame Smith notes, had a "general hostility toward public life" ("Life and Times" 12). Indeed, Dickens was not the only Victorian novelist dissatisfied with photography. George Eliot describes the photographs seen before meeting a person as "detestable introductions, only less disadvantageous than a description given by an ardent friend to one who is neither a friend nor ardent" (5:437). Like Dickens, Anthony Trollope admits, "I hate sitting for a photograph" (682). Yet photographic portraiture was part of Victorian celebrity authorship. Celebrity functions theatrically, as Sharon Marcus puts it, because "it combines proximity and distance and links celebrities to their devotees in structurally uneven ways" (1000). Writing about Victorian celebrity and photographic portraiture, Alexis Easley similarly argues that the discourse surrounding celebrity was "premised on what could be seen and known about popular authors" as well as "the mysterious and unknowable aspects of their lives and works" (12). Indeed, the tension between proximity and distance is spatial and temporal: "although celebrity culture was premised on reconstruction of the past, it was also focused on the ephemeral world of the day-to-day literary marketplace" (11). In the Victorian era, the literary marketplace was becoming more dominated by the visual. In a Victorian culture obsessed with, as Kate Flint puts it, not only what but how it sees, visual media played a crucial role in the cultivation of this elusive, abundant celebrity ("Visual Culture" 151).[11] Despite his reluctance to be photographed, Dickens certainly cultivated both elements throughout his career.

This idea of celebrity frames the controversies surrounding Dickens's images. The Gurney photograph controversy is a case in point. During his second visit to the United States, Dickens apparently promised the Gurneys that they would be the only US photographic studio to record his image during the trip. The Gurneys were scandalized by, as Sidney Moss puts it, "allegations in the press" that Dickens had sat for other photographers, and "To protect their reputation and investment," they ran a notice in the papers:

> In justification of our mercantile honor, which has been assailed by the publication of editorial articles in different Metropolitan journals, which, if true, would tend to place us before the public as imposters, we beg to assert thus publicly that Mr. Charles Dickens has not, and will not sit for any other Photographers but ourselves in the United States; that any pictures of Mr. Dickens, either exposed to view or offered for sale, and not having our imprint, are *copies* of pictures taken in Europe, and that any attempt to advertise them, either by payment or by editorial notice "as originals," is a fraud and imposition to the public. (Moss, 105–6, emphasis in original)

The motivation for this notice makes perfect sense: a great deal of the value of the Gurney image is in its exclusivity. The notice attempts to contain Dickens's images in the name of mercantile honor, but it does so via an appeal to a desired authenticity and originality. Our image of Dickens, the Gurneys declare, is the real image of Dickens in America; everything else you may see is just a copy and, as such, a lie. Embedded in the notice is a desire to declare their image "the" real Dickens image.

An editorial in the *New York Herald* lampoons this somewhat histrionic notice, picking up on the absurd sense of ownership the Gurneys seem to feel toward Dickens's image:

> Alas for these artists ruthlessly forbidden to meddle with the face, notified that those eyes have been secured for the special use of an authorized establishment; that those locks are "private," like the first dish of green peas at a hotel table, and that that jaw is subject to contract! We know not if the sun will be permitted to

> shine on the novelist, lest it might be in league with opposition photographers. (Kappel 169)

This controversy is all the more interesting for how it intersects with Dickens's fight to retain international copyright over his works, demonstrating that the author's desire for control straddled literary works and celebrity image, sometimes to different ends. Dickens's struggle to control the reproduction of his written works mirrors photographers' struggles to retain their own control over his image and is not limited to the Gurney situation: the first daguerreotypist to capture Dickens's image, Richard Beard, owned the patent for daguerreotypy in Britain and controlled his investment very carefully through litigation (Hannavy 127).

The Gurney controversy was one of several disputes surrounding Dickens's image. The Brady photographs, which apparently sparked the Gurney notice, were intended to be made into a stereograph (Moss). Malcolm Andrews describes this as a hoax—the Brady images doctored versions of an earlier Watkins portrait. Nor are the controversies limited to Dickens's photographic portraits: as Andrew Bean and Catherine Griffey write, the Samuel Drummond portrait of Dickens has long been the subject of debate and skepticism. One writer's unexplained doubt that the portrait depicted Dickens became scholarly tradition for the better part of a century. Even the relatively uncontroversial Samuel Laurence portrait has been the subject of some debate, the different versions of the portrait leading to some confusion: which image did Dickens like? Which became the more famous and widely circulating lithograph? These controversies share an investment in controlling a sense of truth or authenticity, concerns we learn (and relearn) to treat with increasing cynicism in our digital age. Jay Clayton lists some of the uncountable, uncontainable, or unknowable number of films, TV episodes, songs, comics, fictions, nonfictions, web sites, stores, and other allusions to Dickens and his novels that are alive and well in our contemporary culture. An important subset of these proliferating allusions is the category featuring Dickens's images. Photographic portraits played a vital role in establishing Dickens's celebrity as an author and continue to play a role in sustaining that celebrity today. Photographic reproductions understandably adorn the covers of Dickens biographies and coffee mugs, hats, T-shirts, plates, and the like.

This Dickens, the Dickens of the coffee mug industry, is in one sense the "right" Dickens in spirit, a postmodern anachronism with an appropriate amount of "allusion, parody, irony, and hyperbole" to do Dickens—the man who "took pleasure in noting the spinoff products from his imagination"—proud, as Clayton suggests (164, 4). In another sense, this endlessly reappropriated face of Dickens holds "No depth—just surface" (102). Although Clayton exalts the Dickensian postmodern, a reading of Baudrillard suggests there is something lost in the postmodern proliferation of the visual. Part of what is lost, according to Baudrillard, is a "definitive ambiguity" between, as he puts it, "art and the real world"; art today is "nothing more than this paradoxical confusion of the two" ("Aesthetic Illusion" 22). People were and are obsessed with capturing Dickens via his image, but while one can collect his image along with Wilkins, one cannot contain the Inimitable.

The idea of the counterfeit—of the not-quite-real, the unobtainable—is crucial to Dickens's realism and his celebrity. Both operate through a combination of restraint and excess: Dickens's realism seems based on withholding a totalizing sense of the real while offering an excess of things, people, places, and scenes; his celebrity on withholding the self while displaying an excess of images. In this way, the photographic portraits do work like his version of realist fiction. The distinction is in perception, and this is at the center of Dickens's line about the counterfeit quality of the photograph. Encountering a photograph and treating it as real is a failure to understand the counterfeit nature of any representation.

Daguerreotypes and Dickens

Famously coy about his own photographic image, Dickens was nevertheless interested in the technology, writing about it in letters and publishing articles about it in various issues of his popular weekly *Household Words* in the 1850s: in 1853, for instance, the journal published an article by Henry Morley and William Henry Wills titled "Photography." This was, observes Arlene M. Jackson, "one of the earliest of the journalistic 'advertisements' for this relatively new invention, and as such ought to be seen as part of the popularizing of photography" ("Dickens and Photography" 148). Shortly thereafter, the articles "The Stereoscope" (Morley and Wills) and "Busy with the Photograph" (Dodd) likewise appeared in *Household Words*. "Busy with the Photograph" describes the difference between the daguerreotype and the calotype in terms of reproduction: "Daguerre's process gives inverted or reverted pictures, without any power of reproduction or multiplication; but in Talbot's process there is a 'negative' produced, whence dozens, or scores, or hundreds of 'positives' may be obtained" (Dodd 243). The number of reproductions possible is inexact and potentially limitless, as Dodd excitedly indicates. Yet such reproductive power makes "the commercial world . . . a little alarmed," for "as photography is copying all sorts of productions, why not copy a Bank of England note?" (244). Photographic reproduction is clearly a cause for concern and "not unreasonably so" (244). Conversely, copies made without a negative—in particular, copies made of daguerreotypes—were difficult to execute and, as Beaumont Newhall writes, "did not lend" themselves "to ready duplication" (28). The negative was seen, for good or ill, as "the all-important element" for photographic duplication, a "necessary component of quick and efficient image reproduction" (Evans 181).

Photography remained a topic of interest in Dickens's subsequent periodical, *All the Year Round.* On June 11, 1859, the essay "Photographic Print" was published along with an installment of *Tale.* "Photographic Print" contributes to and comments on the proliferation of photographic discourse: "Photography has become a science, with a literature of her own. She maintains several journals, and a photographic almanac" (162). The article describes the 1851 introduction of Archer's collodion process and notes that the one drawback of all this innovation is the persistent "want of stability in photography": photographs remain ephemeral (162). The author of "Photographic Print" argues that only Talbot has come close to creating permanent and inexpensive photographs and does so by returning to a "Daguerrean" process of fixing the image to polished metal. The future of photography requires its return to an increasingly outmoded photographic technology noted for unique—rather than reproducible—images.

Daguerreotypes were the first photographic experiments to become commercially successful. Discussing the role of photography in *Bleak House* and Nathaniel Hawthorne's *House of the Seven Gables*, Ronald Thomas suggests that the daguerreotype's "quality of uniqueness" made it the preferable photographic process in North America for more than a decade following the development of collodion negative photography in England ("Double Exposures" 92). Thomas's argument is that US individualism made collodion reproducibility particularly distasteful, whereas in England, "the energies of radical individualism were perceived as a threat equally dangerous to the emerging order as was the oppression of an old aristocratic regime" (92). However, while radical individualism may have been perceived as a threat in Victorian England, the shift from daguerreotype to collodion negative was by no means a solution to this anxiety, nor was it as simple as a tale of two photographic forms. The ambrotype or collodion positive process, for instance, is another unique photographic form, one that emerged contemporaneous with the collodion negative process. An ambrotype is a negative that appears positive when viewed with a dark backing. Rather than directly analogous to radical individualism, unique images such as daguerreotypes and accidentally or deliberately experimental prints can also visually represent a process of individual incorporation into a larger social body. This occurs in two ways. First, in that they photographically represent a scene, these unique images are already mimetic, doubled by their reference to the object they represent. Second, accidental or experimental images frequently acquire their uniqueness from their disruption of the typical photographic uses of light and dark. Thus, while they are themselves original, these images represent the instability of light and dark inherent in all photography.[12]

This instability is reiterated in the temporal flux constitutive of every daguerreotype, for more so than in other art forms, the experience of viewing every daguerreotype is the experience of participating in an anachronism. "The highlights of a daguerreotype were captured in the nineteenth century, but the shadows are from the present day," writes Mark Osterman in "How to *See* a Daguerreotype" (14). This is because the dark spots on a daguerreotype are not part of the recorded image but the absence of image—they are the places where the polished silver of the daguerreotype plate shows through, ready to reflect the darkness of the viewing room.[13] To see any contrast in a daguerreotype, there must be enough darkness in the viewing room for the image to reflect. Placed in direct light, daguerreotypes vanish; they are paradoxically seen mostly clearly when surrounded by darkness. "Without something dark for the daguerreotype to reflect," Osterman observes, "most people simply see themselves reflected in the plate or, even more puzzling, a negative image" (14–15). Light may have been responsible for creating the daguerreotype in the past, but darkness is crucial for viewing it in the present.

Because what may be seen in a daguerreotype is affected by the darkness surrounding the viewer, a daguerreotype becomes a highly volatile, intensely individual image: "Subtle changes of point of view, room lighting, or a slight tilt of the plate create a completely different tonality that is impossible to repeat or recall. Like the fabled blind men describing an elephant, each individual experiences the daguerreotype from their own unique point of view and from a place to which they can never return" (Osterman, "How to *See*" 15). The darkness we see in a daguerreotype is *ours*, a reminder that the daguerreotype is itself an image caught between the time of its capture and the moment of its viewing. Daguerreotypes are photographic products that—in a more extreme, overt way yet nevertheless like all photographs—point to their own subjective construction and resonate historically and formally with the historical novel, a form of representation that is similarly attentive to its own mediation.

Season of Light, Season of Darkness

Dickens's photographic reluctance as a celebrity is reiterated through the photographic sensibility present in his fiction. With his posture of hesitation, Dickens replicates both the contradictory, counterfeit logic of celebrity—that coy attitude that cultivates desire—and the logic of a realism that works precisely by providing details but simultaneously withholding a complete view. In other words, his standoffish availability through photography connects the celebrity artist to his art by mirroring a similar rhetorical structure of suggesting totality while denying it. But whereas many critics link realism to the visual—"realism's 'compulsory and compulsive visibility,'" as Mark Seltzer puts it (95)—the precise nature of the visual in Dickens's fiction gives others pause. Sambudha Sen suggests that Dickens's novels are not realistic because of the way they employ a stereoscopic kind of vision, which has "a determining influence on such vital features of the Dickensian novel as plotting and characterization" (11).[14] Dickens's qualified realism exceeds strict mimesis. Although there is an element of the hyperbolic in his work, easiest to detect in his grotesque or caricaturish characters—Quilp, for instance, Uriah Heep, Miss Mowcher, or Skimpole—Dickens also aspired toward a reality effect. Explaining this in the 1841 introduction to *Oliver Twist*, he writes:

> I had read of thieves by scores. . . . But I had never met (except in HOGARTH) with the miserable reality. It appeared to me that to draw a knot of such associates in crime as really do exist; to paint them in all their deformity, in all their wretchedness, in all the squalid poverty of their lives; to show them as they really are . . . would be to attempt a something which was greatly needed, and which would be a service to society. (457)

Dickens evokes painting to talk about his realist aims, his drive to show things "as they really are,"[15] and he writes this introduction, with its metaphor of painting, in the year he first sat for a daguerreotypist. The author aspires toward a certain reality effect, but he prefers to characterize it through painting rather than photography, that representational form he later describe as counterfeit.

Dickens rarely mentions photography directly in his fiction, yet the photographic imagination spans his oeuvre. Several of his texts set around or after the advent of photography—*Bleak House*, the Christmas books, and *Little Dorrit*, for instance—may be read as abstractly "photographic," while only a few of the novels explicitly mention the technology.[16] In *Oliver Twist*, Mrs. Bedwin compares painters with "the man that invented the machine for taking likenesses": whereas "painters always make the ladies out prettier than they are," "the machine" is instead "a deal too honest" (90). Pip explains on the first page of *Great Expectations* that he does not have a likeness of his parents, "for their days were long before the days of photographs" (3). In *Our Mutual Friend*, Dickens links Reginald Wilfer to photography and cherubim in a convoluted analogy: "If the conventional Cherub could ever grow up and be clothed, he might be photographed as a portrait of Wilfer" (41). These few direct allusions focus on photography's potential "to capture or convey an accurate representation of an object or a person" (Litvack 99). But beyond such minor references, Dickens's treatment of photography remains implicit and his purpose less clearly about verisimilitude. As Nancy Armstrong, Thomas, and Oost have shown us through their analyses of *Bleak House*, Dickens encodes photography more metaphorically into his fiction.[17] Armstrong argues realism and photography were "partners in the same cultural project. Writing that aims to be taken as realistic is 'photographic' in that it promised to give readers access to a world on the other side of mediation and sought to do so by offering certain kinds of visual information. . . . In thus referring to images, realism was therefore referring to something very real" (26–27). I am also interested in Dickens's more figurative treatment of photography, and I explore how this inflects his realism in relation to his treatment of truth and time.

Set during the years of the Revolution and Terror in France, *A Tale of Two Cities* predates the invention of photography by some fifty years. Yet much like *Bleak House* or *Little Dorrit*, *Tale* shares with nineteenth-century photographic discourse a concern with the truthfulness of light and dark, of representation, and of realism and historical authenticity. Dickens's persistent use and deliberate misuse of the light/dark metaphor above all other dualisms draws our attention, as readers of this historical novel, not only to the Enlightenment and the revolutionary reformulation of religious light imagery, but to newer technologies of light and dark. Light and dark imagery pervades *Tale*, and through Dickens's famous dialectical opening, this imagery is tied to a preoccupation with time. The figuration "season of light" and "season of darkness" asks us not only to consider the connection between light and darkness but to read this binary in relation to time. Like a daguerreotype that bridges the time the image was taken with the time it is viewed through its reliance on the play of light and dark at both moments, Dickens's novel also brings together two temporalities through his treatment of light and dark. Not simply anachronistic, novel and daguerreotype are thematically linked through their shared dialectical relation to the past. More specifically, the daguerreotype shares with this historical novel a persistent focus on the unstable relation between these categories of light and dark. The high-contrast illustrations and recurrent use and subversive dismantling of Enlightenment imagery in *Tale* reveals a simultaneous reworking of Enlightenment "truth" and Victorian realism by at once challenging conventional associations between light/truth and the visible certainty that undergirds realism. The novel dabbles in duplication through the doppelgängers Darnay and Carton, but ultimately Dickens privileges a Daguerrean sensibility over a negative-based photographic one. The novel concludes with Carton as an individual who has sacrificed himself for his double and the woman they both love. Carton's words conclude the novel, and his repeated refrain "I see" becomes the final focus. Dickens's turn away from the figure of duplication at the conclusion reiterates his turn away from duplication at other levels of the novel, such as its visual economy.

Light and darkness, past and present: these are *Tale*'s predominant metaphors for duality, and they also mark the disintegration of such binary oppositions. At once light and darkness, this particular season challenges straightforward visual perception. Explicitly, this "season" is the era of the French Revolution. Yet in this historical novel, light and darkness mark the coming together of two related but temporally distinct discourses as well: Enlightenment philosophy and photography. As a technology of light, photography is connected to an established philosophical tradition of using light as a metaphor to express the good, the enlightened, and the true. As Martin Jay observes, visual metaphors permeate Western languages and philosophies, and "there exists a wealth of what might be called visually imbued cultural and social practices," many stemming from the "Hellenic affinity for the visible" (2, 21). The binary metaphor of light and dark is an epistemological touchstone and has been wielded as such in Western culture for centuries: it is, as Jacques Derrida writes, "The founding metaphor of Western philosophy as metaphysics" (27).[18]

For all their associations with the true and good, vision and light are nevertheless volatile substances, put to different uses by science, religion, philosophy, and government throughout history. Tracing this multiplicity of uses, Rolf Reichardt observes that metaphors of light and dark changed over time, associated variously with religion, Enlightenment rationality, and revolutionary propaganda. Reichardt establishes that light and darkness are evolving metaphors: they signify specific forms of the good and true at different moments in history. In the age of photography, this volatility gets beyond metaphoric control. Light's action becomes, as Paul Virilio puts it, "*supernatural*": "the critical problem of the *time-freeze* of the photographic exposure lends daylight a temporal measure independent of the meteorological day. It produces a separation of light and time in a way that recalls the Biblical separation, source of all the visible world's virtualities" (20, emphasis in original). Before the era of photography, light was associated with the natural passage of time, whereas photography's treatment of light challenges the certainty of time itself. "Virtual" rather than directly representative, light is unreliable—and with it, time and nature.

Instability is written into the Bible's first treatment of light and dark: "And God said, Let there be light: and there was light. And God saw the light, that *it was* good: and God divided the light from the darkness. And God called the light Day, and the darkness he called Night. And the evening and the morning were the first day" (Gen. 1:3–5). In this passage, evening and morning come together, the conflation of dusk with dawn forming one day. Thus the Bible describes the condensation of darkness or partial darkness into light within one temporality—even as it describes the separation of these qualities. In the post-Genesis, Victorian age of photography and religious doubt, light and dark are no longer so distinctly separated. Drawing on this biblical passage in his interpretation of Walter Benjamin, photography, and history, Eduardo Cadava writes that "There has never been a time without the photograph, without the residue and writing of light" (5). There is, writes Cadava, a "secret rapport between photography and philosophy. Both take their life from light, from a light that coincides with the conditions of possibility for clarity, reflection, speculation, and lucidity—that is, for knowledge in general" (5). For Benjamin, this light is mercurial, providing "simultaneous illumination and blindness" (Cadava 5). Through Benjamin, Cadava links photography to history, Enlightenment philosophy, and the dialectical complication of that philosophy. We now turn to a similar nexus of illumination, time, and dialectics in Dickens's novel.

Both temporally specific and expressively abridged, *Tale* seems to consciously deploy—rather than unconsciously succumb to—duality. Time, at once "best" and "worst," is after all this novel's first contradiction in terms. But 1775, this year of dualities, is, as Dickens writes, "so far like the present period, that some of its noisiest authorities insisted on its being received, for good or for evil, in the superlative degree of comparison only" (5). Several critics have noted the connection between historical past and compositional present in *Tale* and the larger historical novel genre. For instance, David

Richter writes that as a genre, "Historical novels are set in the past but they always in some sense express the needs of the present" (265). Georg Lukács also writes about this connection between past and present, noting that in the novel and drama, "there is a very complex interaction between [the writer's] relation to the present and his relation to history" (250).[19] But even though the historical novel brings the present with it into its description of the past, this connection of past and present is not, for Lukács, an intentional or successful association: "quite contrary to what so many moderns think, the historical novel does not become an independent genre as a result of its special faithfulness to the past. It becomes such when the objective or subjective conditions for historical faithfulness in the large sense are either not yet or no longer present" (251). In a sense, then, the historical novel is defined by its break from—rather than its continuity with—the past.

This break in turn creates a "dreamlike 'timelessness' " in the historical novel (262). *Tale*, for example, universalizes "purely moral aspects of causes and effects, weakens the connection between the problems of the characters' lives and the events of the French Revolution" (262). The historical novel is thus ironic, for it is more "subjective" and less historical than the social novels of the time. Lukács grounds his critique of Dickens's historical novel in the history of its production. After 1848, he argues, the historical novel genre becomes ever less directly historical and ever more abstract, mediated, and subjective. However, this subjective abstraction is historically tied to the period of the novel's composition: "in the historical novel this tendency of Dickens must necessarily take on the character of modern privateness in regard to history" (263). Lukács responds negatively to the post-1848 historical novel's ironic failure to sustain direct historical specificity and attributes its abstract quality to how post-1848 writers used more of a mediated relationship to history. This leads these writers to "introject" their own "subjective problems into the 'amorphousness' of history" (263). The historical novel's temporal slippage, for Lukács, is a sign of its potential failure to understand the present.

Instead of an aesthetic or historical mistake on Dickens's part, this slippage—between the subjective present of composition and the history that forms its subject—may be read as a manifestation of the broader duality theme foregrounded by the novel. As Richard Maxwell asserts, the destabilization of time forms a larger motif in the novel, exceeding its generic uses of past and present. While the novel keeps careful track of the passage of time, emphasizing, for example, the year "one thousand seven hundred and seventy-five" three times in as many pages in the first short chapter, it also contains several "temporal ellipses," which amount to a "drastic reduction" of the events surrounding the Revolution (Maxwell xi). What Maxwell calls the "condensations of historical time"[20] are paired with a hyperattention to the passage of time back and forth from 1775 to 1794 (xix). For example, setting the scene in Mr. Cruncher's office at the start of chapter 1 of Book the Second (a chapter helpfully titled "Five Years Later"), Dickens documents the time as "half-past seven of the clock on a windy March morning, Anno Domini seventeen hundred and eighty" (57). Descriptions like this make it possible to trace, in several cases, the events contained within the novel down to specific hours as well as days, months, and years.[21]

Rather than an opposition between two diametrically opposed qualities, the treatment of historical time in *Tale* is more about the conflation of past into present—or factually historical into expressively impressionistic—not the contradiction between two uses of time. In fact, writes Grahame Smith in a different context, Dickens has a way of "reading the world in terms of dualities which, although contrasting, are not necessarily oppositional in the binary sense" (*Dickens and the Dream of Cinema* 75–76). Smith's example here is the treatment of light and darkness in relation to London and Paris. According to Smith, the two cities—and the two qualities of light and dark—are equally privileged and are always potentially collapsing into one another. Smith's point is to bring these apparent binaries together and show how they were linked for Dickens. Hence, Dickensian opposites do not conflict so much as they illuminate.

In the case of *Tale*, this revelation is the relation between history and contingency, a relation most clearly articulated through visual motifs. Neither city is described in a way that seems particularly descriptive in a photographic sense. Yet a notion of photography expanded to include the Daguerrean imagination allows us to read the instability between past and present in *Tale* both contextually and thematically. The novel's fourth binary, the "season of Light . . . season of Darkness," weds light to time—specifically the revolutionary timeframe of the novel but implicitly also the Victorian era of the novel's composition. Light and dark are thus not timeless descriptors of visual qualities or metaphors for moral attributes—they are very specifically historically positioned. The evocation of light and dark in the novel is not about light and dark within the story alone but always in relation to a larger historical context and comparison.

Describing eighteenth- and nineteenth-century panoramas and dioramas—the forerunners of daguerreotypes[22]—Richard Altick notes that the first panoramists sought to bring "instant-history painting to a somewhat broader public" or commemorate important historic events as they occurred (136). This documentary impulse persists in photography, yet in photography, writes

Roland Barthes, "I can never deny that *the thing has been there*. There is a superimposition here: of reality and of the past" (76, emphasis in original). The past is captured or commemorated by photography, but the past is no longer "reality" as it is recognized in the present of the observation of the image. Like Dickens's treatment of history, photography captures a reality, but the passage of time transforms that reality: "truth and reality in a unique emotion" (Barthes 77). Rather than directly involved with photography in the way the detective elements of *Bleak House* are said to speak to the documentary uses of early photography, *Tale* engages with this technology on a more implicit level through its illustrations and written descriptions of the relation between darkness and light.

Visual art was crucial to Dickens's understanding of himself and his fiction.[23] In the illustration "In the Bastille," featured on the title page of the first bound edition of the novel, Phiz (Hablot Knight Browne) depicts Doctor Manette sitting in the Bastille, sewing a shoe (figure 1.2). He

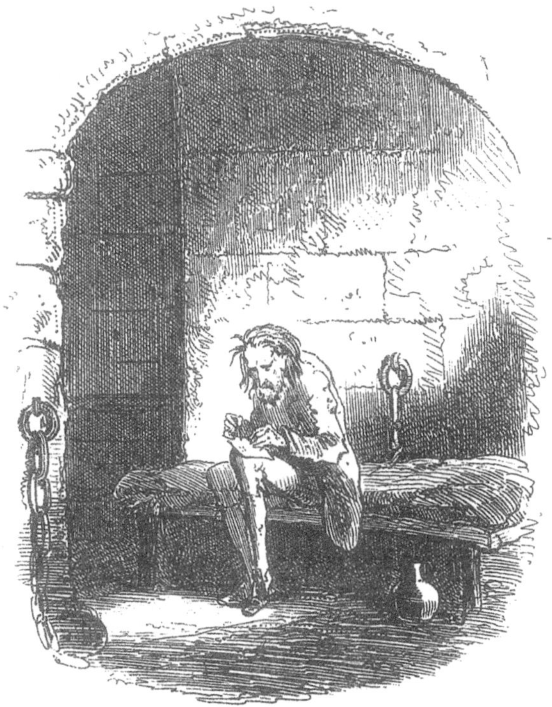

Figure 1.2. Hablot Knight Browne (Phiz), "In the Bastille," title page illustration for *A Tale of Two Cities* (London: Chapman and Hall, 1859). Reprinted by Penguin Classics (New York, 2000), p. 395.

sits with his back to the light, which is coming into the cell from what appears to be a high window beyond the upper right side of the image. This illustration calls to mind Manette's description, analyzed later, of the torturous light of a freedom he is denied. Yet this picture does not depict an individual turning in agony away from the moonlight that represents a liberty withheld from him; it shows the doctor at work. The position the doctor assumes is noteworthy in its spatial orientation. The front of his body is in shadow, confirming that the probable light source is the upper right corner of the image. Yet the shoe he works on is well lit, implying that he is neither facing the light nor facing away from it but positioned diagonally. Following the logic of daguerreotypy, he is in between the light and the darkness, his body position emphasizing this ambivalence. *Tale* was the last of Dickens's novels to be illustrated by Phiz. Whereas in the earlier *Little Dorrit* and *Bleak House* Phiz had used dark plates—a technique that allowed the illustrator to draw on more gradations between dark and light tones and "convey graphically what is for the Dickens novels a new intensity of darkness" (Steig 131)—he returned to simple line drawings in this later work.

Compared with the illustration from *Tale*, the *Bleak House* illustration "A new meaning in the Roman" is more tonally complex (figure 1.3). Although both depict a single source of light illuminating a darkened room, the *Bleak House* illustration uses darker grays along with blacks to give a heightened depth to this dark room. Although the reasons for this shift back away from the "dark plate" method in the later novel have to do with the practical issue of economics and turn-around time,[24] the line drawing's greater emphasis on the binary of darkness and light is, despite the critical disappointment it incited, more resonant with the novel's economy of duality.[25] Read together, *Tale* and its illustrations form part of a Victorian culture in which visual technologies were increasingly important. Less realistic, perhaps, than the more intricate *Bleak House* illustrations, the images in Phiz's last collaboration with Dickens nevertheless speak more to photography. Their stylization and contrast emphasize those two qualities—light and dark—so important to photographic visual representation.

Dickens shows that it is futile to sustain a division between qualities such as darkness and light. In the London of *Tale*, for example, Doctor and Lucie Manette live on a street where "summer light struck into the corner brilliantly in the earlier part of the day; but, when the streets grew hot, the corner was in shadow, though not in shadow so remote but that you could see beyond it into a glare of brightness" (96). The light does not

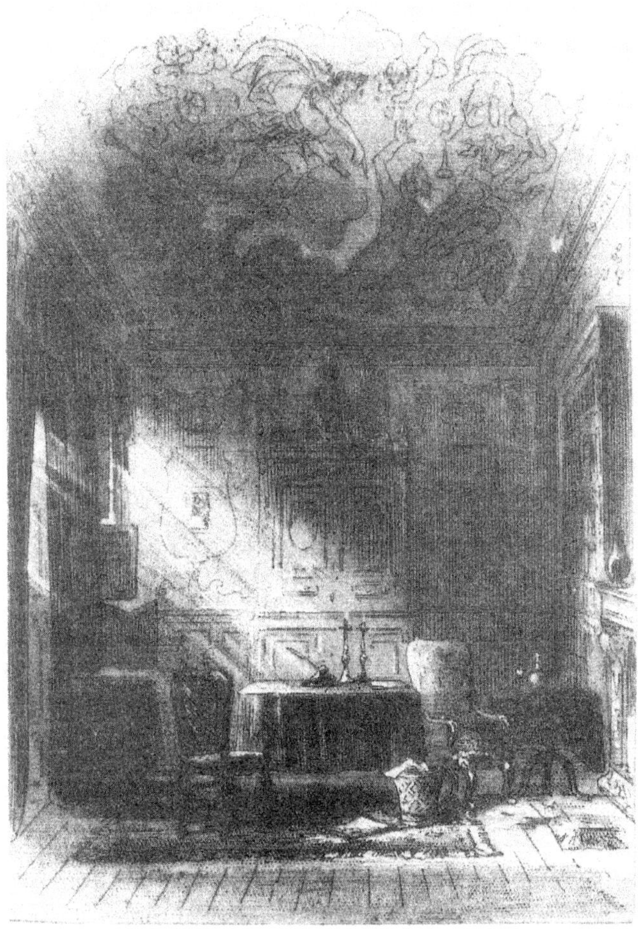

Figure 1.3. Hablot Knight Browne (Phiz), "A new meaning in the Roman," dark plate etching for *Bleak House* (London: Bradbury and Evans, 1853), facing p. 470.

last all day, but despite the shadow that overtakes the bright corner where the Manettes live, it is possible to see beyond the darkness and back to the light. This shadow with the promise of light just out of reach is "a cool spot, staid but cheerful" (96). It remains unclear whether the cheer of this "cool spot" is in its being out of the sunlight and in the shadow or in its proximity to the brightness from which it is nevertheless removed. Taking a closer look at this brief description of the passage of time throughout the day, we see that it could be describing a photographic process: what is light becomes dark, as a light space on a negative will become dark once it is printed. However, this imaginary image is more akin to a daguerreotype than a negative-based photographic print. Like a daguerreotype held in the light, the darkness is eclipsed by "a glare of brightness" (96). There is a partial reversal of darkness and light—or of the introduction of light into something still dark. Read through the figure of the daguerreotype, the light in the street that becomes shadow revealing light introduces us to a spatial and temporal indeterminacy that is both particular to the Manettes and part of the novel's larger comparative historical frame—an image of its past capture and present viewing.

In another instance, Doctor Manette complicates light/dark rhetoric to explain the paradoxical torment of freedom. Using the metaphor of light as freedom, the doctor gestures toward the moon: "I have looked at her from my prison-window, when I could not bear her light. I have looked at her, when it has been such torture to me to think of her shining upon what I had lost" (196). Here the light of freedom is mediated: this symbol representing light as freedom is the moon, not the sun, illustrating the doctor's ironic distance from that very freedom. The moon reflects sunlight (ostensibly the light source that most directly connotes light as freedom), and thus the source of this freedom lies elsewhere—namely, on the other side of the globe. Moonlight here represents a shadowy light—the existence of darkness (as night) in light (as moon). The moon subverts metaphoric expectation by casting a light, the benevolent freedom of which tortures rather than soothes the doctor. Inaccessible, this freedom becomes a terrible light.

In its frequent deployment of metaphors of light and darkness, the novel evokes more traditional understandings of these qualities: for instance, the remains of the Bastille contain the expected Gothic "gloomy vaults where the light of day had never shone," with "hideous doors of dark dens and cages" and "cavernous flights of steps" (227). Such recourses to traditional light/dark categories are just as frequently challenged: in an apparent use of this traditional rhetoric, Dickens notes that in 1775 London, "The highwayman in the dark was a City tradesman in the light" (6). This sentence at once sustains a contrast between the unlawful night and the legitimate day and dismantles the distinction between them, for the same man occupies both positions. The duplicity implied here indicates that while daylight may be a more honest sphere than the treacherous nighttime, the distinction between these two times—and the difference between honesty and treachery—is in fact merely superficial.

In the trial scene at the start of Book the Second, Dickens critiques juridical honesty, exemplifying the ironic dishonesty of the court system through a metaphor of light and mirrors. Charles Darnay is standing trial, and in the courtroom a mirror is positioned over his head "to throw the light down upon him" (66). Rather than the pure light of justice or truth, "Crowds of the wicked and the wretched had been reflected in it, and had passed from its surface and this earth's together. Haunted in a most ghastly manner that abominable place would have been, if the glass could ever have rendered back its reflexions [*sic*], as the ocean is one day to give up its dead" (66). The mirror reflects the ghostly images of past criminals—there is no justice reflected back to Darnay in this court.

The indeterminacy of light and dark is also transferred from Darnay to his doppelgänger, Sydney Carton. Looking at Carton's face near the end of the novel, Mr. Lorry notices, "A light, or a shade (the old gentleman could not have said which)" (321). It is significant that here Carton embodies the impossibility of telling light from dark, for Dickens's system of duality is disrupted, perhaps most strikingly, in the conflation of Darnay and Carton. Because they look so much alike—though they initially represent very different moral motivations—the roguish Carton can conclude the novel cathartically by saving Darnay from an unjust fate. Their similar appearance is thus on one level merely a plot device: to change places with Darnay, it is necessary that Carton look like him. The resolution of the novel thus appears accidental—all contingency and no purpose. At the same time, the novel has foreshadowed this conflation of the two men from their introduction in the court scene. The story of these characters' lives may thus, like a subjective daguerreotype viewing, represent contingency despite an overdetermined sense of purposeful, knowable historical progress. Carton takes Darnay's place in an act that disrupts the complete incorporation of the individual (here represented by Darnay) into the Terror. Though a device, this similarity between the characters is worked into the text figuratively, by way of the novel's larger economy of darkness and light. Mr. Lorry's inability to tell whether light or shade passes over Carton's face registers Carton's change on a metaphoric level, signaling that he can no longer represent the moral opposite of Darnay. Carton adopts some of Darnay's morality, though the indeterminacy of the light or shade on his face registers ambivalence toward this morality. On another level, this scene indicates an inability to tell right from wrong within the context of the French Revolution more broadly—an inability displaced onto the metaphoric system of light and dark.

Of course, in a photographic reading of this novel, Darnay and Carton also represent image multiplication—a more negative-based photographic sensibility. Brought in as a plot device, Carton's similarity to Darnay becomes remarkable to those who know them both. This visual similarity only highlights the character differences between the men. Carton reflects on those differences by looking into a glass: " 'Do you particularly like the man?' he muttered, at his own image; 'why should you particularly like a man who resembles you? There is nothing in you to like . . . You hate the fellow" (89). Looking at Darnay's life—particularly his wife—Carton sees just how far he is from leading the life he would like to lead: his similar outward appearance, he says to himself, "shows you what you have fallen away from and what you might have been!" (89). Darnay looks like Carton and indeed, Darnay is also known as Charles D'Aulnais and Charles St. Evrémonde. This proliferation of names and duplication of appearances recalls Dickens's concern about the proliferation of his own celebrity image. In *Tale*, we have two characters who look alike and are interchanged in the novel's dramatic climax. Who is the authentic individual, the original, in counterpoint to duplications? Is it in fact Carton, who utters the novel's concluding—and most moving—lines? Through Darnay/Carton, Dickens inserts what may be read as a nod to negative-based photographic duplication but then subverts its impact, reformulating this photographic subtext as instead Daguerrean: very much about the play between past and present and ultimately highly individual in its vision.

The novel weaves together history and individual perception of that history: it demands a negotiation of them together; it represents both in a vision of Carton's end. The novel, after all, ends with speculation about what Carton thinks he sees: "I see Barsad, and Cly, Defarge, The Vengeance . . . I see a beautiful city and a brilliant people rising from this abyss . . . I see the evil of this time and of the previous time of which this is the natural birth" (389). This emphasis on Carton's vision is repeated fourteen times in the novel's last two pages, driving the reader visually toward his final "It is a far, far better thing that I do, than I have ever done; it is a far, far better rest that I go to, than I have ever known" (390). Carton's present tense "I do" and "I go to" reflects on and modifies the present perfect "I have ever done" and "I have ever known"; it attains its power as a hopeful finale in the turn away from an old process toward a new future. Of course there is another way of reading the concluding repetition of "I see," which is to emphasize the "I" of the sentence. Throughout the novel Carton has been potentially or actually confused with Darnay, but here he emphasizes the individuality of his vision. Like a person looking at a daguerreotype, Carton sees something no one else can see: the newness, the unexpected turn, the contingent process that forms the image with which the novel concludes.

Understood alongside contemporaneous developments in photographic technology, the play of light and dark in *Tale* reveals the novel's negotiation with the photographic present of its composition and the revolutionary past making up its subject. The daguerreotype does not create the criticism of historical truth and representation, but lends this discourse a particular vocabulary and resonates with mid-Victorian technological developments and Dickens's celebrity. Even though the novel reflects aspects of a negative-based photographic sensibility, Dickens privileges a specifically Daguerrean sensibility, ultimately privileging its logic of singularity. The daguerreotype affords us a new way of accounting for Dickens's symbolic economy of light and darkness, the Enlightenment past he evokes with this symbolism, and the present through which he understands that past.

The Daguerrean imagination allows Dickens to engage with a technology of increasing cultural relevance and yet personal ambivalence—photography—and simultaneously contain its spread. *Tale* affords us an unlikely fictional and metaphoric demonstration of two of Dickens's chief anxieties of photography: the loss of control over one's own image and the lie of visual verisimilitude through the inversion of the image. The novel's treatment of a Daguerrean imagination is entwined with its treatment of history from the first page of the novel, and thus a reading of the Daguerrean trace in *Tale* yields a reading of Dickens's understanding of history. By destabilizing vision in the novel, the author shows the instability of Enlightenment aspirations and critiques the French Revolution while illuminating the extent to which that historic event continues to haunt the present. Dickens allows us to see the present in his vision of the past, just as we catch a glimpse of ourselves in the mirrored surface of a daguerreotype. And, as we will see in the next chapter, *Tale* was not Dickens's only work to address distinct photographic processes obliquely, nor was his fixation on darkness and light confined to a novel about the past.

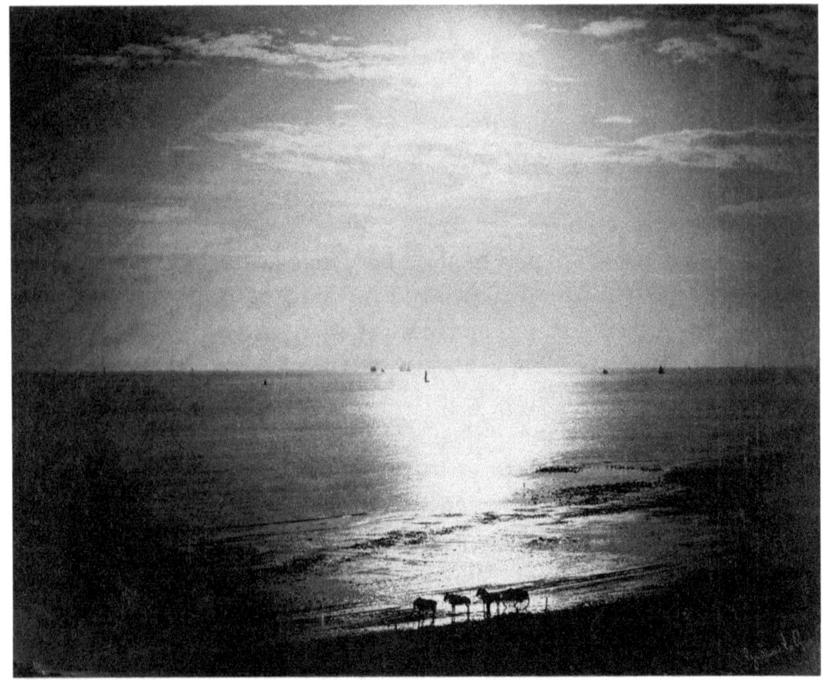

Figure 2.1. Gustave Le Gray, *Le Soleil au Zenith—Ocean* [*The Sun at Zenith, Normandy*], albumen silver print from glass negatives (1856). The J. Paul Getty Museum, Los Angeles. Digital image courtesy of the Getty's Open Content Program.

Chapter 2

The Solarized Print

Little Dorrit's Sun and Shadow

Much has been made of *Little Dorrit*'s shadows,[1] but I am also interested in its light. Dickens opens the novel by describing Marseilles "burning" in the sun (1). This harsh sun stares, exposing everything caught in its rays. There is a curious quality to this light. As Dickens writes, "There was no wind to make a ripple on the foul water within the harbor, or on the beautiful sea without. The line of demarcation between the two colors, black and blue, showed the point which the pure sea would not pass; but it lay as quiet as the abominable pool, with which it never mixed" (1). Sea and harbor are not bleached, as we might expect on so bright a day, but dark—black and blue—with only a "line of demarcation" separating the two. Sea and sky are of a similar hue in this scene, the former "too intensely blue to be looked at" and the latter "purple." This description of a light so intense it looks dark, uninterrupted but for a line of demarcation, parallels the language used to discuss an experimental photographic technique called solarization, itself an example of the unstable distinction between light and dark present in all photography.

Solarized images include qualities of negative and positive in a single positive image and thereby draw together these two qualities often regarded as diametrically opposed. Solarization is not the only technique that brings positive and negative together; the ambrotype is another such example. Yet while an ambrotype is a negative that appears positive, a solarized image appears as positive and negative simultaneously. Here I elaborate on the previous chapter to argue that experimental photography is more central to the history of photography and Dickens's reaction to his own celebrity than we currently acknowledge. A fringe photographic experiment that is not explicitly referenced in *Little Dorrit*, solarization nevertheless shares with this novel a critique of an established metaphoric connection between light and truth, plus a challenge to a nineteenth-century conception of realism understood as photographic objectivity. Dickens's treatment of darkness and light is more experimental in *Little Dorrit* than in *A Tale of Two Cities* and is more focused on the notion of inversion and the negative image. As in my reading of *Tale*, I read in Dickens's treatment of light and dark in *Little Dorrit* a photographic negotiation, one particularly resistant to what we might call the "negative qualities" of multiplication and inversion. In this novel, however, Dickens circumvents inversion through an implicit challenge to photographic objectivity more broadly.

Dickens was in the middle of writing *Little Dorrit* when he declined Mayall's request for another photographic portrait. As we saw in chapter 1, however, his recalcitrance to be photographed did not necessarily translate into a rejection of photography as an aesthetic technique or technology of representation. In his analysis of the photographic imagination in *Little Dorrit*, a novel that, like *Tale*, does not directly address photography, Daniel Novak argues for a more embedded connection between Dickens and photography. According to Novak, *Little Dorrit* "internalizes and dramatizes" photographic and novelistic forms alike without explicitly discussing photographic technology (66). Joss Marsh similarly detects a photographic element in the novel, writing that "much of the visual imagery" identified by commentators demands "a specifically photographic frame of reference if we are to appreciate it in the full" ("Inimitable Double Vision" 266–67). For instance, she writes, the play between sun and shade in the novel resonates with "the dual negative-positive quality of the daguerreotype" (267). This play between light and dark—also present in daguerreotypy, as we saw in chapter 1—is more pronounced in *Little Dorrit*. Light and dark misbehave more dramatically, and the novel's consideration of the visual is less concerned with history and the presence of darkness within light than it is with the utter rupture of the limit between such categories. Rather than oscillate between negative and positive images, *Little Dorrit* gives us an image that is negative and positive at once.

Overexposed to excessive, unfiltered light, solarized negatives and positives look metallic and contain properties of the positive and the negative image at once. These images highlight photography as a mediated representation rather than a faithful depiction of reality. As Melissa Miles writes, solarization "draws on an excessive and volatile light to undermine the relationship between photography, light, truth and presence" (346). To this day, while the technical causes of solarization are known and while software programs have made it relatively simple to produce, a darkroom print solarization is extremely difficult to reproduce consistently. The extra flash of light given to a photograph during the development process or the additional light given to a negative or daguerreotype plate during initial exposure halts the progression of the positive image and introduces an unpredictable negative element. Solarized images thus overtly harness dark and light—both positive and negative—in a single representation. Solarization exposes how fine the line is between the apparent opposites of dark and light.

While *Little Dorrit* does not reference photography or solarization by name, the novel's descriptions evoke photography, and its treatment of light and dark is experimental. In this way, the book troubles the association between truth and light, photographic objectivity and realism. The novel accomplishes this by unsettling traditional metaphoric representations of dark and light, and by highlighting its theme of "unreality" in specifically visual terms. In what follows I begin with a reading of *Little Dorrit*'s unconventional treatment of light and dark before turning to a brief history of solarization. I end by returning to *Little Dorrit* and explore solarization's value as a frame for a reading of unreality in Dickens's novel—a frame that is historically situated and has far-reaching implications for how we understand literary realism and the history of photography alike.

Sun and Shadow

Both light and dark are central metaphors in *Little Dorrit*, but many critics focus on the novel's abundant use of the shadow metaphor. J. Hillis Miller establishes this tradition, arguing that the word *shadow* is the most "frequently recurring" key term in the novel (*Charles Dickens* 230)—a practice Elaine Showalter, Hilary Schor, James Kincaid, and Brian Rosenberg have, with some reservations, developed.[2] Such a focus tends to marginalize the role light plays and how light and dark frequently intersect and complicate one another. Indeed, the *Oxford English Dictionary* illustrates the extent to which dark and light are already contained within the term *shadow* itself. In the primary definition of the noun, *shadow* is described as "comparative darkness, esp. that caused by interception of light; a tract of partial darkness produced by a body intercepting the direct rays of the sun or other luminary." Shadow is not pure darkness but requires the existence of light.

In the novel, references to shadow and light are in a nearly perfect balance, a fact befitting a novel whose first chapter is titled "Sun and Shadow." *Little Dorrit* starts with sunlight but is also full of references to morning light, morning sun, moonlight, watch-light, magic lantern light, flaring gaslight, candlelight, twilight, and sunset, to name a few.[3] A search through Mitsu Matsuoka's "Hyper-Concordance to the Works of Charles Dickens" reveals that *shadow* appears 53 times in the text, the plural 13 times, and associated terms such as *dark*, *darkness*, *moon*, and *moonlight* bring the total up to 206. The total number of references to light in the sense of *lightness*, *illuminate*, *illumination*, *sun*, and *sunshine*, is 208. Although these numbers are inconclusive by themselves, the context in which each term appears indicates a balance between light and dark.

Some critics have analyzed this combination of light and dark. Jerome Beaty, for instance, argues that the novel's light helps to mitigate its darkness, while James R. Zimmerman suggests that "although there are a large number of conventional dark-equals-evil and light-equals-good images . . . Dickens builds a pattern of sun and shadow imagery which sets up both extreme sun and extreme shadow as negative attributes" (94).[4] Emma Hardinge acknowledges an "ambiguous relationship between the key images of darkness and light in the novel" and reads this ambiguity as an index of persona culture (111).[5] Yet the ambiguity surrounding light and dark goes beyond individual personas and affects the novel as a whole: its characters, its settings, and its theme of unreality.

As the novel establishes at its outset, light can be a hostile force:

> A blazing sun upon a fierce August day was no greater rarity in southern France then, than at any other time, before or since. Everything in Marseilles, and about Marseilles, had stared at the fervid sky, and been stared at in return, until a staring habit had become universal there. Strangers were stared out of countenance by staring white houses, staring white walls, staring white streets, staring tracts of arid road, staring hills from which verdure was burnt away. The only things to be seen not fixedly staring and glaring were the vines drooping under their load of grapes. (1)

The repetition of versions of the verb *to stare* ten times in this second paragraph personifies the sun as inescapable and visually intrusive. All this staring produces negative physical effects: the ships blister, the awnings become "too hot to touch," and the "universal stare made the eyes ache." Part of what makes the staring so oppressive is how it has become a "habit" shared by all things in Marseilles. Shade would be a welcome relief, for "everything that lived or grew, was oppressed by the glare," the "very dust was scorched," and blinds were all "closed and drawn to keep out the stare" (1–2).

From this scene of oppressive, glaring light, we move inside a "villanous [*sic*] prison." In counterpoint to the hostile staring outside under the sun, our first characters Cavalletto and Rigaud find themselves in a prison that "received such light as it got, through a grating of iron bars, fashioned like a pretty large window, by means of which it could be always inspected from the gloomy staircase on which the grating gave." The oppressive light outside becomes, within the prison, an object of desire: "To the devil with this Brigand of a Sun that never shines in here!" growls the chilled Rigaud, whose eyes nevertheless somehow "glittered" in the lack of light. This traditional metaphorical allocation—darkness equals "dark" things, such as crime—is nevertheless subtly undercut: "the prison had no knowledge of the brightness outside," but it is not without light altogether—it has a "refuse of reflected light" from outside, enough to allow those outside the cell to inspect the prisoners within (2–3). This (near) contradiction between the bright world without and the dark world within establishes two things: first, the sun is not necessarily a benevolent force or a metaphor for the true and good in the way we might expect by virtue of its contrast to the shadowy prison; second, the division between sun and shadow is unstable. Under the bright sun, the sea reflects black and blue and the sky burns purple; inside the dark prison, reflected light nevertheless makes its way, "languishing down a square funnel that blinded a window in the staircase wall." In drawing a distinction between the oppressive glare of light outside and the oppressive darkness within, Dickens unsettles the expected metaphoric division: both light and dark are distasteful.

At times the novel adheres to a more traditional metaphoric treatment of light and dark. Like the prison in Marseilles, the Marshalsea, with its "blind alleys," is a place whose lamps and candles "had not the air of making it lighter" (48, 67). The morning light "was in no hurry to climb the prison wall and look in at the snuggery windows" (74), and in the evening it "fell dark there sooner than elsewhere" (205). The darkness of the Marshalsea is partly a metaphoric way of describing the people imprisoned therein: "the shadow of the Marshalsea wall," Dickens writes, "was a real darkening influence, and could be seen on the Dorrit Family at any stage of the sun's course" (213). Full of secrecy and deception, Arthur's family house is similarly depicted as a place of literal and metaphoric darkness: "Dark and miserable as ever," Arthur reflects on his return home at the start of the book (25). At the novel's conclusion, Mrs. Clennam defaults to a traditional dark and light metaphoric system in an attempt to explain her family secret: "That Frederick Dorrit was the beginning of it all," she begins, "If he had not been a player of music, and had not kept, in those days of his youth and prosperity, an idle house where singers, and players, and such-like children of Evil, turned their backs on the Light and their faces to the Darkness," Arthur's real mother might not have seduced his father (650).

However, these traditional uses of darkness and light soon begin to collapse in on themselves, much like the Clennam house: the Marshalsea promises to plunge its prisoner inhabitants into the darkness of infamy but fails to live up to this promise. Dr. Haggage understands that the Marshalsea can be a form of "freedom" from debt, rather than incarceration (53). The darkness of the place does not strike all inhabitants equally: as Little Dorrit sits by the window telling Maggy the story of the Princess, the poor tiny woman, and the woman's beloved shadow-memory of a lost love, the sunset shines "very bright upon her," even within the Marshalsea (246). Little Dorrit often finds pockets of sunshine in the prison, as when the "shadow of the wall" makes the room dark, but "in the window, where a little of the bright summer evening sky could shine upon her, Little Dorrit stood, and read" (658). Meanwhile, the darkness of the Clennam house is terrifying to Affery not because of what it hides but because of what it paradoxically makes visible: she is "much more" afraid of seeing something in the darkness "than if it was light" (575). Rather than obscuring her vision, darkness allows her to see mysteries and secrets. Mrs. Clennam's denunciation of the youthful musicians at Frederick Dorrit's home might ring true if she were not the one to turn her face to the darkness both literally (by keeping a dark house) and figuratively (through her own secrets). The novel's conventional treatment of light and dark is frequently undermined by such disruptive descriptions.

The limit between darkness and light does not remain fixed, nor does light behave the way it "should," either literally (as when the sun makes the sea look black and blue) or figuratively (as when the sun "stares" and "glares" so oppressively). Along with many descriptions of light and shadow, references to pictures and images litter the pages—for instance, when Arthur is called on to look at a "natural picture" of Minnie and her dead sister, Lillie (164).[6] The novel's preoccupation with visual representation coincides with a moment in history and in Dickens's life when photography was impinging on the everyday, becoming ever more a part of the lived reality of British people even as experimental techniques like solarization were challenging the authenticity and truthfulness of these representations. Solarization is a particularly rich lens through which to view *Little Dorrit*'s visual negotiations, for the novel's repeated disruption of light and dark mirrors the language and logic of this technique.

Solar Experiments

Solarization illustrates permeability between darkness and light. Figures 2.2 and 2.3 are photographs of a tree in daylight. Figure 2.2 is a traditional print, whereas figure 2.3 has been solarized during printing by exposing the image to a flash of unfiltered light. In solarization, this extra flash of light darkens the image and produces the technique's hallmark metallic effect and often its line of demarcation. Although a complete tonal reversal has transformed the sky into a negative image in the solarized print, the tree in the foreground is not quite a negative, for the center retains its original positive tone. Positive and negative commingle in one image. The movement between positive and negative in a solarization is not as actively volatile as

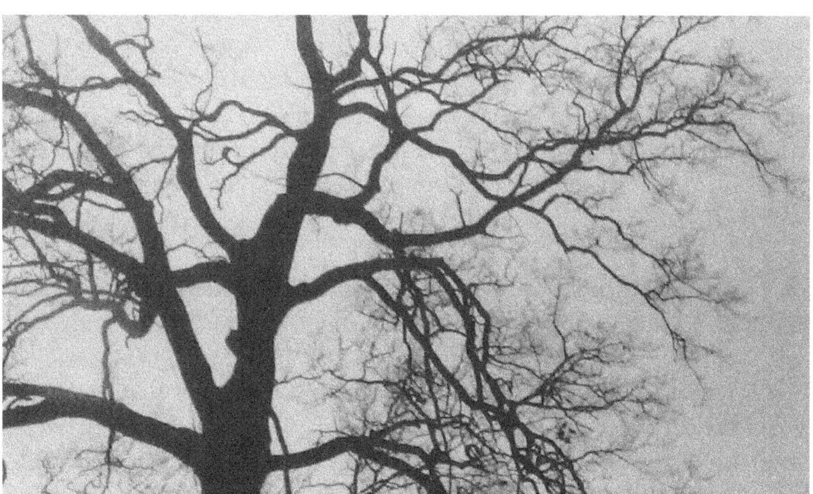

Figure 2.2. Susan Cook, *Oxford Tree* (detail), black and white print (2001). Private collection.

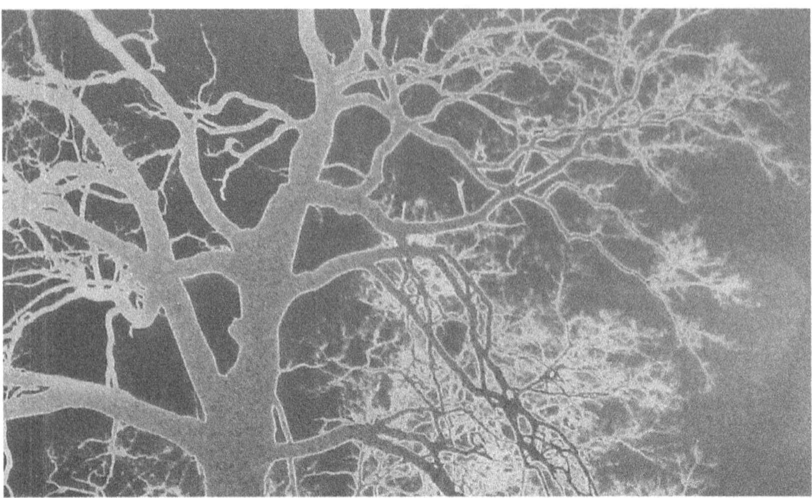

Figure 2.3. Susan Cook, *Oxford Tree* (detail), deliberate print solarization (2001). Private collection.

the quality of darkness in a daguerreotype, but the metallic appearance of the solarization echoes the daguerreotype's perspectival variability. Solarization's emphasis on the conflation of dark and light is also an extreme representation of an inherent quality of all photography: in "Some Account of the Art of Photogenic Drawing," for example, Henry Fox Talbot describes "the art of fixing a shadow," dedicating a section of the essay to this concern and noting "we may receive on paper the fleeting shadow, arrest it there, and in the space of a single minute fix it there so firmly as to be no more capable of change, even if thrown back into the sunbeam from which it derived its origin" (41). The ambiguity surrounding solarization's origins, its precise definition, and even its name, is representative of a larger epistemological instability that remains implicit in photography at large.

Like an uncanny double, solarization has existed as long as photography has, appearing as an unwanted and uncontrollable effect on early daguerreotype portraits, accidentally "discovered" numerous times in collodion wet-plate development in the 1850s and 1860s, and not cultivated as an artistic technique until the twentieth century. The early history of experimental solarization has been largely forgotten; many critics prefer to date its origin to Man Ray's famous images from the 1920s. Yet on September 4, 1857, British photographer William Jackson wrote to the *Journal of the Photographic Society of London* and became the first to publish an account of the phenomenon. The amateur prints he included have not survived, but his letter—for publication, given the title "On a Method of Reversing the Action of Light on the Collodion Film, and thereby producing transparent Positives, at one operation, in the Camera"—announces his discovery of a "solarized" photographic effect (77).

Jackson was cultivating and describing what had been an unwanted effect common to many early or poor-quality daguerreotypes. In daguerreotype portraits in particular, the white areas in the image—such as a lady's white bodice or a man's white shirt—were so susceptible to overexposure that the expression "Blue Bosom Boys" was coined to describe a daguerreotypist whose overexposures produced a bluish bosom (S. White). This blue overexposure is what we would now refer to as solarization, for the white area in the image has started to darken and transform into a negative image. This effect also occurs in daguerreotypes with a bright sky, such as Samuel Bemis's 1840 *Barn in Hart's Location, New Hampshire* (figure 2.4). In this image, the sky begins to turn blue because of the intensity of light captured

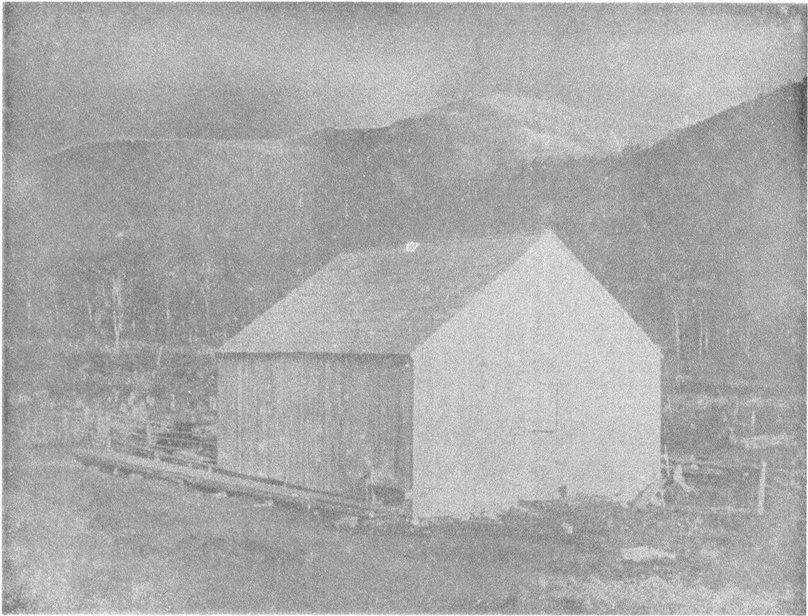

Figure 2.4. Samuel Bemis, *Barn in Hart's Location, New Hampshire*, daguerreotype (c. 1840). The J. Paul Getty Museum, Los Angeles. Digital image courtesy of the Getty's Open Content Program.

by the camera. It is possible the artist cultivated this effect, for the blue of the solarized sky is in fact more "realistic." As in the seascape that introduces *Little Dorrit*, a line—known as a line of demarcation—separates one dark field from the next. In the case of this daguerreotype, a white line of demarcation separates dark sky from dark mountains. In other images, such as Gustave Le Gray's *Le Soleil au Zenith* at the start of this chapter (figure 2.1), the sun alone is solarized. This black sun, which twentieth-century photographers Ansel Adams and Minor White later made famous in their images, captures the hallmark of solarization—a tonal reversal produced by extreme overexposure.

Although it stands to reason that a solarized sky might be cultivated as a desired effect, portrait solarizations were often accidental and treated as mistakes to be avoided. As Grace Seiberling notes in her study of amateur Victorian photographers, early amateurs greatly preferred image stability to "unpredictable patterns created by overexposure and solarization" (28). In 1840, US daguerreotypist John W. Draper instructed that human subjects must temporarily cover their white bodice area with a darker material so that the white area is not solarized by overexposure (217). Sir John Herschel describes a similar effect in 1842, in his personal notes on the cyanotype process: "If *very* long exposed the picture is positive the parts where the light has acted being actually paler than the original formed tint. This I call over-sunning or solarising." In his 1864 *The Silver Sunbeam*, John Towler dismisses solarization as a nuisance:

> This trouble [solarization] does not occur very frequently; it is made manifest by the redness which the high-lights are wont to assume during development, when the exposure has been either too long or the light too brilliant, as in the copying process by the direct rays of the sun. This evil can be remedied by avoiding the causes, or by the use of a *bromo*-iodized collodion, or of citric acid in the developer. (chapter 4)

For Towler and photographers plagued with its unwanted effects, solarization is a "trouble." With language that echoes Mrs. Clennam's excoriation of the young musicians turned to the darkness, Towler describes this disruption of light and dark as an "evil."

The solarized effects on collodion plates Jackson writes about in his 1857 letter were, however, part of a deliberate attempt to turn a negative into a transparent positive. Jackson describes a calculated and careful overexposure to light before the negative collodion plate is fully developed. Overexposure alters the chemical composition of the collodion and produces an image that "appears as a coarse negative by reflected light" or "a faint positive by reflected as well as by transmitted light." In other words, these images were partially negative and partially positive. In his letter, Jackson explains that the sample solarized images he sent to the Photographic Society "may perhaps be regarded rather as curious than of practical use," or useful as "hints" for "how to avoid transparency in negatives" (77). Jackson's experiments with solarization were in the service of transforming his negative plates into transparent positives. Given the finesse required to negotiate the unpredictable process, his assertion that his remarks would be of "practical use" seems disingenuous: "Some practice may be necessary to hit the precise point of development previous to the reversing operations," and even then, "It is difficult . . . to prevent those parts of the picture which border on the sky from becoming negative." Jackson was more inquisitive about this new effect than most, but solarization remained for him an experimental means to an end and was ultimately dismissed as mere unruly curiosity.

The technique continued to attract attention, however. In his 1859 *L'Art du Photographe*, H. de la Blanchere became the first person to discuss this process in a full-length work. Blanchere acknowledges Jackson's letter and notes that he has replicated the experiment. He takes issue with some of Jackson's conclusions and those of his respondents, the members of the Photographic Society, as reported in *The Journal of the Photographic Society of London* ("Proceedings"); he argues that the quality of light, rather than the quantity of light, is of importance to this technique.[7] In this implicit dialogue with Jackson and the editors of the London photographic journal, Blanchere reveals a persistent interest in solarization and its precise causes.

Lack of consistency was one of the evils plaguing solarization for these early photographers. "I have always found it has been impossible to produce a constant result," writes Fenton in his editorial response to Jackson's letter in 1857 (78). Indeed, it has also seemed impossible to establish critical consensus about the history or process of solarization, beginning with the name of the man to whom the process is attributed. The name most affiliated with this technique belongs to a man who famously described the process in 1862 in the meeting notes for the *Bulletin de la Société Française de Photographie*, although he published his findings earlier in an 1860 *Cosmos* article titled "Photographie: Positifs directs sur collodion," or "Photography: Direct Collodion Positives." Sabatier, a doctor and amateur photographer, describes a similar process of deriving direct positives through overexposure, and he calls it "la cursive héliographique"—"cursory sun writing," or "pseudo-solarization" ("Adresse à la Société" 177). Grant Romer for *The Focal Encyclopedia of Photography* identifies Sabatier as "Aramand Sabattier," a French doctor and scientist who established the "pseudo-solarization reversal," which was "exploited for making a positive of a reversal, a second exposure, and development after the first exposure and developing" (132).[8]

The inconsistent naming of the technique—solarization or Sabatier effect—is also a matter of critical debate, and confusion about the exact nature of the process gives solarization "an ambiguity that persists to the present day," as William Jolly writes (chapter 1). According to Michael Langford in *The Darkroom Handbook*, solarization is defined as both the "reversal or partial reversal of the tones of a photographic image caused by extreme overexposure," and a "term commonly applied to partial reversal effects caused by fogging photographic material to light during development (strictly the Sabattier [*sic*] or pseudo-solarization effect)" (345). In other words, *solarization* is defined as extreme overexposure and a misnomer for the Sabatier effect. According to historian Mark Osterman, the term *solarization* is most accurate when describing the process conducted on a daguerreotype or a negative, whereas *Sabatier effect* describes exposure at the printing stage (Discussion).[9] For Jolly, solarization is overexposure before development; the Sabatier effect comes after development. Edwin Buffaloe notes—though Jolly disagrees—that in true solarization, "No second exposure is necessary to produce the reversal." According to Blanchere, it is possible to achieve solarization or the Sabatier effect through chemical means rather than light. This is a finding that, once again, Jolly refutes.

Man Ray's rediscovery of the Sabatier effect with Lee Miller in the 1920s is largely responsible for today's conflation of solarization with this distinct process. Ray describes his process as "solarization" instead of "the Sabatier effect," naming several images accordingly. His experimentations helped establish solarization as an art photography technique, and "Consequently," writes Jolly, "the word solarization has little ambiguity when used by amateur and fine-art photographers; to most the word signifies only the Sabatier effect. Ambiguity is much more probable in discourse with photographic scientists, who are more likely to be aware of, or concerned with, overexposure solarization" (chapter 1). Until Ray and Miller accidentally rediscovered the process, named it somewhat imprecisely, and thereafter used it deliberately,[10] solarization was generally treated as an overexposure mistake, an aberration, or at best an interesting side note to more mainstream developments in the science and art of photography. In the twentieth century, the

Sabatier effect and solarization were continually "discovered" or discovered in new forms. For example, Alfred Stieglitz writes on the back of his 1920 photograph *Hands and Thimble—Georgia O'Keeffe*, "(Historical note): first use of solarization as an integral part of a picture" (Rosenfeld 216).

Understood categorically as an overexposure effect, the term *solarization* can be subdivided more precisely yet: it can refer to the tonal reversal of extreme highlights in an image, such as Adams's and White's black suns; it can describe the tonal reversal, such as in the bluing of daguerreotypes; it can identify the tonal reversal of dense shadow tones in cyanotypes, as Herschel describes; it can similarly explain the tonal reversal of dense shadows in palladiotypes, as in Stieglitz's 1920 image; and it can refer to the Sabatier effect, a fogging of highlight areas on a print along with edge reversal. Walter Woodbury wrote in 1896 that "No satisfactory explanation has ever been given of this particular phenomenon" (462). This statement might be summarizing solarization in toto. Solarization's technique, its history, and the multiple uses to which it has been subjected may all be read as variations on a theme: articulations of ambiguity by definition and practice tied to this technique. The underlying subject of a solarized print is thus always the unstable limit between darkness and light. However marginalized by the recorded history of Victorian photography, solarization captures the uncertainties and instability of that early photography and thus shapes how we might read photography's impact on Victorian culture more generally. Solarization helps us see the contingency and mediation present in all photographic images, as well as the instability of light itself. To the extent that photography and realism are often read in tandem, solarization complicates this relationship.

Solarizing *Little Dorrit*

Jackson's letter appeared in 1857, the same year *Little Dorrit*'s original serialization concluded. The novel's treatment of light—its language of the line of demarcation, its description of a sun that renders the sea black and blue, its fixation on the indistinct limit between light and shadow—never mentions solarization, but I think we can hear echoes of the language used to describe it. Although the critical discussion of darkness has somewhat overshadowed the novel's treatment of light, that light is often a powerful presence: it is figured as a blaze, a stare, and a dazzle. Dickens wields light's power ironically to describe the obnoxiously radiant bride, Fanny, who exudes a glare that blots everything else out: "Few could have seen Little Dorrit for the glare" of her sister (510). For all its power, light does not remain metaphorically stable or otherwise act conventionally in *Little Dorrit.* It is often described as a glare that obscures rather than illuminates. Read alongside solarization, these disruptions register as more than just descriptive oddities—they represent a critique of realistic representation more generally. Jerome Beaty observes that the novel's opening is a "puzzling but emphatic exception to the traditional association of sun with life or the good and shadows with death or evil" (222), while Rosenberg suggests that "shadows are not simply patches of darkness but representations or simulacra . . . images of replication, distortion, and opposition" (43). Each sees part of the whole: the novel uses light and dark to interrogate truth and realism and to suggest a persistent focus on unreality in place of both. This is the project of solarization, rendered in language.

Another approach to these concerns is evident in how bodies of water in the novel frequently challenge the distinction between light and dark, good and evil, and reality and representation. Locked out of the Marshalsea overnight, Little Dorrit and Maggy wander over London Bridge, observing "little spots of lighted water where the bridge lamps were reflected, shining like demon eyes" (148). This reference to demon eyes joins the novel's opening description, discussed above, of a light that glares and stares in undermining the traditional association between light and the true and good. The River Saone reflects darkness as well: "like a sullied looking-glass in a gloomy place, [the stream] reflected the clouds heavily; and the low banks leaned over here and there, as if they were half curious, and half afraid, to see their darkening pictures in the water" (104).

Further into the novel, Arthur is unable to detect a distinction between land and water as he walks to the Meagles' home the day he learns of Minnie's engagement to Henry Gowan. He walks during sunset and observes that all of nature seems to be in a perfect state of equilibrium: "Between the real landscape and its shadow in the water, there was no division; both were so untroubled and clear" (280). Reality and representation are perfectly equated here, yet by the end of the chapter we learn that reality has not dominated in the comparison. Putting Minnie's roses in the river, he watches as "Pale and unreal in the moonlight, the river floated them away." He goes indoors while, Dickens repeats, "the flowers, pale and unreal in the moonlight, floated away upon the river; and thus do greater things that once were in our breasts, and near our hearts, flow from us to the eternal seas" (284). Rather than reflecting reality, the river is superimposed with "unreal" flowers. Instead of reinforcing the unreality of representation, the juxtaposition of reflective water and unreal flowers in this scene suggests an unreality in all things.

The novel also challenges the reality of visual perception in temporal terms. Submerged in one of Affery's dream chapters, Dickens describes the "mental unhealthiness" confronting recluses and invalids: "Pictures of demolished streets and altered houses, as they formerly were when the occupant of the chair was familiar with them; images of people as they too used to be, with little or no allowance made for the lapse of time since they were seen; of these, there must have been many in the long routine of gloomy days" (284). An invalid views static images very much like photographs—as frozen moments in time. The oppression of the first chapter's sunny glare occurs amid precisely this kind of arrested motion: "There was no wind to make a ripple on the foul water within the harbor, or on the beautiful sea without" (1). This motionless image follows what Roland Barthes describes as a realist understanding of the photographic: "The realists do not take the photograph for a 'copy' of reality, but for an emanation of *past reality* . . . The important thing is that the photograph possesses an evidential force, and that its testimony bears not on the object but on time" (88–89, emphasis in original). Traditionally understood, photography arrests motion, fixing reality as a thing experienced in the past.

Little Dorrit's photographic evocations follow an experimental logic. The novel's first words suggest movement by introducing the play between light and dark as a play between determinate and indeterminate, specific and vague: "Thirty years ago, Marseilles lay burning in the sun," Dickens writes, fixing the scene's temporal and physical location. But this is not the end of the sentence: "Thirty years ago, Marseilles lay burning in the sun, one day" (1). The added "one day" is out of place, awkwardly separated from the time "thirty years ago" by the location, "Marseilles." It also undermines the relative specificity of the first part of the sentence. This shift between the specific and the vague is a subtle reminder that what we take for realistic precision can be efficiently undercut with a comma and two small words. In contrast to the seascape that introduces the novel, *Little Dorrit* concludes on a "healthy autumn day," when "from the sea-shore the ocean was no longer to be seen lying asleep in the heat, but its thousand sparkling eyes were open, and its whole breadth was in joyful animation, from the cool sand on the beach to the little sails on the horizon, drifting away like autumn-tinted leaves that had drifted from the trees" (679). Static images are not dependable, for they make "little or no allowance" for the lapse of time; the only realistic kind of image is an unstable one—in constant motion between dark and light. *Little Dorrit* does not pretend to give us a picture of past realities but rather an image of the unrealities into which its characters are plunged.

The novel's illustrations are another crucial element to consider in this discussion of the way *Little Dorrit* asks us to see. Hablot Knight Browne portrays one such image of unreality in his title page etching (figure 2.5), which, as Elaine Showalter has observed, depicts Little Dorrit coming into the Marshalsea's "permanent shadow world" from the world of light outside (21). To portray the "shadow world" of the Marshalsea, Browne backlights Little Dorrit. Yet she is incompletely backlit: her face is somehow illuminated, indicating a light source coming from within the Marshalsea. Ostensibly, the image depicts the Marshalsea's position within a metaphoric dark/light binary, but Little Dorrit's illuminated face disrupts the opposition. Her cloak betrays a line of demarcation. Perhaps this is only the light from the outside world shining on her back as she enters the (not quite) darkness, but in the first bound edition, this image appeared at the start of the novel and frames Dickens's reference to the line of demarcation separating sea and harbor. Light, as we saw in the description of Little Dorrit inside the prison, intrudes on the Marshalsea's darkness. Sometimes, it also intrudes within the Marshalsea's darkness, as when the imprisoned Arthur sits in "the shadow of the wall," and "the shadow fell like light upon him" (633). Read metaphorically, this passage describes how the tables have turned. Because of a failed speculation, Arthur is now imprisoned; in this prison, shadow now falls like light. Treating shadow as a simile for light complicates the divide between the two. It also describes something very similar to photography—wherein the shadow on a negative becomes light in a print—and it describes solarization more specifically as the technique that highlights this play between darkness and light. Darkness may largely prevail inside the Marshalsea, but the limit between inside and outside is anything but firm: because it is a debtor's prison, family members such as Little Dorrit can of course leave the Marshalsea each day. A child born in the prison yet not a prisoner herself, Little Dorrit constantly traverses the boundary between the two—and as she does so, her presence in word and image alike trouble the distinction between light and dark, the laws of physics, and the unreal visual economy of the novel.

Our eponymous character questions visual reality when she finds herself suddenly wealthy at the start of book 2. Now out of the Marshalsea for good, Little Dorrit and her family travel to the Continent: "It was from

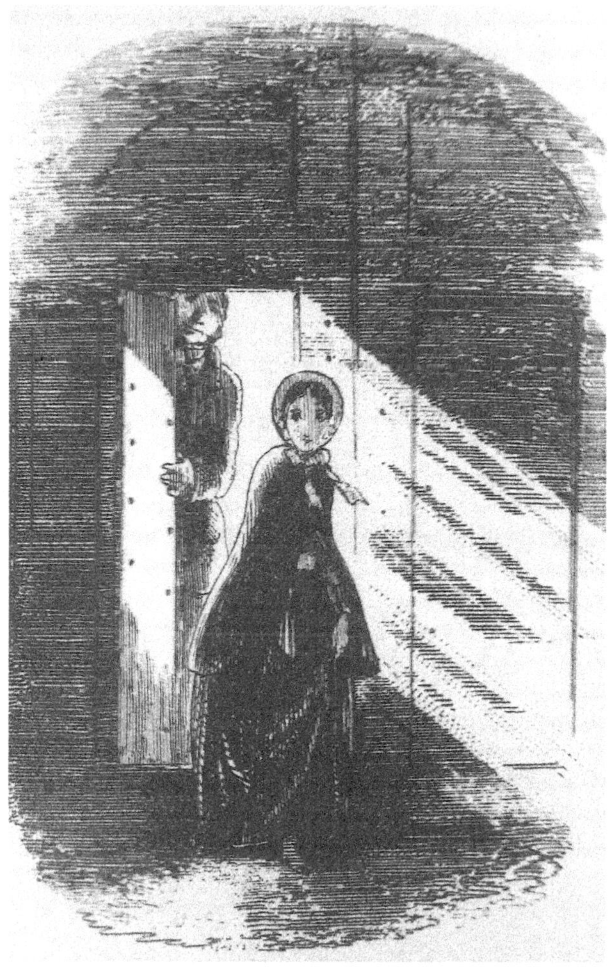

Figure 2.5. Hablot Knight Browne (Phiz), "Title Page," etching for *Little Dorrit* (London: Bradbury and Evans, 1857).

this position," sitting in a luxurious carriage traveling into Italy, that all Little Dorrit sees "appeared unreal; the more surprising the scenes, the more they resembled the unreality of her own inner life as she went through its vacant places all day long." Everything she experiences abroad is a series of "unrealities," "only the old Marshalsea a reality," but even then, only a reality with her father inside (387–88). The "crowning unreality" is Venice, "where all the streets were paved with water" (389). Little Dorrit muses that the residents of Venice "were not realities . . . such people were all unknown to her," for the only "lasting realities" are the fellow prisoners of her former life. As she gazes on the other unreal people around her, she watches the sunset, "in its long low lines of purple and red, and its burning flush high up into the sky." The sun is "so glowing on the buildings, and so lightening their structure, that it made them look as if their strong walls were transparent, and they shone from within" (390). As in a solarized image, light follows an alternative logic. Underscoring the scene and the people, the light performs an unreal trick, functioning not as something projected by the sun onto the building but from the building out. Like the blazing sun at the start of the novel, this unreal light emphasizes the theme of unreality Little Dorrit experiences all around her. Dickens uses light to radically question what we think we know about reality and representation.

The novel concludes with a description of Little Dorrit and Arthur going "quietly down into the roaring streets, inseparable and blessed; and as they passed along in sunshine and in shade, the noisy and the eager, and the arrogant and the froward and the vain, fretted, and chafed, and made their usual uproar" (688). Unlike the litany at the start of *Tale*, this is emphatically not a series of opposites but a cacophony of stimuli. Echoing the first chapter title, "Sun and Shadow," this "sunshine and shade" sustains the play between the two to the end. Decide for yourselves, Dickens seems to be saying to his reader: will you go "quietly" into a "blessed" life, despite the roar? This shared self-possession—this inner sense of "usefulness and happiness"—is not given by the external world but is experienced in spite of that world. The external world—the world of the roar, the noise, the sunshine, and the shade described throughout the novel—is, *Little Dorrit* insists time and again, best understood as an unreal world. It is a world that does not obey the logic of metaphysical truth or photographic objectivity; it is an experimental world through which our main characters must make their own way. Little Dorrit and Arthur spend the novel at odds with one another—Little Dorrit living in the prison with her father, while Arthur is free and in love with Minnie, Arthur imprisoned once Little Dorrit is free—but they come together at the end for all their differences, themselves like sunshine and shade combined.

Little Dorrit reimagines truth and realism in its play of light and dark. Solarization was the nineteenth-century name for the technique that most overtly challenged the separation between light and shadow, the truth metaphorically connoted by light, and the objectivity implied by photographic representation. These are challenges contained within every photograph, but they are highlighted in solarization. Analogously, *Little Dorrit* does not portray vision according to the conventional logic of photographic objectivity. The world of this novel is one where light does not illuminate the truth but blinds, where the limit between light and dark is not always distinct, and where what is seen is sometimes unreal. For all of *Little Dorrit*'s light, the novel gives us a dark view of illumination—but, the novel insists, that is not necessarily a negative thing. Challenging illumination in this way allows Dickens to implicitly challenge the authority of photography, including, by extension, the photographs of himself he found to be so counterfeit.

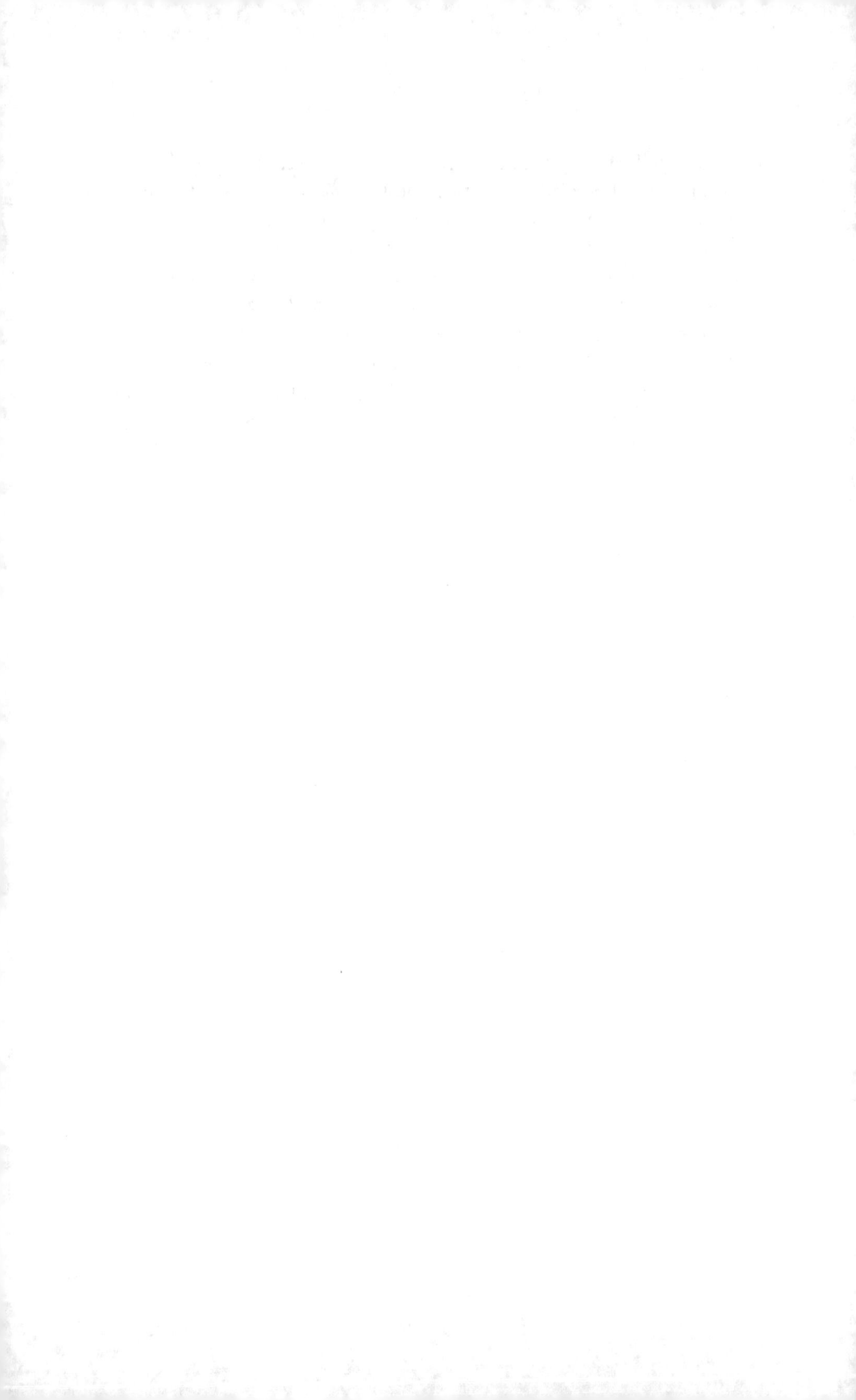

Chapter 3

The Forensic Photograph and the Cabinet Card

Failing to Observe with Sherlock Holmes

At the start of Arthur Conan Doyle's third short story, "A Case of Identity," Holmes and Watson ponder the nature of reality and representation. "Life," Holmes insists,

> is infinitely stranger than anything which the mind of man could invent. . . . If we could fly out of that window hand in hand, hover over this great city, gently remove the roofs, and peep in at the queer things which are going on, the strange coincidences, the plannings, the cross-purposes, the wonderful chains of events, working through generations, and leading to the most *outré* results, it would make all fiction with its conventionalities and foreseen conclusions most stale and unprofitable. (Conan Doyle, *Sherlock Holmes* 1:287–88)

Watson disagrees. He believes that such strange occurrences are far from the stuff of fiction: "We have in our police reports realism pushed to its extreme limits, and yet the result is, it must be confessed, neither fascinating nor artistic" (1:288). Watson finds that such police reports are "perfectly familiar" in that they follow a predictable pattern. His view is that the police reports provide a catalog of sameness, a litany of reports each just like the last, whereas Holmes insists that life is more interesting than fiction or the imagination.

This conversation initially appears predictable. Holmes's method, after all, depends on the observation of minute details and deductions based on such observations. Meanwhile, Watson—as Holmes's foil—allows us to learn about the mind of the great detective. Yet the conversation soon turns its focus away from the value of observing detail and toward the role of detail and observation in the creation of reality and art. During his conversation with Watson, Holmes reveals a desire to "peep in" at the things people do in the privacy of their homes and their "purposes," "chains of events," "plannings," and happenings "working through generations"—in short, details privy to the psychologies of the people involved, details from a portion of the narrative that exists outside the frame of the picture. These internal details are the things that supersede "all fiction with its conventionalities." Holmes admits that "A certain selection and discretion must be used in producing a realistic effect," a selection and discretion wanting in police reports, with their mere catalog of details.

What makes this tête-à-tête worth pausing over is that throughout their conversation, Holmes and Watson exchange their more conventionally understood roles. Watson focuses on the details of the police report, whereas Holmes pays lip service to details and emphasizes the virtues of selection and discretion—of going beyond those details. In this scene, Watson describes contemporary police work as operating like what we may think of as traditional detective practice, whereas Holmes gives us a view that is much more internal, holistic, and artistic. Holmes provides a theory of the nineteenth-century scientist, as well as the literary realist, as a discriminating observer, picking and choosing the things worth noticing. On one hand, his discriminating view is shared by the trained judgment of scientists described by Lorraine Daston and Peter Galison in their history of objectivity; on the other hand, he expresses such selective judgment in romantic terms, expressing the desire to fly out into the city to view queer things that make works of fiction stale and pale in comparison. Holmes presents a theory about the discretion and artistry of details. This, he suggests, is what grounds his own detective practice—not the sheer volume of those details.

The conversation between Holmes and Watson at the start of "A Case of Identity" frames a critique of vision that also proves central to the first short story of the Holmes canon, "A Scandal in Bohemia." An exemplar of scientific practice, Holmes is typically read to have what Elizabeth Miller describes as "professional objectivity, paralleling contemporary efforts to define science in these terms" (32). Yet Holmes fails to live up to this ideal. In "A Scandal in Bohemia," his fallibility is first and most famously expressed through an exchange with a scandalous celebrity photograph, but it also compels a rethinking of vision altogether, for vision itself proves to be suspect. This fallibility is a sign of the times: as Jordan Bear notes, during the first decades of photography, "What constituted 'the real' was undergoing a thorough reevaluation" (24). In a discussion of combination photography, Bear explains how "the properties of neutrality and objectivity were quickly undermined by images that had no holistic referent in reality" (32).

With a few notable exceptions, photography is marginalized in the detective's investigative repertoire, fleeting and largely incidental to the story's plot and theme; in all but one case, photography is a practice Holmes observes rather than an essential technique in which he participates. Significantly, those instances of photography within the Holmes canon are themselves undermined, as though to contain the anxieties of unmitigated reproduction and the inversion of truth inherent in negative-based photographic processes. Holmes appears in place of these processes: like a camera himself, complete with a photographic memory, the detective seemingly has little need for photographs. Photography is most thoroughly undermined in its appearance through the cabinet card of the king of Bohemia and his celebrity mistress Irene Adler in "A Scandal in Bohemia." This story's resolution hinges on photographic failure, a failure enabled by the negative through both the unacknowledged multiplicity of the missing photograph that makes the containment of the image an impossibility, as well as the inversion of Holmes's and Adler's roles in the course of the case. Whereas at the time photography was routinely deployed as an objective science in its application to detective work, and whereas Conan Doyle himself upheld the truth value of photography in his own life—even to the point of adamantly championing the occult represented through evidence of the spirit world shown in spirit photographs—the most quintessential detective in literary history shows photography to be a source of deception in some instances. This deception is effective because it places Holmes in the position of the fan, captivated by Adler's celebrity image.

Although he problematizes vision via photography with a distinctly fin-de-siècle flavor, Conan Doyle's detective shares with Dickens's literary works a challenge to photographic objectivity writ large. This challenge is similarly articulated along the fault lines of reproducibility and inversion, thus suggesting in Conan Doyle's work a connection back to earlier photographic discourses and forward to more sweeping theories about optics. Indeed, in the later decades of the century, the New Physics continued to challenge established visual epistemologies. The New Physics, which in the early twentieth century led to quantum mechanics, was in the latter decades of the nineteenth century characterized by a questioning of the physical properties of light: was light comprised of particles, or did it operate as a wave? The failure of vision in "A Scandal in Bohemia" is not simply about the fallibility of photography but also a larger perceived threat, expressed contemporaneously in discourses surrounding the nascent New Physics, to the meaning of vision and truth itself.

I begin with a consideration of the role of photography in forensic science and the spiritualist movement—both significant for Conan Doyle—before analyzing how photography is mobilized in the Holmes canon. Across the Holmes canon, photography operates as a contradiction: it is a science yet somehow beyond science, it is a marker of objectivity yet also the vehicle through which Holmes's objectivity is undermined, and it is a source of truth, yet specifically in "A Scandal in Bohemia" it is rejected for another form of evidence—the written word. Photography's contradictions in "A Scandal in Bohemia" coalesce around the specter of image reproducibility and the theme of inversion, which are encoded metaphorically into the story's questioning of truth. In short, they emerge in those qualities enabled by the negative, using a technology often wielded as a vehicle for objectivity to undermine that objectivity. Notably, the photograph in "A Scandal in Bohemia" is a celebrity photograph of not one but two celebrities: the king and the actress—and although the king clearly outranks the actress, it is Adler's celebrity that reigns supreme. The image functions as a celebrity photograph ought, which is to say it promises proximity to the celebrity but then denies that very proximity. In Holmes's failure, we see the fusion of scientific theory and celebrity culture, represented by a photograph. The implications of this failed vision stretch beyond photography and celebrity culture, to scientific debates about the nature of light.

Photography and Detection

While photography's dual roles in both forensic science and the spiritualist movement may seem incongruous to modern viewers—the one interested in documenting fact, the other in faking it—they share more than a cursory glance acknowledges. Both reflect a preoccupation with objectivity and an implicit challenge to that objectivity. This contradiction is essential to Conan Doyle's use of photography in his detective stories. As a trained ophthalmologist and photographer who wrote about a detective, Conan Doyle was steeped in the world of photographic objectivity.[1] However, his photographic writings and his famous literary detective serve as critiques of photographic objectivity from the inside out.

From its earliest days, photography was lauded for its scientific promise, including its promise to aid the field of forensic science. As discussed in the introduction, photography received a mixed reception in its earliest years, with some critics considering it a science and others somewhat controversially treating it as an art. Scientific photography was a dominant species: Keller observes that "science ranked high among the applications first proposed for the nascent photographic medium, as so many of its early practitioners were scientists themselves" (21). Yet Bear notes that photographic objectivity was from photography's inception a matter for debate: "The first decades of photography were contemporary with a period of extraordinary ambivalence about the nature of illusion and its role in a modern urban culture whose identity consisted in large part of the revelation of those forces—physical, chemical, and biological—which undergirded the lived experience of its populace" (24). The exact nature of photography was a matter of discussion, in other words, and it oscillated somewhere between science and art, occupying neither space absolutely. One of photography's first applications was portraiture, a form of documentation that nevertheless often exists in the service of affect. Lady Eastlake notes this in her 1857 essay "Photography," when she writes of the photographic portraits that dominate the photographic sphere. For Eastlake, photography's value lies in the communication it forges between individuals; she rhetorically asks, what are "nine-tenths of those facial maps called photographic portraits, but accurate landmarks and measurements for loving eyes and memories to deck with beauty and animate with expression, in perfect certainty, that the ground-plan is founded upon fact?" (65). She does not view photography as an art, but rather than considering it a dispassionate science, she reads in portraiture the expression of individuals' desires to connect with one another. Photography therefore inhabits a space between art and objective documentation—a space Conan Doyle uneasily depicts in his detective fiction.

Family portraits were a dominant photographic genre throughout the century. Photography's popularity in England and the United States was immediate and pervasive: "portrait studios abounded in almost every city, and itinerant photographers moved from town to town to meet the seemingly universal demand," as Ronald R. Thomas writes (*Detective Fiction* 113). Yet this was not the only way people were captured on film. Thomas continues,

> Virtually from the moment of its invention . . . photographic portraiture was also deployed in an entirely antithetical way. Not only an ideal medium for personal celebration, photography

> offered the perfect technique for public surveillance as well. . . . The immediate adaptation of photography to the bureaucratic procedures of personal documentation and identification in police work seemed as natural as its rapid rise to popularity among the middle classes as an inexpensive form of personal portraiture. (113)

Beginning in the 1840s but starting more systematically in the 1880s, photography was used to aid in law enforcement, most overwhelmingly in the form of mug shots. Henry Fox Talbot writes in *The Pencil of Nature* that photographs could be used to document images of valuable property in the event that the property was stolen,[2] but the primary use of photography in police work was through images taken of suspects and criminals. In 1846, US photographer Mathew Brady was asked to contribute to Marmaduke Sampson's *The Rationale of Crime and its Appropriate Treatment* with an appendix of New York prisoner portraits. These portraits represent the first mug shots, a trend that picked up steam in the 1850s with "rogues' galleries" of criminal portraits kept by law enforcement in Europe and the United States. In 1870, notes Stephen Monteiro, "the British government required all prisoners to be photographed, with additional prints sent to Scotland Yard for a national archive" (345).

Most famously, photography was put to forensic work by an English statistician and, quite differently, by a French physical anthropologist. Whereas Francis Galton developed a system of photographic composites to derive a criminal type from the superimposition of many criminal portraits, Alphonse Bertillon created for each suspect a separate full-face and profile photographic image plus additional statistical information. Galton was interested in discovering the criminal type, but Bertillon sought to document as many criminals as possible—as many as 4,500, according to his claim in 1893 (Monteiro 345). These uses of photography—as classification and division—were noteworthy at the time: Bertillon's innovations make their way into Conan Doyle's *The Hound of the Baskervilles* and the story "The Naval Treaty." Holmes is impressed by Bertillon's system in "The Naval Treaty," expressing to Watson "enthusiastic admiration of the French savant" (1:723). Crime scene photography was another forensic use of the technology, although as Monteiro writes, "Despite occasional examples reaching as far back as the 1860s, crime scene photography only became standard practice in the closing years of the 19th century, as police departments hired staff photographers and the invention of flash photography made on-the-spot field work practical" (345).[3] By documenting evidence, recording crime scenes, and cataloging suspects and criminals, photography had proven indispensable to police work by the end of the century.

Critics link the development of the detective novel in part to the rise of forensic science and more specifically to the increasing role of photography in this science—detective fiction and the development of modern police force were "coincident," as Thomas writes (*Detective Fiction* 4).[4] Edgar Allan Poe, who authored what is widely held to be the first modern detective story in English, "Murders of the Rue Morgue" (1841)—brings photography and the work of the detective together in his description of "The Daguerreotype." This essay, written a year before his famous short story, extolls photography's proximity to truth even under the scrutiny of "a powerful microscope":

> If we examine a work of ordinary art, by means of a powerful microscope, all traces of resemblance to nature will disappear—but the closest scrutiny of the photogenic drawing discloses only a more absolute truth, a more perfect identity of aspect with the thing represented. The variations of shade, and the gradations of both linear and aerial perspective are those of truth itself in the supremeness of its perfection. (5)

Citing Poe's enthusiastic statements about the absolute verisimilitude of photography "and its capacity to capture rather than simply to represent the real," Thomas notes statements such as these "not only anticipated the talents of his fictional private eye, they also heralded the almost instantaneous deployment of the camera in actual police work" (*Detective Fiction* 114). Literary works did not simply reflect the rise of the detective—they helped shape that figure.

From the early 1840s on, photography, police work, and literature were entwined in a self-creating and self-sustaining project. Photography's resonance with both scientific and artistic communities makes it a fitting compatriot of the developing genre of detective fiction, itself a combination of art and forensic science. Moreover, as Thomas argues in another study, photography and literary art share a preoccupation with photography's central concern: light. "Together," writes Thomas, "camera and literary detective developed a practical procedure to accomplish what the new discipline of criminal anthropology attempted more theoretically: to make darkness visible—giving us a means to recognize the criminal in our midst by changing the way we see and by redefining what is important for us to notice" ("Making Darkness Visible" 135). Photography and literary works both function by eradicating darkness and shedding light on plot, scene, or criminal; both photography and detective fiction serve the pursuit of truth. Yet photography troubles this pursuit in Conan Doyle's detective fiction.

The idea of photography as objective illuminator certainly seems to have appealed to the young Conan Doyle, who developed an avid interest in photography while studying to be a medical doctor. Between 1881 and 1885 he published fourteen articles in the *British Journal of Photography* and the *British Journal Photographic Almanac for 1883* about his experiences with and observations of the technology. Biographer Martin Booth argues that he "had a firm ground knowledge of photography but, in his straitened circumstances, he could not afford expensive equipment," perhaps accounting for the drop in his interest in the mid-1880s (65). Even so, several of Conan Doyle's articles describe his own experiments, so he must have owned or borrowed photographic equipment. He writes in "After Cormorants with a Camera" about manipulating negatives to create the best effect of "artifice" (534). However, most of his writings on photography support the view that he considered it a technology with which to be experimented, not a means of trickery. In another article, "On the Reproduction of Negatives," he weighs in on the question of negative duplication, a question "of no little importance at the present day, owing to the large number of prints now so frequently required for publication and other purposes, and which it would be impossible to produce within reasonable period from one negative" (535). This essay, as I discuss below, indicates that Conan Doyle was aware duplication was a key aspect of photography. Other titles such as "A Few Technical Hints," "Trial of Burton's Emulsion Process," and several travel pieces for the *British Journal of Photography*'s "Where to Go with the Camera" series support a view of Conan Doyle as a proponent of photography's documentary and scientific uses.

In later life, Conan Doyle rarely mentioned these earlier articles. As Booth writes, this could be part of a larger effacement of his early life and difficult circumstances or possibly his response, in the *British Journal of Photography* in 1883, to another essay, "a piece concerning psychic photography and a psychic force known as Od" (65). Conan Doyle is critical of this essay, and here we begin to see the origins of his rationally minded detective. He excoriates the piece based on its corruption of the scientific method: "Mr. Warner cites as facts things which are incorrect," he writes, "and that in a crisp and epigrammatic way which is delightful. From these so-called facts he draws inferences which, even if they were facts indeed, would be illogical, and upon these illogical inferences draws deductions which, once more, no amount of concession would render tenable" ("The 'New' Scientific Subject" 418). Sounding a bit like his future famed detective, Conan Doyle champions a scientific approach and uses it to critique the article: when "a communication which abounds in scientific errors appears in an eminent scientific journal, it is not right that it should be allowed to pass uncorrected or unchallenged. Let Mr. Warner mature his views for another twelve years or so, and then give them light more logically and less dogmatically" (418). This is clear critique of psychic photography as described in the *British Journal of Photography* article.[5]

However, spirit photography was not, as Conan Doyle and others would have seen it, necessarily incompatible with the younger writer's views. Tim Gunning writes, in "Invisible Worlds, Visible Media," that "from the middle of the nineteenth century on, photography intertwined with other visual devices not simply to record a recognizable world, but also to provide images of a previously invisible one" (54). Whether this previously invisible world featured microbes shown through microphotography or the spirit world captured by spirit photographs, the message for many viewers remained the same: photography allowed one to see that which had not been seen before. The use of photography to capture spirits was not necessarily something that should be accepted without proper recourse to the scientific method and appropriate uses of logic, but it was often accepted as part of a larger catalog of objects and phenomena that had been previously unseen and unknown, and that science and the technology of photography was making more visible every day. Conan Doyle became interested in spiritualism in 1886, according to Georgina Byrne, and he joined the Society for Psychical Research in 1893.

In his *History of Spiritualism*, Conan Doyle frequently wields logic to frame his defense of the movement. In his chapter on spirit photography he writes that

> Modern researches have proved that these psychic results are not obtained, in some instances at least, through the lens of the camera. On many occasions, under test conditions, these supernormal pictures have been secured from an unopened box of photographic plates. . . . Whatever the eventual explanation, the only hypothesis which at present covers the facts is that of a wise invisible Intelligence. (2:147, 149)

He "cannot deny, however, that it has been occasionally made the tool of rogues, nor can we confidently assert that, because some results of any medium are genuine, we are therefore justified in accepting without question whatever else may come" (2:151). Yet he argues, "In pointing out the evidence for the psychic cocoon, the author hopes that he has made some small contribution to the better understanding of the mechanism of psychic photography. It is a very true branch of psychic science, as every earnest investigator will discover" (2:151). These are not the words of someone who sees photography as nonscientific.[6] Indeed, Srdjan Smajic notes that both "ghost and detective fiction are structured by and in conversation with contemporary philosophical and scientific work on visual perception" (3). Just as the literary genres are linked through this interest in visual perception, so are contemporaneous views of detection and observations about the spirit world. The two converge in fiction and photography; as Christopher Rovee suggests, "Between empiricism and impressionism, materialism and spiritualism, science and art: the predicament of photography in its halting first half-century is persistently its uncertain ontological location" (392).

To the end of his life, Conan Doyle insisted on the veracity of spirit photography and the spirit world it documented.[7] Biographers generally agree that the deaths of his wife, son, brother, two brothers-in-law, and two nephews in the early twentieth century gave Conan Doyle an incentive to overlook arguments against spirit photography. But even before these tragic decades, according to Booth, "For Conan Doyle, science could not exist without there being some spiritual quality to it. Existentiality was not enough" (61). Conan Doyle's belief in spiritualism and spirit photography often remains an embarrassment to fans who see in Sherlock Holmes the antithesis of these views,[8] yet for Conan Doyle the world of the detective and the world of spirits were not incommensurate.

Nevertheless, there is an incompatibility buried in Conan Doyle's works about Holmes—a contradiction surrounding the seemingly infallible detective and his machine-like reasoning skills. This contradiction pivots around the uses of photography in the stories, but rather than suggest that the detective's world and the spirit world are incompatible, I argue that the conflict resides in photography itself. Conan Doyle shows us via a limited treatment of photography throughout the Holmes canon that the technology is—for all its acclaim as, as Poe puts it, "truth itself"—often a source of unease for the famous literary detective ("The Daguerreotype" 2). Occasionally used by the detective and others in their work, photography's most famous appearance in the Holmes canon is in "A Scandal in Bohemia," where it challenges Holmes, that "perfect reasoning and observing machine," by undermining his skills of detection (1:239). Instead of illuminating man's fallibility in comparison to the superior technology, photography slinks out of the story's frame—ultimately of little use in the resolution. A technology that should logically play a major role throughout the Holmes canon is in fact very limited, controlled, and at times undermined.[9]

The Private Eye

In many of the Holmes stories, photography—when it is present at all—appears in a very limited way as a naturalized technology of forensic science. It is sometimes wielded as an objective form of visual proof, which we see in "Silver Blaze," "The Yellow Face," "The Second Stain," "The Adventure of the Cardboard Box," and "The Adventure of the Illustrious Client." In "Silver Blaze," for instance, Holmes uses the photograph of the murdered John Straker to help prove the man had been leading a double life and thus help confirm that he had intended on maiming the racehorse Silver Blaze so as to bet against him and defraud other gamblers. Photography is also used as proof of a double life and affection in "The Yellow Face": suspicious of his wife, Grant Munro goes to a nearby house where "all my suspicions rose into a fierce, bitter flame when I saw that on the mantelpiece stood a copy of a full-length photograph of my wife, which had been taken at my request only three months ago" (*Sherlock Holmes* 1:558). The photograph seems to prove that Munro's wife has been loose with her affections, though we later learn that she was previously married to a black American man and kept her child, a "little coal-black negress," forced to wear a mask to help hide her mother's shame, in the house across the street, unbeknownst to her second husband (1:563).

Photography is proof of identity in "The Second Stain," proof of familial relationship in "The Adventure of the Cardboard Box," and proof of debauchery in "The Adventure of the Illustrious Client." In this last story, a "beastly book" of "Snapshot photographs" proves that Adelbert Gruner is a sinful womanizer (2:523). The album is, as Holmes puts it, a "lust diary" and even inspires the unemotional detective to "plead" with Adelbert's fiancée "with all the warmth of words that I could find in my nature" to leave the man (2:536, 525). These words do not have the desired effect, but the book of photographs proves to be a "tremendous weapon," for if photographic evidence "will not break off the marriage, nothing ever could"

(2:536). These examples of photographic objectivity clash, however, with its most sustained treatment in "A Scandal in Bohemia," where its purported objectivity is undermined within the plot, challenged by its own technical processes of reproducibility and inversion.

While photography peppers the Holmes canon more subtly than one might expect given its use in forensic science at the time, it is simultaneously so naturalized in the world of forensic science that Holmes is described as being like a camera himself. Watson describes Holmes at the start of "A Scandal in Bohemia," explaining his emotions for "*the* woman" Irene Adler could not possibly be love:

> It was not that he felt any emotion akin to love for Irene Adler. All emotions, and that one particularly, were abhorrent to his cold, precise but admirably balanced mind. He was, I take it, the most perfect reasoning and observing machine that the world has seen, but as a lover he would have placed himself in a false position. He never spoke of the softer passions, save with a gibe and a sneer. They were admirable things for the observer—excellent for drawing the veil from men's motives and actions. But for the trained reasoner to admit such intrusions into his own delicate and finely adjusted temperament was to introduce a distracting factor which might throw a doubt upon all his mental results. Grit in a sensitive instrument, or a crack in one of his own high-power lenses, would not be more disturbing than a strong emotion in a nature such as his. And yet there was but one woman to him, and that woman was the late Irene Adler, of dubious and questionable memory. (1:239)

Here love is the antithesis of the mind of the scientist—it is grit or a crack in the lens of the mind of the detective, a veil blurring the instrument, which is the mind of the reasoner. The lens metaphor may easily indicate a magnifying glass or a microscope, but the story's subsequent focus on photography prompts the deduction that Watson is comparing Holmes to a camera. Indeed, given his precise recall of visual evidence when piecing together solutions to his cases, Holmes may be said to possess a photographic memory. The *Oxford English Dictionary* informs us that the term *photographic memory*, which in the twentieth century became known as eidetic memory, was first used in print in 1884, in the Dunkirk, New York *Saturday Evening Observer*. The concept thus predates Holmes and reasonably explains his visual precision.

In other stories, it becomes clear that photography is not only a metaphor for the detective but a technology on which he relies. In "The Adventure of the Lion's Mane," Holmes takes a photograph of the strange marks on the deceased McPherson. "I have examined them very carefully with a lens," he declares, and bringing out a photographic enlargement, states, "This is my method in such cases" (2:686–87). As Allen H. Butler deduces in his speculation for the *Baker Street Journal*, given Holmes's acumen as a chemist and his "natural unwillingness to possess less than total control of his detective methods," it stands to reason with "plausible probability that he did have photo-processing capability at the Villa" (160). In this one story, Butler shows, it follows that rather than simply being acquainted with photography or using photography as a detective method, Holmes may have been a photographer. Nevertheless, this thread is never revisited, and photography once more fades into the background.

Although it would appear that photography is the perfect metaphor and tool for a machine-like detective, in several instances photography is not purely objective but obscures, distracts, or otherwise operates as a red herring in the case. For example, in "The Red-Headed League," photography is a ruse. The pawnbroker Jabez Wilson is under the impression that his assistant goes to the cellar to develop photographs at the most inconvenient times, when in fact photography is a cover story to obscure the tunnel to a nearby bank he is helping construct. A photographic darkroom is also used as an excuse in "The Adventure of the Copper Beeches," with the intent of keeping a suspicious governess out of a section of the house. As well as occasionally obscuring the truth, photography appears as embellishment in the case—inessential to the case's resolution, it nonetheless contributes gravitas. In "The Adventure of Charles Augustus Milverton," a woman blackmailed by Milverton kills her blackmailer and Holmes lets her escape. Walking along Oxford Street at the end of the story, Holmes and Watson encounter "a shop window filled with photographs of the celebrities and beauties of the day" (1:924). One photograph in particular, "a regal and stately lady in Court dress, with a high diamond tiara upon her noble head," makes them pause, for it is an image of the blackmailed woman. This photograph, and "the time-honoured title of the great nobleman and statesman whose wife she had been," serve as the story's conclusion. Although not essential to the resolution of the case, the celebrity photograph makes it clear just how dangerous the blackmailer had been—and how high up the social ladder he was able to reach with his noxious influence.

This story from 1904 was not the first time Conan Doyle brought together photography and celebrity. "A Scandal in Bohemia" offers the most sustained and complete critique of photography across the Holmes stories and novels in that it sets up photography as a mechanism of objectivity and then undermines that objectivity. In the process it mobilizes concerns about not only multiplication and inversion but also the impact of those techniques on celebrity and the realism demanded of detective fiction. "A Scandal in Bohemia" is a unique story within the Holmes canon. Whereas Conan Doyle's two previously published Sherlock Holmes novels, *A Study in Scarlet* and *The Sign of Four*, could only claim moderate success, with "A Scandal in Bohemia" Holmes "blazed into popularity" (Carr 64). "A Scandal in Bohemia" and the stories that followed engaged the public in a way the novels had not and helped produce a readership, or more appropriately a fan base, still famous for its intensity and longevity.

The story is also unique because it represents a rare example of a suspect besting the detective, and it marks the only time Holmes is tricked by a woman. Near the start of the story, Holmes is hired by the king of Bohemia to retrieve an incriminating cabinet card of the king with a woman, Irene Adler. The king is betrothed to a woman of his own rank, and his former lover Adler has blackmailed him with the photograph. Holmes connives to trick Adler into disclosing the location of the photograph and then take it from her but finds himself outsmarted: Adler has disguised herself by dressing in men's clothing and escaped, along with the image. She leaves behind a photograph of herself and note for the king, promising she will not use the incriminating image against him.

The story begins by foreshadowing Holmes's failure. As Watson narrates,

> To Sherlock Holmes she is always *the* woman. I have seldom heard him mention her under any other name. In his eyes she eclipses and predominates the whole of her sex . . . there was but one woman to him, and that woman was the late Irene Adler, of dubious and questionable memory. (1:239, emphasis in original)

Holmes does not love Adler, Watson suggests, because love is abhorrent to him; it is "grit" in the sensitive instrument of his perfect reasoning mind. Adler comes to represent the whole of her sex; yet as the story will show, Holmes's high-power lens manages to crack. He is no ordinary detective—he is a perfect observing machine, and for that the failure is more significant. "A Scandal in Bohemia" reveals Holmes's fallibility and the fallibility of vision more broadly in the form of the photograph. Somewhat against the grain of critics, such as Thomas, who identify the story's central drama as the failure of the detective, I suggest that Holmes's failure signals a much larger failure: the failure of visual evidence. Holmes fails because he relies too much on visual evidence—what he thinks he sees of Adler and a photographic record he thinks he must trust. In the story, visual evidence reaffirms gender stereotypes and supports a technical trust of photography but simultaneously undermines both. Even though Watson establishes our intrepid detective as the flawless observing machine, vision fails Holmes and the story in two significant ways and thus illustrates an unease with epistemologies of vision. This fictional unease is vectored through photography in the form of a photographic image that cannot be contained and a photographic subject who cannot be accurately seen. Resonating with contemporaneous developments in optics, the story uses photography to represent a larger anxiety about the truthfulness of what we see. "A Scandal in Bohemia" expresses the visual instability of its historical moment and positions Holmes not as a new model of observation but as a product of his time—one particularly skeptical of photographic truth claims. Unable to evolve his form of vision, Holmes fails to see the solution to or implications of this case—all he can see is the celebrity Adler.

Before the king of Bohemia pays Holmes and Watson a visit near the start of the story, Holmes explains to Watson why Watson fails as an investigator: he sees but he does not observe. Rather than seeing the seventeen steps making up the staircase in his house, Holmes knows they are there, "because," as he says, "I have both seen and observed" (1:242). *Observe* is the right term for what Holmes does: he watches things, he inspects, he detects scientifically. From these observations, he derives deductions: answers resulting from a process of reasoning and inference. He does not simply see or literally perceive—a word that can connote the imagination, dreams, visions, and, in a definition coined a few years after this story, the operation of cameras themselves. While sight emphasizes a single sense, observation includes sight and other senses and cognitive abilities. Most of Holmes's evidence is visual, but he uses multiple senses simultaneously to arrive at the most accurate result. Explaining to Watson how he knows the doctor has started working again, Holmes lists the scent of idioform and the sight of a black mark of nitrate silver as his primary clues. Scent aids sight, and they reinforce one another to produce the observation. Although he asserts the value of sight and observation more generally—and, indeed, the dependence of observation on sight—the story that follows suggests that instead of an aid to knowledge, sight is a hindrance.

The opening situates Holmes as the quintessential observer who goes deeper than sight alone. However, instead of observing, he merely sees when it comes to Adler. She addles him and leads him to misjudge her. He initially stereotypes her based on her sex, declaring to Watson, "When a woman thinks that her house is on fire, her instinct is at once to rush to the thing which she values most." This, Holmes continues, "is a perfectly overpowering impulse" for women, and "I have more than once taken advantage of it . . . A married woman grabs at her baby; an unmarried one reaches for her jewel box" (1:258). Leaving aside all the gender assumptions and logical leaps at play in this passage, we can observe that Holmes has clearly misread this particular unmarried woman. He is right in the sense that the threat of fire drives Adler to her hiding place, but he fails to see beyond the stereotype after this scene. He merely sees her as she appears in her cabinet card. He does not recognize her disguised as a man or realize that she has read through the situation, evaded him, and escaped. He has been seeing her as a stereotypical woman, a celebrity on a card—not a woman who dresses like a man and thinks like him. Elizabeth Miller suggests that "Conan Doyle's stories put forth a far more compound and ambivalent theory of gender, vision, and the public than has been previously acknowledged; they support the authority of the gaze and locate ontology in image, *except* when depicting women criminals" (69, emphasis in original). Yet rather than maintaining an objective view except when challenged by women, the challenge gender poses to Holmes throws the rest of the scientist's powers of vision into question. Although this gendered "grit" in his lens likely exists because of contemporaneous feminine disobedience, as Miller notes, that is not the end of the story. This visual disruption is mobilized by gender but not confined to it—rather, this gendered moment of anxiety opens up an instability of vision that exceeds gender and, indeed, all subjectivity.

Holmes's failure to go beyond sight alone and really observe Adler perhaps makes sense in a story where visual evidence holds such pride of place. Early on, the story establishes a photograph—a technology of sight—as the ultimate evidence: indisputable proof. The king hires Holmes because he is concerned about the scandal that may erupt when a photograph of himself and the lower-class actress surfaces. Initially, Holmes dismisses the scandal: "Was there a secret marriage?" he asks, "No legal papers or certificates?" Without these, he continues, "If this young person should produce her letters for blackmailing or other purposes, how is she to prove their authenticity?" The king suggests that "there is the writing." "Pooh, pooh! Forgery," responds Holmes. "My private note-paper," the king continues. "Stolen," Holmes answers. "My own seal," says the king. "Imitated," offers

Holmes. "My photograph," the king goes on. "Bought," concludes Holmes. "We were both in the photograph," continues the king. This stops Holmes: "Oh, dear!" he responds, "That is very bad! Your Majesty has indeed committed an indiscretion" (1:246–47). The indiscretion, as Holmes frames it, is not the affair but the existence of visual evidence of it. Handwriting, private paper, and personal seals alone are not solid enough evidence, but a photograph of the two together—well, Holmes cannot explain away this type of proof. Photography here is presented as unquestionable, hard visual evidence.[10]

It does not seem to matter to anyone in the story that the photograph in question is a cabinet card, a professionally produced print created from a negative and designed to be reproduced. Cabinet cards came into vogue in the 1870s, taking over from the earlier and smaller cartes de visite that had dominated the market in the 1860s.[11] Like cartes de visite before them, cabinet cards were primarily portrait photographs, commercially sold by studios across Europe and the United States. In the earliest years of photography, Claudet's calotype portrait studio advertised that "when a portrait is once obtained, an unlimited number of copies can be made from the original" (qtd. in Taylor 18).[12] A single portrait, advertised the studio in 1844, cost £1, 1 shilling, while subsequent copies cost 5 shillings. The possibility of duplicate copies was a selling point for consumers.

The complete elision of the negative in the instance of the king's cabinet card is strange, particularly considering the fictional Irene Adler was, according to William D. Jenkins, based on the real-life Adah Isaacs Menken. In his argument for Menken as the template for Adler, Jenkins describes two photographic scandals featuring Menken with famous literary men: she posed with Algernon Charles Swinburne, who "distributed so many copies of their photograph that it became an article of commerce, sold as a postcard in London stationery shops," and numerous times with Alexandre Dumas (11). Menken's "many scandalous photographs" with Dumas were taken by photographer Alphonse Liébert (see figure 3.1 for an example), and "were widely distributed by both subjects as well as the photographer who sold them for publication all over the world. . . . Dumas tried to get a court injunction against further publication but his petition was denied until it was too late to mean anything" (14). He later won a court battle "banning the display of the photographs and turning the negatives over to him" (Foster and Foster 271).[13] In a travel memoir, Dumas writes about his "horror" of being photographed:

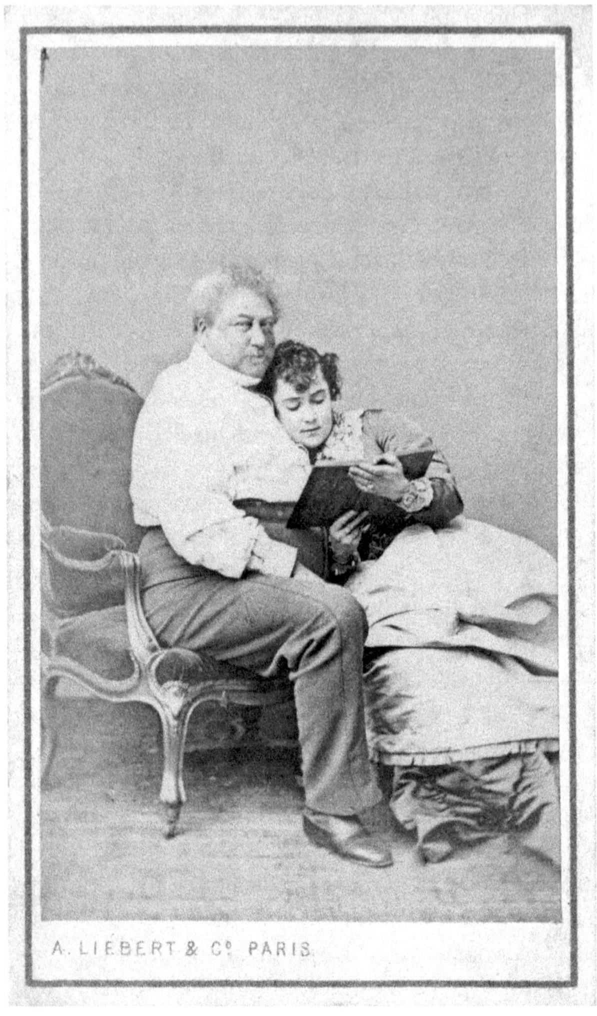

Figure 3.1. Alphonse Liébert & Co., albumen carte de visite of Alexandre Dumas *père* and Adah Isaacs Menken (c. 1867). Private collection.

> Formerly, when people gave their portraits, they could not give them profusely; they were so valuable that they gave them only to those persons whom they dearly loved. . . . Now all that is passed. One gives portraits to those who ask for them as we would alms to a mendicant; and if the portrait is not given to a person to whom we are altogether indifferent, it is made a

> matter of exchange, and we give one portrait with a stipulation that we receive another. . . . All kinds of people, who are the most indifferent to you, include you in their collections. . . . You are arranged like a collection of butterflies or moths. (75)

In this passage, Dumas echoes Dickens by expressing his concern about the reproduction of his image. If Jenkins is correct that Adler is a fictionalization of Menken, the existence of only one photograph (and no negative) of Conan Doyle's literary version is narratively convenient, although a significant enough departure from fact to beg notice, notwithstanding the fact that virtually all cabinet cards were made with reproduction in mind. Presumably in the world of this story, the king controls the negative and any other copies; at any rate, this one, purloined image is apparently all the evidence Adler needs to blackmail the king and ruin his reputation with visual proof of their "indiscretion."[14] Holmes has already introduced the concept that sight alone is not a strong enough foundation on which to build reasoned deductions, but the teacher forgets the lesson, as we see in the case of the photograph and Adler.

Holmes's inability to see Adler for who she really is and the failure of the photographic image to "count" as evidence in the final analysis mark this story as a broader critique of visual evidence. This critique is not particular to photography alone: Sidney Paget's original illustrations reproduce Holmes's failure to see Adler. Of the ten illustrations accompanying the story, Adler only appears in three: numbers six, eight, and nine. In illustrations six and eight (figures 3.2 and 3.3), Adler is part of the background: veiled and visible in profile along with Holmes and Norton in illustration six, and nearly obscured in the shadows while she sits in the carriage in illustration eight. In illustration nine (figure 3.4), the only illustration in which Adler is foregrounded, she is disguised as a man, walking along the street past Holmes and Watson undetected. As Elizabeth Miller notes, nothing in this illustration hints at Adler's true identity. Illustration must work alongside text to give us a complete picture of Adler: "Without the words of the story, one would never know the walker is a woman," writes Miller, "Without the picture, one would never grasp the disarming menace of Irene Adler's transsexual performance" (26). Miller uses this scene to describe how Holmes, "the expert eye, finds his visual acumen continually thwarted by the female body's resistance to interpretation" (26). Indeed, illustration and text reinforce one another in showing the extent to which Holmes fails to see Adler accurately—or more precisely, the extent to which he is able to

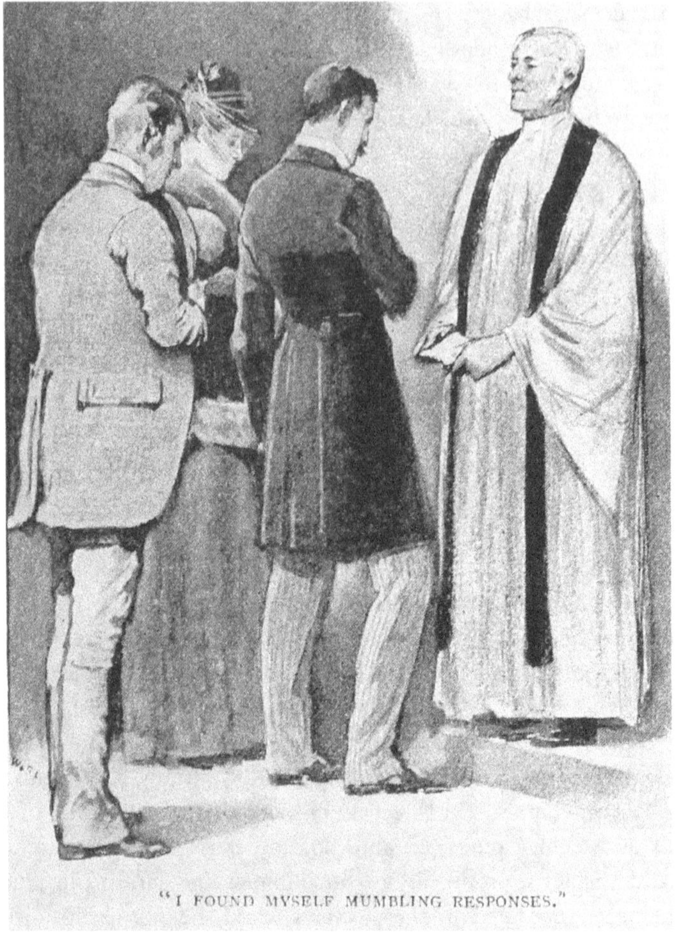

Figure 3.2. Sidney Paget, illustration number six for "A Scandal in Bohemia," "I found myself mumbling responses" (*The Strand* Magazine, vol. 2, London: George Newnes, 1891), p. 69.

see beyond the disguise. Image and text may operate from two perspectives, each giving us a view the other does not, as Miller suggests, yet they also reinforce each other by challenging visual certainty. Adler remains visually distanced from us throughout the illustrations. Furthermore, her disguise in illustration nine puts us in Holmes's position, looking at who we think is a man on the street. The illustrations ask us to see like Holmes, denying us visual certainty.[15]

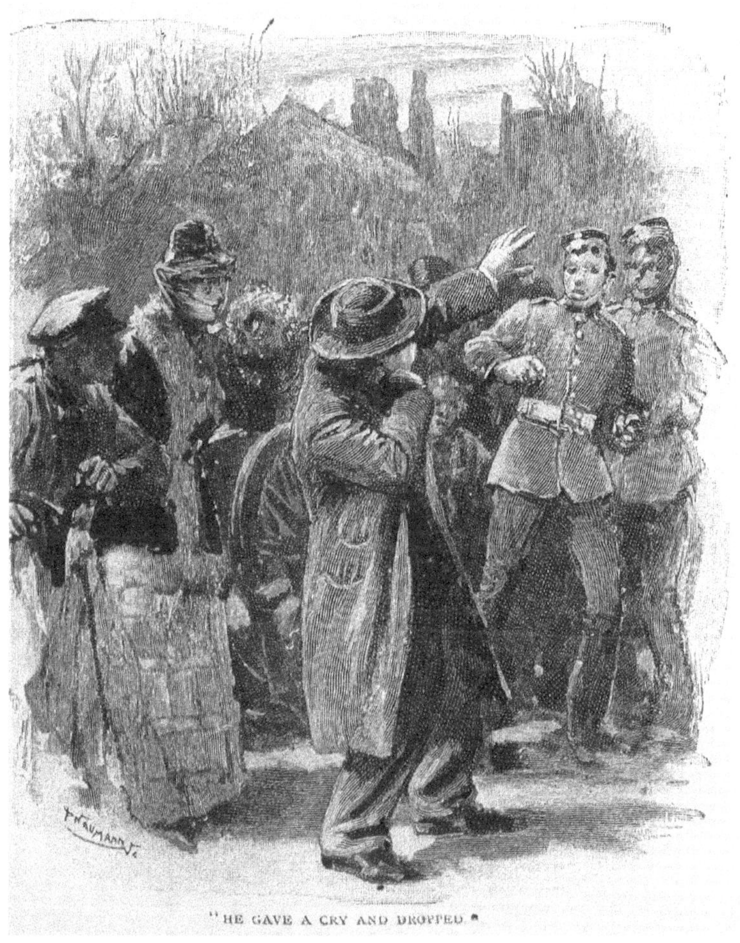

Figure 3.3. Sidney Paget, illustration number eight for "A Scandal in Bohemia," "He gave a cry and dropped" (*The Strand* Magazine, vol. 2, London: George Newnes, 1891), p. 71.

The story continues to undermine the significance of photography as evidence all the way to its final page. After escaping Holmes's clutches, Adler leaves behind a photograph of herself and a note, declaring that she no longer wishes to blackmail the king, for "I love and am loved by a better man than he." She keeps the original, incriminating photograph, she declares, merely "to safeguard myself, and to preserve a weapon which will always secure me from any steps which he might take in the future" (1:261).

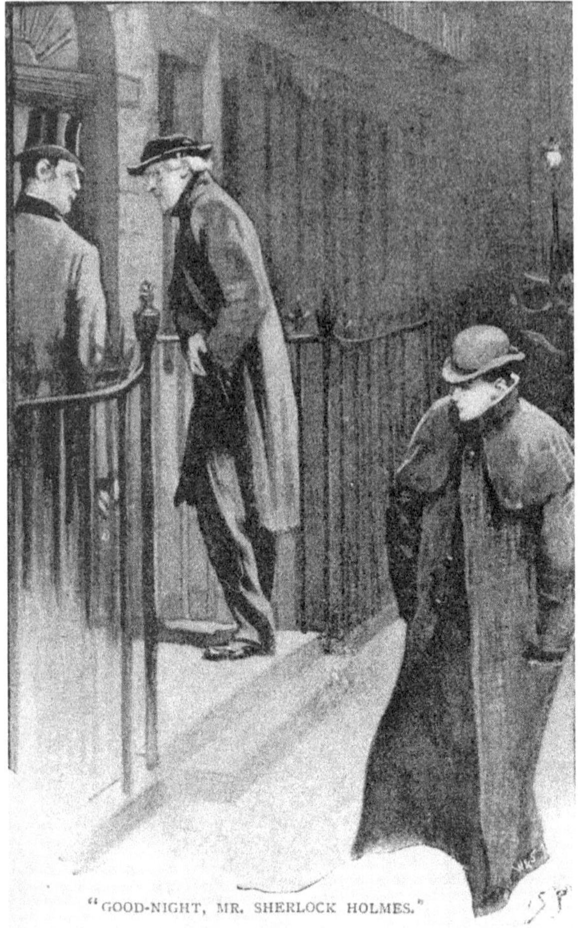

Figure 3.4. Sidney Paget, illustration number nine for "A Scandal in Bohemia," "Good night, Mr. Sherlock Holmes" (*The Strand* Magazine, vol. 2, London: George Newnes, 1891), p. 73.

Adler's description of the photograph as a "weapon" is ominous indeed, yet the king's reaction is immediate and surprising: "I know that her word is inviolate. The photograph is now as safe as if it were in the fire" (1:262). The king's response is an abrupt reversal. Until this point in the story the photograph has served as an unassailable piece of evidence that Holmes and the king have been pursuing like a fetish object, and it is suddenly determined to be inconsequential. Adler's promise—her word—replaces it.

Whereas Holmes notes all sorts of problems with the written word at the start—it might be forged, the paper could be stolen, the seal could be imitated—here word supersedes image and the king is content. The story ends on this note, albeit somewhat abruptly and unsatisfactorily because we have been anticipating a resolution in visual terms. Through the king's discussion with Holmes near the start, the story locates control and knowledge in the photographic image, so that like Holmes, we spend the story searching for a visual solution. Yet at the end the story returns us brusquely to Holmes's opening dialogue with Watson, reminding us that seeing is only one aspect of observation—only one way of knowing.

Photography and the New Physics

The story challenges the truth claims of photography and at the same time joins a larger debate about the meaning of vision and a skepticism of the nature of light that extends into the twentieth century. "A Scandal in Bohemia" shares continuity with literary predecessors also interested in how photography affects vision, culture, and realism more broadly, but at the same time, its contributions are of a distinctly late-century tenor. The story's treatment of the failure of visual objectivity links it to contemporaneous discussions about the nature of vision, discussions that would result in the establishment of the New Physics and quantum theory in the first decades of the twentieth century. Conan Doyle was writing in the 1890s, when scientists and the educated public were actively engaged in debating vision via the nature of light. This debate furthermore affected photography as a related science. Many pioneers in nineteenth-century photography were scientists—chemists, physicists, or both. German scientist Hermann von Helmholtz, for instance, developed theories of optics and color vision, and taught Alfred Stieglitz and Gabriel Lippman, who each went on to impact the history of photography (O'Connor 647). The cross-pollination between physics and photography occurred not just in the academy but also in the press: a glance through the *British Journal of Photography* throughout the century indicates by way of its repeated references to physics and optics the extent to which developments in physics continued to affect photographic practice.

Although his early conversation with Watson suggests otherwise, Holmes in fact appears ill equipped to manage either this new woman or the New Physics and the challenge to traditional epistemologies of vision it portends. At the turn of the twentieth century, optics was a field in flux, the nature of light itself a source of centuries-old ambiguity and controversy debated with new fervor. From the sixth through the seventeenth centuries, light was thought to be composed of particles; it had matter. This long-held conception formed the foundation for a particle theory of light. In 1637, however, René Descartes upended this theory in *Discourse on Method, Optics, Geometry, and Meteorology*, effectively beginning modern optical physics with the notion that rather than being particulate, light is wave-like. For the next two and a half centuries, scientists debated this point back and forth. Much work on physics in the nineteenth century was Cartesian in that it was dedicated to proving the wave-like nature of light and thereby disproving particle theory—indeed, in the September 6, 1867, issue of the *British Journal of Photography* William H. Harrison uses wave theory to explain the "phenomena of photography," suggesting "no other hypothesis attempts to explain the return of a dry plate after exposure to its original sensitive condition by lapse of time . . . the idea that the invisible image is 'motion' deserves consideration" (425). By the end of the nineteenth century, scientists had come to realize that wave theory could not account for all the properties of light. Wave theory was increasingly seen as an insufficient paradigm—phenomena such as black-body radiation and the photoelectric effect suggested a material quality of light that could not be understood by classical wave theory alone. C. E. Kenneth Mees acknowledges the insufficiency of wave theory in his article "The Photography of Coloured Objects in Principle and Practice" in 1906, writing, "Light cannot consist of waves in the air, partly because we know that it travels through interstellar space, where we imagine that there is no air, but also because the velocity of light, nearly 200,000 miles per second, is so great that it is impossible that it could consist of a wave in any material substance with which we are acquainted" (735).

At the start of the twentieth century, Max Planck revolutionized modern physics with his theory of quanta and thermal radiation—a theory predicated on a wave/particle duality. This was developed further—and more famously—by Albert Einstein and eventually theorized as quantum mechanics later in the twentieth century. The groundwork for this revolution had been laid in the nineteenth century, through the work of James Clerk Maxwell on electromagnetism in the 1860s and 1870s,[16] and Heinrich Hertz on electromagnetic radiation in 1888. Simply put, it was increasingly clear in the latter decades of the nineteenth century that the physical properties of light were not completely known and thus a traditional metaphoric link between vision and knowledge was destabilized. Because of photography's proximity to developments in the field of optics, photography was implicated in the more philosophical implications of this destabilization of vision and knowledge.

Conan Doyle's treatment of sight in "A Scandal in Bohemia"—and the story's upending of visual proof *qua* photography in favor of what it posits as an alternative solution—one's word—makes sense for this moment in the history of science when the nature of light (and thus optics more generally) was actively debated and questioned. Nor was this debate restricted to a specialized scientific community. As Geoffrey Cantor et al. remind us in their introduction to *Culture and Science in the Nineteenth-Century Media*,

> Science formed a fundamental and integral part of the cultural economy of nineteenth-century Britain . . . readers outside the relatively small and elite intellectual community depended largely on magazines, periodicals, and newspapers for their understanding of contemporary cultural issues. Before rigid disciplinary specialization, these sectors of the nineteenth-century print media not only provided information about science and related areas of cultural debate, but also played a major role in shaping public attitudes towards these historically important subjects. (xvii)

"Victorian science," James Mussell similarly argues, "was part of Victorian culture. . . . It was not unusual for literary authors to engage with scientific ideas in their work; nor did scientists ignore the concerns, forms or techniques of literature" (326).[17] In other words, the wave/particle discussion would not have been limited to the scientific elite but would have been part of a broader public discussion in the periodical press. It also makes sense that this discussion would connect back to the side of optics with which the public had arguably the most familiarity: photography.

It is thus consistent with public optical debates of the period that Holmes initially discredits the preeminence of sight and that in the final analysis, the story undermines the validity of strictly visual evidence. Throughout the stories and novels, Holmes's powers of observation are repeatedly linked to optical devices, including the microscope, the magnifying glass, eyeglasses, and the telescope. But the photograph truly seems to disrupt his vision. It is instructive to consider Scottish Enlightenment philosopher Thomas Reid here: "The eye is a machine most admirably contrived for refracting the rays of light," he writes, "and forming a distinct picture of objects upon the retina; but it sees neither the object nor the picture. It can form the picture after it is taken out of the head; but no vision ensues. Even when it is in its proper place, and perfectly sound, it is well known that an obstruction in the optic nerve takes away vision, though the eye has performed all that belongs to it" (247). Like Holmes, the eye is a machine of sight. Yet this machine alone is not enough, as Reid and this inaugural Holmes short story both explain. The eye is easily distracted.

In his focus on the visual aspect of his work, Holmes forgets to observe Adler or the status of the photograph. The photograph becomes a hollow fetish object—an object that is not actually the evidence it purports to be. It represents the threat of a woman—a woman who cannot be contained through vision alone—and the threat of celebrity through uncontrollable photographic reproduction. It also represents the threat of inversion by showing the inversion of gender roles and roles between detective and subject. In this story, Adler does not remain visible as she ought; unrecognized through the unexpected inversion of roles, she escapes the detective. Holmes fails here, despite the story's somewhat upbeat conclusion. He tells us what it means to observe, but he does not seem to observe that his own investigative methods are becoming outmoded, his views of women stale, and his faith in vision itself obsolete despite his affinity for photography. Fifty-seven subsequent Sherlock Holmes stories and novels suggest he overcame these challenges, but this oft-anthologized failure provides a striking critique of visual evidence and its value for the modern detective.

Chapter 4

The Double Exposure

Double Negatives at the Fin de Siècle

Although today the double negative is typically interpreted as a sign of grammatical ignorance—or a play on that perceived ignorance, as in the Rolling Stones' "I can't get no satisfaction"[1]—this negative connotation is a relatively recent construction. Prior to the 1700s, the double negative was not read as an error. William Shakespeare used double negatives in his writing as a point of emphasis, employing such constructions as "You know my father hath no child but I, nor none is like to have" (*As You Like It* I.ii.16).[2] More recent grammarians argue that this syntactic construction has no place in modern English. As Christine Timmons and Frank Gibney explain in the *Britannica Book of English Usage*, "At one time the double negative was acceptable in English. . . . However, today in Standard English the use of two negative terms in one sentence brands the writer as uneducated" (qtd. in *Oxford English Dictionary*). This modern attitude in fact derives from the influential *Short Introduction to English Grammar* of 1775. In this tome, Robert Lowth argues that "two Negatives in English destroy one another, or are equivalent to an Affirmative" (162). Lowth dismisses the double negative as unnecessary and goes on to establish a rule that it should be avoided. It was widely denounced throughout the nineteenth century and into the twentieth. Henry Louis Mencken exemplifies this ongoing position in his 1921 study *The American Language*, asserting, "Syntactically, perhaps the chief characteristic of vulgar American is its sturdy fidelity to the double negative" (310). Yet neither this rule nor its underlying definition stood completely unchallenged: in 1917, for instance, Otto Jespersen suggested that "the double negative always modifies the idea, for the result of the whole expression is somewhat different from the simple idea expressed positively"

(63). From this brief history, we see three definitions of the double negative emerge: two negatives emphasize the negation, two negatives cancel each other out, or two negatives produce an alternative that is not quite the same as a mere reversal of the negative idea expressed.

This chapter demonstrates how the different uses and interpretations of the double negative mirror the logic of the photographic double exposure, a technique that fuses two negatives to achieve different effects. Double exposures are formed when two photographic negatives or images are combined to create a single positive image. The combination may occur within a single print or plate, as in some spirit photography, or it may occur in the eye, as in the image viewed through a stereoscope. Double exposures form one type of composition photography, a technique that, as Daniel Novak suggests, enables an "impossible literary and pictorial body-in-pieces" that is "central both to a Victorian technology of realism and to the Victorian realist novel" (1). Novak argues that the abstraction and combination of disparate elements intrinsic to composition photography lie at the heart of the realist project; the fiction of manipulation, he suggests, is ironically central to realism. I also see in double exposures—a type of composition photography—a broader implication for Victorian fiction, and I argue that this broader implication demands more attention to the technology that produces double exposures than it has heretofore received.

My argument focuses more on the negatives that make such fragmented, abstract images possible than it does on the resulting composite images. I am interested in the underlying structure—the grammar—of the photographic image and how this structure affects the way the photographic image is culturally regarded. Like the syntactical structure of the double negative, the double exposure combines two negative elements. The rhetorical effect of the resulting positive image may be strengthened by the combination of negatives (a stereoscopic view, for instance, functions through the combination of two images, side by side), it may be completely undermined by the combination (often the case in accidental double exposures, which ruin both compositions), and in some cases, it may create an image altogether distinct from the sum of its negative parts (as seen in spirit photographs or photography using composition techniques).[3]

The double exposure and the double negative contain cultural implications as well as grammatical ones, as I show in my reading of late-century texts by E. W. Hornung, Cyril Bennett, Robert Louis Stevenson, and Oscar Wilde. This chapter moves from concrete discussions of double exposures in

Victorian short stories of the 1880s to figurative representations of double exposures in well-known Gothic tales. It ends by considering how the second of these tales, *The Picture of Dorian Gray*, takes on notoriety, sharing a bit of the celebrity status of its author. By representing double exposure literally and figuratively, these late Victorian authors demonstrate the ways in which two negatives might emphasize negation, cancel each other out, or reveal another image altogether. Each narrative shares an interest in doubleness and singularity, of two images combined into one. This motif of combination furthermore gives each author a figurative vocabulary for exploring questions of identity and reputation. Individual identity depends on singularity, but as we have seen, celebrity in the age of photography depends partly on the multiplicity of the image. Reputation occupies an uneasy space in between the individual and her or his image and becomes a central motif in each of the fictions explored in this chapter.

Exposed Reputations in Late Victorian Short Fiction

E. W. Hornung's "A Spoilt Negative" and Cyril Bennett's "Spirit Photograph" depict double exposures—or the potential for double exposures—as tricks or mistakes that nonetheless facilitate each story's resolution. In both stories, the question of feminine propriety and reputation hangs in the balance, and this threat to reputation is resolved after the development of the image. Rather than produce a social scandal similar to Irene Adler's photograph in "A Scandal in Bohemia," the double exposure eludes that scandal. Double exposures are depicted as lies that nonetheless lead the main characters to a truthful revelation and happy ending. Indeed, the resolutions playfully conflate multiple meanings of positivity. The stories' double exposures function much like the conventional double negative construction of two negatives forming a positive and thereby cancel each other out, although Bennett's story takes a few more twists and turns along the way.

By the mid-nineteenth century, the general public was familiar with the idea that photography could be and was often manipulated in specific contexts. Manipulation was common in the spheres of art photography and spirit photography, and the manipulative techniques common to these spheres were frequently communicated to the public. For instance, in his July 1, 1851, article "On the Application of Science to the Fine and Useful Arts," Robert Hunt notes that "with the advance of this beautiful art [photography] there appears to be progressively increasing desire to produce more artistic results; and numerous manipulatory improvements have recently been introduced" (188). William John Hubbard's instructions for negative manipulation, cited in the introduction, represents just one instance of the many articles and books designed to teach professional photographers and amateurs how to modify images, thereby improving their fidelity to reality or emphasizing their artistic effects: Conan Doyle's first publication in the *British Journal of Photography*, "On the Reproduction of Negatives," similarly advises readers how to manipulate the negative to create beautiful clouds on the print. Manipulations including overexposing, underexposing, solarizing, combination printing, and coloring the negative or the print were often the subject of informative how-to articles and other print discussions, indicating the nonspecialist public was fairly acculturated to the manipulative effects of photography more generally. As Stephen Petersen notes, "The initial celebration, by William Henry Fox Talbot and others, of the superior 'truth and fidelity' of photography gave way in the second half of the nineteenth century to an increasing awareness of the potential duplicity of photographic images and of photographic operators" (552). Faith in the truth function of photography increasingly declined from the 1860s through the end of the century,[4] with Eduard J. Steichen going so far as to claim in 1903 that "faking" existed since photography's "very beginning" (107).

From photography's earliest decades, amateurs were active participants in the development of photographic practices, as Grace Seiberling documents in *Amateurs, Photography, and the Mid-Victorian Imagination.*[5] Photography was a democratizing activity, and this democratization increased following the wet-plate and dry-plate developments, as amateurs and specialists contributed to photography's discourse.[6] General interest in and widespread familiarity with technical processes would have alerted a savvy public to the possibility of manipulation and fraud. Beyond this, public enthusiasm for photography and amateur investment in the practice means that photographic manipulation was not a top-down affair but one practiced by people with varying degrees of photographic expertise and shared with the public more generally.

Sir David Brewster describes one method of photographic manipulation in his 1856 book on *The Stereoscope: Its History, Theory, and Construction*—notably before the first publicized spirit photographs. Brewster describes double exposures that are essentially combination printing at the level of the negative. He introduces this technique "for the purpose of amusement," explaining that through these double exposures "the photographer might carry us even into the regions of the supernatural" (205). He describes an image in which "a female figure appears in the midst of" a group of people "with all the attributes of the supernatural. Her form is transparent, every object or person beyond her being seen in shadowy but distinct outline" (205). He demystifies the image, explaining that "to produce such a scene, the parties which are to compose the group must have their portraits nearly finished in the binocular camera, in the attitude which they may be supposed to take, and with the expression which they may be supposed to assume, if the vision were real." At this point,

> When the party have nearly sat the proper length of time, the female figure, suitably attired, walks quickly into the place assigned her, and after standing a few seconds in the proper attitude, retires quickly, or takes as quickly, a second or even a third place in the picture if it is required, in each of which she remains a few seconds, so that her picture in these different positions may be taken with sufficient distinctness in the negative photograph. (205)

This "experiment" may be varied: "One body may be placed within another . . . Any individual in a group may appear more than once in the same picture, either in two or more characters, and no difficulty will be experienced by the ingenious photographer in giving to these double or triple portraits, when it is required, the same appearance as that of the other parties who have not changed their place" (206). This description details for the reader how a photographer might create a supernatural "appearance," or a scene staged as if "the vision were real" (205). The description painstakingly explains the way such an image might be created, thereby working to demystify the process step by step.

The double exposure phenomenon Brewster describes is akin to the process by which an individual sees a single image when looking through a stereoscope. In Brewster's terms, the stereoscope allows us to see two different images simultaneously: "When we look with both eyes open at a sphere, or any other solid object, we see it by uniting into one two pictures, one as seen by the right, and the other as seen by the left eye . . . we not only see *different pictures* of the same object, but we see *different things* with each eye" (5, emphasis in original). This is not an observation particular to professional photographers. Instead, as Brewster puts it, it is "a fact well known to every person of common sagacity that *the pictures of bodies seen by both eyes are formed by the union of two dissimilar pictures formed by each*" (6, emphasis in original). In other words, the mechanics of stereoscopy were obvious to the general public. The purpose of this technology was experimentation: through the stereoscopic camera, Brewster writes, "the photographic artist can make experiments, and try the effect which will be produced by his pictures before he takes them. He can thus select the best forms of groups of persons and of landscapes, and thus produce works of great interest and value" (126). Far from a mysterious, de facto sign of the spirit world, double exposures function similarly to popular stereoscopy, the mechanism of which is quite literally out in the open.[7] The idea that two images could be combined into one would have been widely understood, particularly after the "stereoscopic mania" of the early 1860s ("Commercial Photography" 47).[8]

By featuring double exposures—or the possibility of double exposures—Hornung's and Bennett's late-century short stories speak to a general cultural awareness of this technique. Furthermore, they use the double exposure as a device to reassert romantic resolution and propriety. Each introduces the technique as or alongside a potential challenge to social decorum, then resolves the tension through a traditionally happy ending. Two negatives, in other words, equal a positive—in this case, a positive in romantic plot terms. In her article "Domesticity in the Darkroom: Photographic Process and Victorian Romantic Narratives," Susan Shelangoskie examines the extent to which these stories explore the romantic plot through/alongside photography. "Victorian discourse surrounding photography emphasized not just photographic images, but all aspects of the photographer's work from the glasshouse to the darkroom," she notes, and by relocating the sphere of photography from the commercial to the domestic, works like these "contest the photographer's authority over the image he or she develops, sometimes advocating strong models of shared rights between photographer and sitter" (93–94). Although I share Shelangoskie's interpretation that these stories ultimately "restore social stability" through their uses of photography (108), I note that they do so primarily through their use of or reference to the double negative. In other words, the specific technology shared by these stories matters. These are not simply stories about photography but ones where the specific negative technique described affects plot and form. Double exposures influence the plot of each story, while double negatives reiterate this effect on the level of narrative structure.

The first of these stories, "A Spoilt Negative," was penned by Conan Doyle's friend and eventual brother-in-law, E. W. Hornung. This story features a photographer by the name of Dick, introduced to us in the first line as "an artist: not a painter, nor a sculptor, nor a musician, nor, indeed, a devotee at the shrine of any Fine Art—yet an artist" (2). Dick is an amateur, but he takes his Art with a capital A very seriously and attempts to follow it "for its own sake" (3). He often finds himself invited to parties only to be asked to serve as group photographer, a role he hates—he would much rather be photographing individual portraits. One morning at his uncle's villa, he is asked to photograph a cow and calf. Later in the day, he finds himself alone with his love interest, Elsie, who is sleeping in a hammock. He thinks that he would have "exchanged his complete apparatus for the gratification of obtaining one good negative of Elsie Keswicke" (5). He photographs Elsie sleeping (or so he thinks). In actuality, she is aware she is being photographed, and when he offers to show her the negative plate as it develops, "doubtless intending it as a huge surprise," she plans "to let him know that it was no surprise: to smash his negative—nip in the bud the sequel he had in view—and leave him heaped with contumely and utterly annihilated!" (10). She intends to do this to find out whether he really cares for her, or "whether, after all, it was not simply his so-called Art that he was in love with" (10). The plot seems to drive toward an unpleasant conclusion for Dick.

Dick constructs a portable darkroom so they can see the development of the negative at the same time: a "double-dark-tent," and the only one of its kind in the world, according to Dick (11). As he develops the plate, it becomes clear that he has taken a photograph of Elsie but while her "form and face" were most conspicuous in the image—"black as ink, of course, with the usual reversal of the lights"—from her head "protruded two great horns—from the feet hung an unmistakable tail—she was plainly supported on four cloven hoofs—her hand rested on the back of what appeared to be an ill-shapen black dog! . . . The enthusiast had committed the prime blunder in photography—he had taken two photographs on one plate" (14). Dick is horrified that he has ruined his photograph of Elsie and offended her at the same time; meanwhile, she bursts into tears because she perceives his mistake to be a trick—a deliberate manipulation of the negatives to make her look like a cow. Dick and Elsie are operating under heightened emotions, and Dick threatens to drink the developer. This threat calms her, and after a telling ellipsis, the reader discovers the two have come to a romantic understanding.

The double exposure error facilitates the story's romantic conclusion, but before doing so it operates as a metaphor for Elsie's imperiled social reputation. She is horrified when she sees the developed double negative, for she feels herself the victim of "a low, vulgar trick—a trick that no *gentleman* could play" (14, emphasis in original). Feeling degraded and made a fool of, she repeats this appeal to propriety again, declaring Dick to be "an *apology for a gentleman*" (14, emphasis in original). Elsie does not regard the double exposure as true for an instant but immediately interprets it as a cruel joke—a manipulation that breaks the rules of social decorum. She believes it is done to make her look a fool, and this distresses her because it is an affront to her reputation. It does not seem to matter that she and Dick are together in a dark tent, or that the textual break before the story's happy conclusion suggests they have shared a kiss or other romantic exchange. The true threat to social reputation, the story suggests, is a double exposure no one could mistake for reality.

After Elsie and Dick's unnarrated romantic resolution, the meaning of the photographic double negative shifts. "We'll preserve the negative for ever and ever," says Dick to his "darling" in the story's final lines: "It shall go down to posterity as an unbroken record" (15). The couple keeps the double exposure because it is itself a marker of their romance, thus operating, in other words, like a double negative in one sense of the term. All Dick will tell others about the encounter is that "he had spoilt a negative." "And so," Hornung reiterates, in case his reader missed the import of this line, "indeed he had—in more senses than one" (15). Dick has spoiled a negative—literally ruined the negative of Elsie—and in doing so has ruined a negative situation, creating a positive romantic outcome in its place. Photographic negative and grammatical negative coincide here, as the two negatives make the story's positive romantic outcome possible.

Bennett's 1888 story, "The Spirit Photograph," similarly uses the double exposure as a plot device to arrive at a positive conclusion, as well as a metaphor for the grammatical figuration of the double negative. In its reference to spirit photography, the story also speaks to a specific subset of double exposure images. Perhaps the most famous type of double exposure is the spirit photograph, and for that reason double exposures and spirit photography are frequently discussed together.[9] In the nineteenth century, spirit photography attracted popular attention for its use of manipulation. As noted in chapter 3, Arthur Conan Doyle maintained a long-held personal belief in the veracity of spirit photography and fairy photography, a belief that was sometimes an embarrassment to fans of the rationally minded Sherlock Holmes. Conan Doyle was not alone in his concurrent advocacy of spirit photography and rationality, and he numbered among those Victorians who recognized spirit photography for the manipulation that it was—and yet had no trouble doubting the truthfulness of the photographic image. In 1869, photographer William H. Mumler was arrested in New York for fraudulently staging his spirit photographs. Conan Doyle himself writes about this case as well as the case of M. Ed. Buguet, a French spirit photographer who was arrested and charged with creating fake spirit photographs and thereby defrauding the public (*History of Spiritualism* 2:136). These instances mark the beginning of a "realisation that fakery was quite possible in the apparently immutable photographic image," as Chris Webster puts it (1333). The faking intrinsic to spirit photography is curiously poised in a position of both/and: spirit photography makes use of double exposures, which were generally understood to be manipulations. At the same time, double exposures are again and again represented—in spirit photography and other contexts, as we will see—as tricks: lies that work as tricks precisely because it was intended that viewers would believe them. Rather than an exception to a general rule about the truthfulness of photography, then, spirit photography serves as an index of the extent to which photography could be used as a trick.

"The Spirit Photograph" begins in medias res on a Himalayan climbing expedition, focusing a limited omniscient perspective through an English climber by the name of Mansell. The climbers are roped together during a climbing accident, and when the guide returns to camp and explains that everyone else fell to their deaths, Mansell is presumed dead as well. The next chapter of the story details the circumstances of Mansell's wife, Fanny, who is convinced her husband is dead and becomes friends with her neighbor, amateur photographer Lord Undercroft. Undercroft begins to teach Fanny how to take photographs, and she laments that she has no photographs of her husband "with which to refresh her memory. Never had she succeeded in prevailing upon him to have his likeness taken. . . . So even that small consolation was denied to her" (365). One day Lord Undercroft shows Fanny some spirit photographs, explaining the spiritualist's theory that "we are constantly surrounded by spirits, invisible to the naked eye, yet sufficiently substantial to affect the highly sensitized photographic plate" (365). "You don't believe in them, do you?," asks Fanny. "No more than I do in flying pigs," Undercroft replies, and proceeds to demystify the photographic process: "I dare say they are easy enough to manufacture. We will have a try one day if you like. I have often obtained very funny results by taking two pictures one over the other on the same plate," while the bereaved sitter "makes up his mind that he is going to see the shade of some particular defunct individual, and then he recognizes the apparition, no matter whether it is recognizable or not" (365–66). In this conversation, Undercroft straightforwardly explains the double exposure manipulation underlying spirit photography, and his explanation does not seem to surprise Fanny.

Undercroft's romantic overture later in this conversation does come as a surprise. In the following chapter, Fanny unhappily mulls over this conversation and decides she must turn him down. As she is thinking through this development, she photographs her house and then retreats to her darkroom to develop the plate. As she looks at the developing plate, she finds herself shocked: "The outline of the house formed a frame round a portrait. *She was gazing at her husband's face*" (369, emphasis in original). Because of her husband's aforementioned aversion to photography, Fanny knows there is no likeness of him "in existence" (369). She interprets this as a sign from beyond the grave: "She had sinned. She had been unfaithful to the memory of her husband. She had dared for one moment to entertain Lord Undercroft's offer. This was a judgment on her for her wickedness" (369). For a moment, readers and Fanny alike are meant to believe that Mansell's face is proof that the spirit photographs Fanny has been learning about are in fact truly signs from the spirit world. Fanny faints, overcome with terror. When she wakes she discovers her husband sitting beside her. A perfectly rational explanation ensues, and husband and wife are happily reunited. It turns out Mansell survived the climbing accident and recovered slowly in a hut "far from civilized regions" before returning home (370). A lengthy illness kept him from sending a telegraph, and after recovering he heard that his wife was "consoling herself" with Lord Undercroft (371). Jealous, Mansell decided to keep his survival secret and return home to discover the situation firsthand before disclosing his identity. He was in the yard when his wife was photographing the house and ended up in the frame as Fanny, who had turned away to look at her watch, took the photograph.

The photograph of Mansell framed by the house is thus not a double exposure. Rather, it is a regular photograph that appears to Fanny, on first glance, to be a spirit photograph. Even though she knows that spirit photographs are double exposure tricks, she also knows her husband never sat for a photograph in the past, so she immediately interprets his face in the image as a metaphysical "judgment." Indeed, "it could never be ascertained positively whether Mansell was really so ignorant" about photography that he was "unaware that he was taking his own likeness when he put his head in front of the camera" (372). For his part, the manservant Saunders believes that Mansell decided to "take a mischievous revenge on Fanny for the readiness with which she had consoled herself" during her husband's absence (372). In other words, Mansell feigns a double exposure by inserting himself into the image, like a ghost in a spirit photograph. The story thus negates two possibilities: that the image is the legitimate photograph of a spirit and that the image is a spirit photograph—a photograph derived from multiple images recorded on the same plate. The image is instead the product of improbable happenstance, for Fanny happens to look down for three seconds precisely as her husband momentarily enters the frame.

In "A Spoilt Negative," the image is perceived all along as a manipulated double exposure (although it is an accidental double exposure), but "The Spirit Photograph" toggles between several options. Is this a ghost story? Is someone manipulating Fanny's emotions through the trick of the double exposure? Bennett negates both possibilities by offering up a third solution. This solution—and the story's resolution—points to a complete reunion between husband and wife. Mansell promises to give up mountain climbing, he allows his photograph to be taken, and Undercroft moves out of the neighborhood. Undercroft unwittingly facilitates the reunion between husband and wife, but he must leave the scene so the couple can complete their happy resolution. Fanny's social exposure to any sort of impropriety and the possibility that the image is a double exposure are both negated, and domestic harmony is reinstated. Although this story's treatment of photography highlights manipulation and thus cynically questions the realism of photography, photography becomes the story's vehicle for confirming the "truth" of the situation and resolving tension. Social calamity is averted through a photographic image that appears to be either otherworldly or two images in one, but that negates both possibilities. As "The Spirit Photograph" shows us, double exposures need not directly materialize in a story for this technology to influence a narrative and evoke the logic of the double negative. Indeed, as *Strange Case of Dr. Jekyll and Mr. Hyde* and *The Picture of Dorian Gray* illustrate, the double negative may function without a sustained, direct reference to photography. At the same time, photography pervades the culture surrounding these texts and influences the logic by which each tale articulates duplication and negation.

"It Is Hyde Now That Controls Jekyll"

In *Jekyll and Hyde* and *Dorian Gray*, there are no literal photographic double exposures; Instead, double exposures function more as a figurative structure, providing a frame of reference for the doubleness explored in each text. These stories are more properly Gothic than realist, and this genre gives the writers the means of exploring themes of doubleness and inversion more metaphorically than literally. The supernatural frame of these stories allows each author to delve into these concepts on a metaphoric level while introducing similar concerns about reputation shared by Hornung's and Bennett's short stories.

Jekyll and Hyde's Gothic revelation is, of course, that Jekyll and Hyde are two individuals inhabiting one body, like two negatives creating a single image, only one of which may be seen at a given time while the other remains latent. From start to finish, the novel is structured to slowly expose the truth of the case to the reader. Much like Hornung's and Bennett's short fiction, Stevenson's novel is concerned with reputation. But whereas double exposures lead away from scandal in the short fiction, in *Jekyll and Hyde* the double exposure is itself the great scandal of the text. In the novel, Hyde is the negative figure: a dark double of Jekyll who allows Jekyll to remain respectable while Hyde can enjoy all the depravity life has to offer. However, although Jekyll may have created Hyde as the inverse of his own psyche so that he might simultaneously enjoy propriety and a more debauched lifestyle, in actuality Jekyll is not wholly the good counterbalance to Hyde's dark depravity. The two are separate but linked, sharing a single body but not wholly synced to form a whole person. Showing that he is not beyond duplicity himself, Jekyll is yet one more negative, and by way of its conclusion the tale illustrates that two negatives (Jekyll and Hyde) do not make a single (positive) individual; rather, the evil Hyde takes over and completely dominates. Jekyll and Hyde die, unable to sustain themselves as a single figure. Furthermore, Jekyll cannot control his transformation into Hyde at the end of the novella because he can no longer access a particular chemical, a detail that resonates with photochemical processes. Ultimately, the outcome of this double exposure is a negation of life itself—Shakespearean in its employment of the double negative as emphasis to show the dark limits of double exposure.

Jekyll and Hyde's theme of doubleness is illustrated beyond the limits of Stevenson's narrative. From 1887 to 1888, American actor Richard Mansfield starred in Thomas Russell Sullivan's stage adaptation of Stevenson's novel, first in Boston and then in London. The adaptation opened a year after the initial publication of the novel and quickly made its star infamous for his transformation from Jekyll to Hyde. Mansfield's performance was called an "embodiment of evil" by the *Daily News* ("The Theatre"). His performance lasted the 1888 season at the Lyceum Theatre, but in October the *Daily Telegraph* announced he was to "abandon the 'Creepy Drama,' evidently beloved in America, in favor of wholesome comedy" (qtd. in Corton 121). His performance was apparently too "creepy" for a public then experiencing a series of violent and unsolved murders, for that was the autumn of Jack the Ripper. Lurid details about the Ripper murders were often published in the same newspapers as reviews and other information about Mansfield's performance of Jekyll and Hyde: the *Daily News*, the *Daily Telegraph*, the *Echo*, *Morning Advertiser*, the *Pall Mall Gazette*, the *Star*, and the *Times* all published reports about the Ripper murders and Mansfield's performances concurrently in this timeframe. Writing for the *Pall Mall Gazette*, W. T. Stead made more of a direct connection in the article "Another Murder—and More to Follow?," published on September 8:

> This renewed reminder of the potentialities of revolting barbarity which lie latent in man will administer a salutary shock to the complacent optimism which assumes that the progress of civilisation has rendered unnecessary the bolts and bars, social, moral, and legal, which keep the Mr. Hyde of humanity from assuming visible shape among us. There certainly seems to be a tolerably realistic impersonification of Mr. Hyde at large in Whitechapel. (1)

In this article about the Ripper murders, the "revolting barbarity" of real life is likened to the work of "Mr. Hyde." Later in the same issue, "Mr. Richard Mansfield as Dr. Jekyll and Mr. Hyde" is listed under "To-Night's Entertainments." In an anonymous letter sent to the City of London Police, Mansfield was accused of actually being the Ripper: "when I went to see Mr. Mansfield take the part of Dr. Jekel [*sic*] and Mr. Hyde," writes the informant, "I felt at once that he was *the Man Wanted*" ("Anonymous Letter to City of London Police," emphasis in original). Mansfield was rumored to abridge his Jekyll and Hyde act because the public felt such a convincing performance would—or perhaps already had—incited murder

(C. Morley). Another rumor suggested the actor was questioned by Scotland Yard in connection with the Ripper case ("Seeing Double"). The salacious news coverage, and the rumor mill more broadly, thus attempted to fuse the fictional Hyde with the factual Ripper via Mansfield.

Mansfield was made famous by his depiction of Jekyll and Hyde, and he reprised the role intermittently until 1907 (Linehan 170). Photographer Henry Van der Weyde commemorated his transformative performance by creating a double exposure cabinet card to depict the actor's dual roles in the adaptation (see figure 4.1). The title given to this cabinet card prioritizes the name of the actor—"Mr. Mansfield" over Jekyll and Hyde—as though reinforcing rumors that Mansfield's performance bled over into life. This image was reprinted in *The Richard Mansfield Calendar for 1900: showing pictures of his favorite characters with some appropriate quotations and good wishes for each month.* The quotations, in his handwriting, for the month of December include "a merry Christmas! Work never killed anybody but a

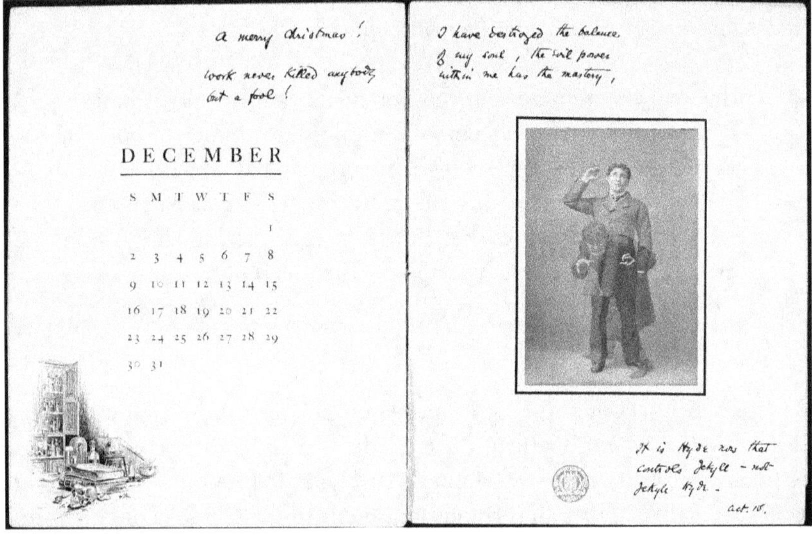

Figure 4.1. *The Richard Mansfield Calendar for 1900: showing pictures of his favorite characters with some appropriate quotations and good wishes for each month.* Richard Mansfield, English actor, (1857–1907) as Jekyll and Hyde. A photograph and a calendar, for December. New York: D. Appleton, [c. 1899]. Photograph by Henry Van der Weyde. Reproduced by permission of The Image Works. © British Library/ The Image Works."

fool!," and "I have destroyed the balance of my soul, the evil power within me has the mastery, it is Hyde now that controls Jekyll—not Jekyll Hyde. Act IV." The Christmas wish is placed in jarring juxtaposition against the observation that "Work never killed anybody but a fool," and an even stronger tonal juxtaposition is created by the *Jekyll and Hyde* quotation. Indeed, this pair of quotations creates a Jekyll-and-Hyde–like dichotomy of dark and light. Yet the quotation from the stage adaptation suggests the dichotomy cannot remain in balance: Hyde reigns supreme. While *Jekyll and Hyde*—both Mansfield's performance and Stevenson's novel—are ostensibly about "the thorough and primitive duality of man," in fact they show the extent to which Jekyll and Hyde are negative copies of one another, in the end producing a negation of life itself: a double negative reinforcing negativity.

It is conventional for contemporary critics to focus on *Jekyll and Hyde*'s theme of duality. Karl Miller, for instance, suggests the story is part of the tradition of "the modern double" (49). Arguments that pivot around the story's treatment of evolutionary biology, political anxiety, social propriety, and the Gothic tradition often turn to the significance of the doppelgänger or dark double and the role this played in the culture writ large.[10] The notion of two conflicted entities coexisting in a single individual captivated—and still captivates—the imagination. As Miller writes, "There can be no satisfying short description of what doubles are, or of what they have become in shedding some part of their supernatural origins, as harbingers of evil and death, and growing into an element of individual psychology," yet "they have often been about running away, and revenge. . . . One self does what the other self can't" (416). It is fair to say that doubles tend to appear as negative inversions of the self, or parts of the self that are permitted to be bad while the "normal" part of the individual must be good. "Man," Jekyll thinks, "is not truly one, but truly two," moral and amoral at once (Stevenson, *Strange Case* 48).

However, the figure of the double in Stevenson's novella is not as simple as a diametric opposition. Jekyll's objective is to separate the two extremes of his identity and thus liberate them—to allow "the unjust" to "go his way, delivered from the aspirations and remorse of his more upright twin; and the just" to "walk steadfastly and securely on his upward path, doing the good things in which he found his pleasure, and no longer exposed to disgrace and penitence by the hands of this extraneous evil" (49). But in practice, he succeeds in maintaining his complicated self and also separating out his negative side. Evil is truly extraneous, for it forms another person alongside and not bifurcated from the original Jekyll. Perhaps because Jekyll feels he has spent "nine tenths of a life of effort, virtue and control," there is nothing remarkable about the new Jekyll once Hyde has been removed: he retains his name, and no one remarks that he appears any more virtuous than before. Hyde, on the other hand, "alone in the ranks of mankind, was pure evil" (51). Any attempted balance is further undermined when Hyde begins to take over the pair: "whereas, in the beginning," reports Jekyll in his written statement of the case, "the difficulty had been to throw off the body of Jekyll, it had of late, gradually but decidedly transferred itself to the other side. . . . I was slowly losing hold of my original and better self, and becoming slowly incorporated with my second and worse" (55).

Jekyll is a complex individual who both fears and appreciates the "pleasures and adventures of Hyde," whereas Hyde is simply bad (55). Jekyll is motivated to conduct his experiment because of his concern for his social reputation, not necessarily because he fears his "impatient gaiety of disposition" is objectively wrong. Instead, he finds his disposition "hard to reconcile with my imperious desire to carry my head high, and wear a more than commonly grave countenance before the public" (47–48). Being good entails having a conscience and a general awareness of good and bad, whereas being bad is blissfully unaware and not conflicted. Above all, Jekyll has a sense of social decorum. Unlike in Hornung's and Bennett's short fiction, such social niceties buckle under the weight of this very different double negative. Rather than Jekyll and Hyde forming two sides of a whole individual, then, Jekyll contains all or part of the negative qualities he is so eager to compartmentalize.

Although the two are not so diametrically opposed, physically they are quite distinct. It seems their different appearances, like the different appearances Mansfield was so famous for evoking on stage, are what most emphatically differentiate them. Whereas Jekyll is more or less depicted as a regular, complex individual, "a large, well-made, smooth-faced man of fifty, with something of a slyish cast perhaps, but every mark of capacity and kindness," Hyde is of another order altogether (19): he is "pale and dwarfish," gives "an impression of deformity without any nameable malformation," is "troglodytic," and appears like Satan himself (17). He is "hellish," not "like a man" and "so ugly" he makes people hate him at first sight and "turn sick and white with the desire to kill him" (9). Those who encounter Hyde stack similes and metaphors on top of imprecise descriptions, in an apparent attempt to articulate the inarticulable—to describe a quality so horrible it cannot be described. There is something about Hyde's appearance that horrifies those who come into contact with him, and that "something" is baffling, for it is visual but indescribable. For instance, Enfield tells Utterson that Hyde "is not easy to describe":

> There is something wrong with his appearance; something displeasing, something downright detestable. I never saw a man I so disliked, and yet I scarce know why. He must be deformed somewhere; he gives a strong feeling of deformity, although I couldn't specify the point. . . . I can't describe him. And it's not want of memory, for I declare I can see him this moment. (11–12)

The visual representation of evil, though difficult to describe, is what makes Hyde so terrible. As Utterson thinks to himself, "It was already bad enough when the name was but a name of which he could learn no more. It was worse when it began to be clothed upon with detestable attributes; and out of the shifting, insubstantial mists that had so long baffled his eye, there leaped up the sudden, definite presentment of a fiend" (13). For all who see him, Hyde's appearance confirms his evil nature, but in a way that cannot be articulated. In other words, Hyde is a doubly negative image: first in the sense that he appears to others to be everything that is negative, and second in the sense that he forms no easily describable image at all and is thus a negation of the image altogether.

Whereas Hyde's visual appearance differentiates him quite forcefully from Jekyll and the rest of humanity, the two nevertheless remain visually linked, two dissimilar images coinciding like a double exposure. Indeed, they do not look alike, but their handwriting does. Utterson looks at a letter signed by Edward Hyde and determines it is written in "an odd, upright hand" (26). The clerk asks whether the letter is from Dr. Jekyll, for he recognizes the handwriting. Placing two sheets side by side, the clerk concludes there is "a rather singular resemblance; the two hands are in many points identical: only differently sloped" (28). Using "two hands" metonymically for handwriting, Stevenson suggestively implies that the two bodies are identical but "differently sloped," as though the same body viewed from a different perspective. The novella does not ask us to see different men so much as it asks us to see the extent to which these different men may be seen concurrently. Similarly, Van der Weyde's photograph asks us to consider what it means to see two distinct individuals at once. The scandal of *Jekyll and Hyde* is not that Jekyll has created a monstrous alter ego/body that goes around killing people and trampling small children; rather, the scandal is that the monster operates as a double exposure, not severed from Jekyll at all. Rather than mitigate scandal, as Jekyll hopes it might, double exposure proves to be the very source of that scandal in Stevenson's novella.

Unlike Hornung's and Bennett's short fictions, where photography is featured prominently, *Jekyll and Hyde* laments the absence of this technology. Hyde cannot be easily captured following the murder of Sir Danvers Carew, for "he had never been photographed; and the few who could describe him differed widely" (24). Yet while photography may only be mentioned as an unfortunate absence in Stevenson's novella, the text is steeped in late Victorian visual culture: heavy emphasis is placed on sight and how Hyde looks, and words such as *picture*, *image*, *look*, *appearance*, and *sight* abound. As Owen Clayton suggests, the novella has close ties to photography: reading the author's experiences with the darkroom and photography around the time he was writing the novel, he argues that Stevenson's "understanding of the divided self had a close connection to photography" (61).[11] The horrifying climax comes when Lanyon sees Hyde drink his concoction and notes the physical transformation of Hyde into Jekyll: "as I looked there came, I thought, a change . . . his face became suddenly black and the features seemed to melt and alter. . . . I saw what I saw, I heard what I heard, and my soul sickened at it; and yet now when that sight has faded from my eyes, I ask myself if I believe it, and I cannot answer" (47). The transformation of Hyde's face to "black" functions on several registers simultaneously. On the most basic metaphoric level, his blackened face connotes the darkness of his soul, his evil interior. Yet this metaphor is also historically specific, freighted with connotations of racial degeneration popularized at this time. Finally, it is technologically evocative: Hyde's face becomes "black" as though going through a process of photographic negative inversion, a transformation like a reverse photographic development from positive into negative. Although the horror Lanyon experiences is based on what he sees and hears, the only description passed on to us is rendered in visual terms.

Beyond the visual economy pervading the novel, the text is surrounded by a late-century photographic literary culture, as evidenced by Van der Weyde's image and Stevenson's own numerous experiences sitting for his photographic portrait, dating back to his early youth.[12] Skeptical of the ability of photography to capture his likeness, Stevenson echoes Dickens's distrust of his photographic image when writes to art student A. Trevor

Haddon in 1883, promising to send a photograph of himself but noting that when he does so, "It will not be like me; sometimes I turn out a capital, fresh bank clerk; once I came out the image of Runjeet Singh; again the treacherous sun has fixed me in the character of a travelling evangelist. It's quite a lottery . . . The truth is I have no appearance; a certain air of disreputability is the one constant character that my face presents: the rest change like water" ("Letter to A. Trevor Haddon" 149). Stevenson characterizes himself like Jekyll and Hyde: he has no constant appearance, save a certain disreputability.

The novella does not lead us to the conclusion that two negatives form a positive as in Hornung's and Bennett's short fiction; instead, we are asked to consider a different figuration of the double negative. Jekyll and Hyde represent the tale's metaphoric double exposure—two individuals occupying a single image, each negating respectability to different degrees. Jekyll acknowledges that while man is not truly one but two, "the state of my own knowledge does not pass beyond that point. Others will follow, others will outstrip me on the same lines; and I hazard the guess that man will be ultimately known for a mere polity of multifarious, incongruous, and independent denizens" (48). Instead of a resolution of opposites, Stevenson imagines a different conclusion for Jekyll and Hyde. They ultimately die because they are unable to sustain their split existence. Hyde takes over and threatens to destroy Jekyll, who has no choice but to end them both. This Shakespearean conclusion makes use of a Shakespearean double negative. Rather than the two negatives forming a positive, they compound. These two negative are not resolved into a single positive individual but reinforce the negative aspects of each. Jekyll cannot reconcile himself with Hyde or destroy just one without the other. The double exposure fails, for the two cannot coalesce into a single image but must remain separate, the complexity Jekyll yearns for forever compartmentalized into two distinct selves. The only possible outcome is a negation of Jekyll, Hyde, and the composite Jekyll/Hyde alike.

The Uses of the Double in *The Picture of Dorian Gray*

As Walter Pater notes in his review of *The Picture of Dorian Gray*, the novel takes as its focus "that very old theme . . . of a double life" (132).

Like *Jekyll and Hyde*, *Dorian Gray* features a metaphoric treatment of the double exposure and ends with the demise of the subject of that exposure. Rather than reconciling (or attempting to reconcile) the two Dorians, the novel has them trade places. The picture of Dorian is Dorian's ugly but true inverse, and it is a negative that represents reality more than Dorian himself. Together, Dorian and the picture represent both surface and symbol in a feedback loop of reproduction that devolves into the negative alone: destroying his picture at the end of the novel, Dorian is exposed as an alternative to his ostensible self—dead, disfigured, and an inversion of his former appearance. Dorian and his picture are both negatives, coalesced as a single image only at their moment of origin. As though telling the story of a double exposure in reverse, the two—individual and representation—are one at the start of the novel but grow ever more apart until they are no longer recognizable as the same image/person. The doubles in *Dorian Gray* cannot come together as a single image again, so Dorian must die, and the Dorian/painting reversal must revert back again.

This novel's extratextual life—specifically, how it was used in Wilde's trial for gross indecency—adds a final spin to the novel and its meditation on art and life. As in *Jekyll and Hyde* but to a greater degree, fiction seeps into life, affecting those affiliated with this text. In 1895, *Dorian Gray* was brought into Wilde's first trial and used as evidence of the author's moral depravity. By using the novel this way, attorney Edward Carson argued that fiction is not separate from reality. This history has become a staple among literary critics, many readings of the notorious novel and its celebrity author hinging on the novel's extratextual history. Unlike the other texts examined in this chapter, then, Dorian and Dorian's picture are not permitted to collapse in on themselves or produce a positive image; Carson drew the double negative firmly out of fiction and into the world, asking that double negative to stand as evidence of something beyond the limits of the text. In addition, the novel reflects back Wilde's preoccupation with doubling and its impact on the individual during the early 1890s, a preoccupation reflected in his other writings around this time. The photographic negative, specifically the double exposure, allows us to see this interplay of doubling, identity, novel, and celebrity author through a new frame.

The individual is negated in *Dorian Gray*, as the novel's Faustian plot drives relentlessly toward its inevitable final lines: "Lying on the floor was a dead man, in evening dress, with a knife in his heart. He was withered, wrinkled, and loathsome of visage. It was not till they had examined the rings that they recognized who it was" (251). Nearby sits "a splendid portrait of their master as they had last seen him, in all the wonder of his exquisite youth and beauty" (251). Although Dorian has spent the majority of the novel watching his painting change to reflect his increasingly depraved life, he maintains his "pure, bright, innocent face, and . . . marvelous untroubled youth" (181). Like Jekyll's Hyde, the painting is Dorian's dark double, a physical manifestation of everything in Dorian that is negative; as Basil notes, "Sin is a thing that writes itself across a man's face. It cannot be concealed" (181). Sin must manifest physically, and in this Gothic tale it can do so through Dorian's portrait. The individual is depicted as split into two, metaphorically articulating the logic of the photographic double exposure. Yet on closer inspection, this proves to be an incomplete inversion. Dorian switches places with his painting, and although he looks innocent and young but is nevertheless evil, his painting does not completely invert those characteristics: he looks evil in the painting, but this does not mean the painting itself is necessarily innocent or young.

While visuality is central to *Dorian Gray*, photography is at first glance little more than an afterthought. There is one direct reference to photography in the novel, and it is relegated to the level of a witticism. In chapter 4, Lady Henry meets Dorian and remarks, "I know you quite well by your photographs. I think my husband has got seventeen of them." "Not seventeen, Lady Henry?," asks Dorian, to which she replies: "Well, eighteen then" (85). This banter communicates Henry's interest in Dorian—or perhaps reveals Henry to be a hoarder—and echoes back to the original representation of Dorian: the picture. According to Novak, photography pervades the novel beyond this single reference. Basil's picture of Dorian and Dorian himself "represent two competing discourses and fantasies about photography in Victorian culture. In one sense, Dorian's body represents a fantasy about the innocence and inviolability of the photograph and photographic 'truth' . . . in another sense, Dorian's body is photographic, because it is at once impossible and 'real,' abstract and material" (138). Furthermore, as Novak argues, "having *become* the portrait, Dorian turns Basil's painting into a reproducible work of art. That is, he turns painting into photography" (139, emphasis in original). Lord Henry's seventeen or eighteen photographs of Dorian do not merely refer to the central art piece in the novel—they signal a broader, metaphoric engagement with photographic technology. This engagement extends to our interpretation of the painting and Dorian. Novak observes that Dorian is "like a photographic negative" (142) insofar as Henry's words make a "sudden impression" on him, which he reflects physically through what Basil takes to be "the most wonderful expression" (Wilde, *Dorian Gray* 60). While Novak locates the photographic in Dorian, the logic of photographic negativity extends beyond this single character. In her reading, Jane Gaines argues that the novel as a whole is a "metaphor for photography," the narrative elucidating "problems posed by the invention of photography" by dramatizing "the relationship between the painting and its object, suggesting as they do an analogy between photographic portraiture" as well as raising the issue of "authorial originality as a claim to ownership in a work" (42–43).

The negative allows us to read the photographic trace in *Dorian Gray* as a comment on originality and duplication, within and beyond the text. On its surface, Wilde's novel seems to duplicate Stevenson's motif of a single individual represented by two visibly dissimilar figures. Also as in *Jekyll and Hyde*, these figures cannot ultimately resolve, except with the destruction of the individual. Insofar as Dorian and his picture reference one another and form a single image of the individual—beautiful yet rendered ugly through sin—they are akin to the negatives that form a double exposure. The novel pivots on Dorian's exchange with his painting. This is true even before Dorian's Faustian deal. When Basil first meets Dorian, he discovers "someone whose mere personality was so fascinating that, if I allowed it to do so, it would absorb my whole nature, my whole soul, my very art itself" (48). Dorian is more than Dorian to Basil: "He is all my art to me now," explains the painter, articulating the extent to which Dorian and art are fused in the painter's mind (51). Indeed, Basil's painting is admired as "a wonderful work of art, and a wonderful likeness as well," and Lord Henry announces that "it is the finest portrait of modern times. Mr. Gray, come over and look at yourself" (64). Called to look at his image as himself, not merely a representation of himself, it seems to Dorian that "he had recognized himself for the first time" (65). Dorian's painting, in other words, is a perfect representation of the young man. As the novel goes on and Dorian becomes corrupted, he gradually looks less and less like the painting. The painting famously takes on his negative attributes while he remains the perfect image of handsome youth. The painting is Dorian's negative in the sense that it displays his negative conduct. Yet he is also the negative, in the sense that he performs these corrupt deeds. The novel, then, offers us two negatives without a true positive.

Dorian is "jealous of the portrait," for it depicts a beauty that will not die, and at this moment he swears he would give his soul to trade places with the image so as to never lose his youth (66). Since this is a Gothic parable, Dorian's wish is granted, and the man and painting are entwined for the remainder of the novel. As Dorian sins by being cruel to others, starting with Sibyl Vane, and generally leads a life of moral depravity, the painting changes to reflect his fall, a "most magical of mirrors" that will "reveal to him his own soul" (141). Dorian and picture are each the negative, the origin, of the other. Dorian is the original subject, but by exchanging the reality of aging and physical impact of the world for the picture's qualities of permanent youth and beauty, he trades his status as an original for that of a copy. In photographic terms, he is the original negative but exchanges that position for a reproduction.[13] The original thus only signifies in relation to its copy, creating a negative feedback loop in which the individual needs the copy to exist at all. As though validating Dickens's concerns about photographic reproduction, in many ways Dorian has *become* his image, negating the negative as an origin. Although he claims "each of us has a Heaven and Hell in him," it appears his heaven remains in his uncorrupted past, whereas his hell increasingly takes over after he is corrupted by the yellow book (188). The truth of this corruption is exposed in the novel's final scene, where the return of his actual physical appearance is an abrupt and decisive judgment on his life for all the world to see. Here the two Dorians appear as they ought, illustrating for those who gaze on the dead man and his portrait the truth of the individual in a single tableau.

This was not Wilde's only exploration of the theme of split subjectivity: in his 1891 children's story, "The Fisherman and His Soul," a fisherman falls in love with a mermaid, who tells him they cannot marry unless he sends away his soul. A witch teaches him how to accomplish this, informing him, "What men call the shadow of the body is not the shadow of the body, but is the body of the soul. Stand on the sea-shore with thy back to the moon, and cut away from around thy feet thy shadow, which is thy soul's body, and bid thy soul leave thee, and it will do so" (180). The fisherman excises his soul and goes into the sea to marry his mermaid. Unsurprisingly, because it is characterized as a shadow with all its associated metaphoric implications, his soul goes on to do corrupt things. The fisherman has not given his soul a heart. He is finally drawn out of the sea by his desire to dance, but once reunited with his soul, he cannot sever the bond again. Ultimately, the fisherman's heart breaks and he dies. Whereas *Dorian Gray*'s connection to the art world comes in the form of the painting and by extension photography, as another mode of reproduction "The Fisherman and

His Soul" articulates its theme of duality through dark and light, tapping into a metaphoric system as we saw in Dickens. The shadow representing the fisherman's soul evokes the light/dark dialectic of *Tale* and *Little Dorrit* but applies this dynamic to the individual. The individual's soul is his shadow—or negative—but it is not until he negates the negative that the individual's own self is threatened.

On the surface, "The Fisherman and His Soul" reads like a moral tale, its message one of the importance of the heart and the danger inherent in neglecting the soul. *Dorian Gray* also holds a moral lesson, as Wilde repeatedly argues. In his June 26, 1890, letter to the editor of the *St. James's Gazette*, for instance, Wilde explains that "the moral is this: All excess, as well as all renunciation, brings its own punishment" (240). Yet both "The Fisherman and His Soul" and *Dorian Gray* may be conversely read as the undoing of morals: both focus on moral questions but also offer a cynical view of the world, foreclosing any sort of positive resolution and subtly mocking other, more traditional moral tales.[14] In his 1891 preface to *Dorian Gray*, Wilde resists the search for morality in art, warning, "Those who read the symbol do so at their peril" (42). In "The Decay of Lying," published in revised form in 1891, Wilde suggests through the character Vivian that "lying, the telling of beautiful untrue things, is the proper aim of Art" (320). His novel at once demands a moral interpretation but then resists that interpretation, positioning itself as a paradoxical aphorism that sounds like truth yet is difficult to sustain. Indeed, the aphorisms that abound in *Dorian Gray* are most frequently paradoxical. Henry's quips—such as "Nothing can cure the soul but the senses, just as nothing can cure the senses but the soul" or "It is only shallow people who do not judge by appearances. The true mystery of the world is the visible, not the invisible"—present seemingly contradictory or shocking statements as matters of fact (61, 62).[15] They appear antithetical to truth, but as the character Mr. Erskine explains, they are "the way of truth. To test Reality we must see it on the tight-rope. When the Verities become acrobats we can judge them" (79). Henry's declaration that the visible world is more mysterious than the invisible, and Wilde's seemingly paradoxical preference for surface over depth, subvert what we think of as foundational. Thus the negative, implicitly thought to be foundational to the photographic image, is instead, by this aphoristic logic, refigured as derivative of its resulting image. In other words, the negative gives this apparently paradoxical logic a material referent as well as a grammatical precedent.

Throughout *Dorian Gray* Wilde's wit seems devised to test reality or challenge traditional assumptions, but at times his language comes closer to that of double negatives, such as the double negative Lord Henry repeats, with variation, three times: he tells Dorian that "With your personality there is nothing you could not do," and shortly thereafter thinks to himself "There was nothing that one could not do with him" (63, 76). After Sibyl's death, Henry says again, "There is nothing that you, with your extraordinary good looks, will not be able to do" (138). The focus of the double negative shifts, across these examples, from personality to appearances, but the double negative is consistent. Initially this double negative seems to conform to the simplest definition, whereby two negatives make a positive. Yet the most apparent positive to emerge from this double negative is the construction that Dorian will be able to do anything. Try as he might to truly test the social limits and do just that—anything he wishes—his life catches up with him. In this sense, the meaning that emerges from the double negative appears darkly prophetic: there is nothing, it seems, Dorian cannot do, yet the realization of this will become his undoing. He will be unable to sustain "anything," because "anything" relies on a suspension of reality. Dorian will not be able to live with his portrait reminding him of everything he has done while he remains unchanged—which is to say, there is nothing he is unable to do except do nothing. The double exposure in this case functions like the grammatical understanding of the double negative popularized around the turn of the century: it modifies the original statement, representing something new. It does not reinforce the negative or contradict it—it creates an alternative meaning. Like Dorian's picture, these double negatives change the original subject. Just after the Sibyl scene, Dorian begins using double negatives of his own: "If one doesn't talk about a thing, it has never happened," he tells Basil (142). If one talks about a thing, however—for instance, in a novel—this is not the same as suggesting it has happened in real life. After all, as Wilde suggests, "Life imitates Art far more than Art imitates Life" ("Decay of Lying" 320). The meaning that emerges from *Dorian Gray* is that of a novel that demands to be read as art and not life, and which was, and is still, often read alongside the life of its author. It is a meaning that always misses its mark—a taunt to realism and representation. Which is to say, the double negative here produces a paradox.

The novel's paradoxical aphorisms are, as Joseph Bristow explains, inversions that may be read as "part of a politically oppositional reverse-discourse. . . . Lord Henry's eloquence overturns commonly held assumptions to reveal the unethical bases of values all too readily deemed fit for young minds" (Bristow, "Wilde" 54). The very construction of Lord Henry's speech is a threat to the public, because through paradoxical aphorism he is able to undermine morality. The aphorisms "invert given values and make other meanings possible" (54). *Dorian Gray* mobilizes paradox as subversive subtext. Jonathan Dollimore observes that this aesthetics of inversion extended beyond the limits of Wilde's texts: "One of the many reasons why people were terrified by Wilde was because of a perceived connection between his aesthetic transgression and his sexual transgression. 'Inversion' was being used increasingly to define a specific kind of deviant sexuality inseparable from a deviant personality" (67).[16] As Dollimore argues, grammatical inversion and sexual inversion were read as following similar logics. The novel's relationship to sexual inversion is of course part of its infamy and cultural/critical legacy—part of the reason the text was brought into Wilde's trial. This use of the text, coupled with the preface's demand that the novel be treated as art and nothing more, ironically form yet another paradox. Here the double exposure follows the third logic of the double negative, in which two negatives are neither reconciled into a positive nor reinforced by one another. Instead, they create an alternate meaning.

The novel was famously used as evidence to prove its author's immorality. In *Regina (Wilde) v. Queensberry*, the novel was treated as a negative example of its author's sexual proclivities, and selected passages from the periodical edition were read aloud in court. In his examination of Wilde, Edward Carson cites Wilde's preface to *Dorian Gray*—"There is no such thing as a moral or an immoral book. Books are well written, or badly written"—and suggests dangerous real-world implications for this attitude (Wilde, *Dorian Gray* 41). "The affection and love of the artist of *Dorian Gray* might lead an ordinary individual to believe that it might have a certain tendency?" asks Carson, who proceeds to read three long passages from the novel depicting interactions between Basil and Dorian (Hyde 110). The in-court references to the more suggestive *Lippincott's Monthly Magazine* edition of the novel are, as Norman Page puts it, "extensive" (29).[17] Carson uses these references to ask whether the novel's "description of the feeling of one man towards a youth just grown up was a proper or an improper feeling?" and to establish a connection between Basil and Dorian's relationship and that of Wilde and Lord Alfred Douglas (Hyde 111). In other words, the novel was used to expose its author, duplicating Dorian's exposure on an extratextual level.

Reading *Dorian Gray* beyond itself despite Wilde's requests to the contrary, we encounter, besides the infamy of Wilde's trials, the author's image. Like Dickens, Wilde was photographed to excess, and those photographs were widely reproduced and circulated. He was, as David M. Friedman writes, the creator of "the value system we now call celebrity culture" (16).[18] Despite the figure of the celebrity predating the 1870s—as we see with Dickens, for instance—Wilde constructed his own celebrity with a distinctly modern flourish, creating "a flashy new category incorporating the best and worst of notoriety *and* fame" (19, emphasis in original). Just as photography was essential to earlier Victorian formulations of celebrity, so too was it essential to Wilde's. Twenty-seven of Wilde's arguably most famous photographs were taken by celebrity photographer Napoleon Sarony, a New York photographer known for his portraits of famous entertainers—and for the creation of fame through his portraits (88). As Novak puts it, Sarony's photographs "often created as much as they recorded celebrity status" (131). Like Dickens, Wilde understood his image to be central to his fame, but whereas both authors acknowledged that image reproduction—authorized or not—escaped the control of the photographic subject, Wilde aspired to "use photography to regain control of his public image" (Friedman 93). He did this by calculatedly posing for the Sarony photographs to establish an image of his own design, to create an "aura of celebrity" through the reproduction of his own image (95). Another important distinction between the authors is that Dickens's numerous portraits came after he had achieved fame as an author; the photographs solidified and perhaps extended his celebrity. Wilde, however, was notorious for his epigrams and aphorisms and for being caricatured in the press; his literary career largely followed, rather than preceded, the Sarony photographs. As Michael North puts, it, "Wilde was famous because he was widely pictured and not vice versa" ("The Picture of Oscar Wilde" 185).

Wilde's photographs raise questions about celebrity photography, reproducibility, and control over one's own image. His photographic image became infamous in 1883, when Sarony filed a copyright infringement suit against the Burrow-Giles Lithographic Company for its production of 85,000 unauthorized copies of one of Wilde's photographs. The case went to the US Supreme Court, which found in Sarony's favor and thereby affected future copyright issues at large in the United States (Gaines 51). Arguing that photography is an original work of authorship, Sarony simultaneously reduced the concept of originality to "nothing more than a point of origin" (51). Claiming authorship of the portraits, Sarony relegated Wilde to the position of passive subject, rather than active agent in the establishment of his celebrity. Essentially, the Supreme Court decision suggests that "photography could be an art of fiction, but that Wilde's famous 'pose' was hardly his own property" (Novak 122). In this case, the image of Wilde was granted more protections than the human subject Wilde, who was treated as a product of Sarony's art. The Sarony photograph of Wilde confirms Dickens's fear about the loss of control of the photographed celebrity author, just as the use of *Dorian Gray* in a court of law confirms Wilde's concerns about the reception of his infamous work of art—a work of art itself endowed with a kind of negative celebrity status.

Several of Wilde's photographic portraits were used as the basis for "etchings, advertisements, and even newspaper drawings of Wilde during his trials" (Novak 118). These appeared alongside voluminous reports and editorials of the trials. David Schulz argues that Wilde had "parlayed the growing technology of newspaper reproduction and distribution to enhance his celebrity persona while aligning himself with a culturally dissident avant-garde" (40). Perhaps because "Wilde was a known commodity to the press," that press was all the more prepared to mediate his downfall (40). Notably, the newspaper accounts "provide the only surviving 'firsthand' documentation of the event," and "by deliberately invoking performance tropes . . . the newspapers attempted to write into their accounts an immediacy" (44). Newspaper reports thus featured descriptions of Wilde's body, descriptions that changed as the trials went on. Accompanying many of these descriptions, the illustrations repurposed what were often images taken years earlier. Thus recycled, the photographs were made to trouble the distinction between fame and infamy. The repurposed images at his trials were extracted from their original context and conflated celebrity with suspect—like an Irene Adler, but one who did not manage to escape. Like the novel used as evidence in the trial, these photographs were reappropriated as a form of evidence: an attempt to make Wilde's queerness legible.

In addition to a focus on negativity, each of the stories analyzed in this chapter grapple with the issue of control over image. In Wilde's novel, the only way to exert control over an image is to make that image into a work of art. Yet as Wilde's trials reveal, there can be no full control over art. In the age of photographic reproduction, the image is too easily repurposed. Wilde sets up his novel to be doubly impervious to critique: first, via the preface's art for art's sake defenses and second, through the novel's apparent moral message. The tragic paradox of *Dorian Gray* is that neither defense succeeds. "To reveal art and conceal the artist is art's aim," writes Wilde, but in this case the celebrity artist works at cross-purposes to his own art in that his reputation hinges on the exposure of his own image. As Sarony's case proves, only the artist (but really no artist) can control the art and its reproductions. Of course, "No artist desires to prove anything"—except perhaps that he is a celebrity (*Dorian Gray* 41). Wilde's language turns us around and around, negations compounding and revealing alternate interpretations—the novel opening up into life, signifying otherwise.

Chapter 5

The Postmortem Photograph

Photographing (in) Wessex

Bennett and Hornung were not alone in linking photography to issues of feminine reputation and propriety in their late Victorian fictions. Amy Levy similarly thematizes such concerns in her 1888 novel, *The Romance of a Shop*, a book about four sisters who open a photographic studio to make ends meet. In the eyes of friends and family, the studio is a scandal, the Lorimer girls perceived as "naughty children, idle dreamers" (65). The scandal of the arrangement is that it brings the sisters into the world of commerce, an unfortunate change in social status. As one sister, Fanny, asks at the outset, "need it come to that—to open a shop?" (54). Another potential scandal soon presents itself. Gertrude reveals that they have been asked to perform "rather a dismal sort of job. It is to photograph a dead person" (84). Although this type of photography, Gertrude notes, "is quite usual," to Fanny it seems strange that Lord Watergate "should select ladies, young girls, for such a piece of work!" (84). This job of photographing the dead, which was by no means exceptional in Victorian England, nevertheless exacerbates the threat to the sisters' reputations.

This threat is ultimately evaded through a marriage plot conclusion. By photographing Lord Watergate's dead wife, Gertrude first meets the man who eventually becomes her love interest. Photographing the woman "lying dead or asleep, with her hair spread out on the pillow," Gertrude also sees Lord Watergate as though she is photographing him: "The broad forehead, projecting over the eyes; the fine, but rough-hewn features; the brown hair and beard; the tall, stooping, sinewy figure: these together formed a picture which imprinted itself as by a flash" (87). The postmortem photograph could be mistaken for a photograph of a sleeping subject; likewise, the postmortem photograph and Gertrude's first glimpse of Lord Watergate are described in similar terms, which has the effect of blurring the boundary between private memento mori and public view of an individual, normalizing the death photograph as yet another way an individual is viewed in this photographic culture. Death photography functions in the novel as a plot device in aid of the story's romance, and thereby Levy's novel reinforces a normalizing view of death photography entwined with life.

In Bennett's, Hornung's, and Levy's texts, photography expresses the high stakes of women's reputations in late Victorian England, and it ultimately helps facilitate each story's emotional romantic conclusion. Likewise, in Thomas Hardy's works, photography is a highly malleable sign of affective attachment: a technology that is not always trustworthy but is repeatedly emotionally charged. Rather than featured as double exposures, as in Bennett and Hornung, in Hardy's work, photography imagines the visual as absence itself. This brings it into closer alignment with postmortem photography—which is the photography *of* absence—Levy describes. Whereas in Dickens photography signals a questioning of visual certainty, and in Conan Doyle it poses a critique of visual evidence—the questioning and ultimately the dismantling of visual objectivity—in Hardy photography frames the visual as the negation of such evidence. In other words, it manifests as the antithesis of its intended use by Conan Doyle's famous detective. In Hardy's work, photography is treated as both more important and less trustworthy than it ought to be, and it is given a significance that exceeds representation and is treated with a skepticism that undermines its attempts at verisimilitude. The twining of these contradictory treatments gives photography its haunting, mournful appeal across Hardy's works. Photography promises presence to characters and readers but instead provides a record of its own failure to provide that presence. I argue that Hardy uses photography to negate presence itself. He depicts photography but then undermines its ostensible recording function. The visual record vacated by photography is instead displaced to Wessex, Hardy's fictional/factional palimpsest of southwestern England that forms the settings of most of his literary works, and that is reproduced visually over and over again through maps and photographs.

The characters in Hardy's poems and fiction often treat photography like it is not just a representation, but actually is the represented person or place. Hardy critiques photography as realism in his fiction, undermining photographic objectivity in *A Laodicean* and visual certainty in "An Imaginative Woman." In *Jude the Obscure*, he goes a step further by first offering several images and then refusing us the image—a postmortem photograph—that the novel conditions us to anticipate. Instead of registering a discomfort with photographic reproduction and inversion, Hardy circumvents the photographic record altogether. It reemerges, a trace that haunts the world of his texts in the form of photographic frontispieces. Hardy features photographs of Wessex locations—themselves famous locations to which people did and do take tours—in each volume comprising his collected 1912 Wessex edition of the novels. These photographs represent places that do not exist, causing us to question photographic truth and its relationship to the real. As such, the Wessex photographs reiterate the challenge to photography Hardy poses in *Jude* and show presence itself to be a lie—a negation.

Photography repeatedly signifies affective attachment and the loss of intimate connection across Hardy's works. In *A Laodicean*, which features one of most plot-driven and direct treatments of photography in Hardy's oeuvre, photography nonetheless functions as a divisive force, nearly disrupting the marriage plot. In "An Imaginative Woman," photography is also divisive, facilitating the rift between husband and wife and ultimately creating erroneous familial discord at the end of the story. Yet Hardy's interest in photography extends beyond the limits of realism, and in fact we can see the affective power of photography most succinctly in his poems "The Photograph" and "The Son's Portrait." In each, the photograph of a loved one becomes more than image on card stock or paper—more than a representation of the real—but the person him- or herself. In "The Photograph," the act of burning a photograph of a lost lover feels to the surviving speaker "as if I had put her to death that night" (l. 20). The speaker imagines that the destruction of the image impacts the subject in the photograph, wondering "if on earth alive / Did she feel a smart, and with vague strange anguish strive? / If in heaven, did she smile at me sadly and shake her head?" (ll. 23–25). In "The Son's Portrait," Hardy continues to explore a subject initially developed in *Jude*: namely, the discovery in a shop of a familiar photograph and the realization that this photograph was therefore discarded by a beloved. The narrator in this poem is a mother who sees her dead son in a framed photograph in a lumber shop. The shop owner explains, "A lady—I know not whence— / Sold it me, Ma'am, one day, / With more. You can have it for eighteenpence: / The picture's nothing; / It's but for the frame you pay" (ll. 11–15). The photograph, the mother realizes, was sold by her son's former wife after his death in the war, and she buries it "as 'twere he" (l. 22). In these poems, the photograph signifies not a mere representation but an absent presence. The photograph represents the subject—indeed, it *is* the subject of the poems—but it is a subject[1] that has been lost.

In focusing on affective attachment and its absence, this chapter is also in many ways about mourning and the extent to which photography facilitated mourning practices in late Victorian culture. Rather than solidifying interpersonal attachment as we might anticipate, photography makes that attachment more elusive and less substantial, particularly in Hardy's final novel. Photography haunts *Jude*, suggesting a connection that cannot be, functioning as a placeholder for what is missing. This haunting desire is duplicated in the establishment of Wessex throughout Hardy's canon, most powerfully through the photographs that stand in for Wessex locales in the Wessex edition. In Hardy, Wessex is the celebrity figured most prominently, a place represented over and over again in illustration, cartography, and photography, as well as a place that can never be visited, no matter how accurate the map. I trace the effect of the photographic negative through motifs of reproduction and inversion across Hardy's literary treatments of photography and the solidification of his fictional locale through the 1912 Wessex edition. I use the postmortem photograph—a particular type of memento mori popular in the nineteenth century—and then frame my discussion of the immaterial in relation to Hardy's photographic imagination. My discussion of the negative thus shifts from the material process of photography to the more metaphoric negation Hardy's photographs evoke. Through *Jude* and the Wessex photographs, we are left to contemplate the emptiness of a truly negated image.

The Failure of Photography in Hardy

Photography figures prominently in *A Laodicean*, and critics analyzing the role of the technology in Hardy's work often focus their attention on this novel and his shorter fiction and poetry, where references to photography are most explicit. The plot of *A Laodicean*, for instance, pivots in key ways around photography. The novel represents the tension between modern realism and a more medieval romanticism through the modern architect George Somerset and the former noble Captain De Stancy, and it is infused with modern technologies such as photography and telegrams, which effectively threaten the budding romance between Somerset and Paula Power. While these technologies are treated as dangers, the novel's marriage plot sees Paula ending up with Somerset—and thus the book expresses ambivalence around the modernity Somerset represents. Photography is also central to "An Imaginative Woman," where a woman falls in love with a man she does not know through his photograph. In both *A Laodicean* and "An Imaginative Woman," photography questions reality.

Critics have long noted Hardy's uneasy relationship to realism, referring to his statements on the literary convention. As Roger Webster summarizes, Hardy's essays on fiction published between 1888 and 1891 express a rejection of realism in preference of "a more impressionistic and visionary mode" (25). Rejecting realism as "copyism" and sight as "acquired by the outer sense alone" and close to photography, Hardy values a partial and distorted vision of art: "To see in half and quarter views the whole picture . . . is the intuitive power that supplies the would-be storywriter with the scientific bases for his pursuit" ("The Science of Fiction" 137). These partial views and this scientific basis, Hardy writes here, are enough. "Visual thinking," notes Sheila Berger, "is at the cord of Hardy's aesthetics," and indeed, "Seeing for him is not a metaphor for knowing; it is a form of knowing" (xii). Along with this visual thinking "a sense of contradiction—unresolved tensions, incongruity, ambiguity, ambivalence—rests at the core of his writing" (xiii). In other words, Hardy's aesthetic system is highly visual but does not provide a complete or simple picture.

In describing Hardy's debt to the visual arts, critics often note that his writing adopts painterly qualities rather than photographic ones: "Hardy distinguishes between two conceptions of truth," writes Jane Thomas: "the objective, photographic 'truth' of realism, and the subjective, more painterly truth of art" (443). According to Thomas, Hardy favors this second truth. Photography gets wrapped up in this critique of realism, according to Jennifer M. Green, who notes that Hardy "criticizes" photography in his work "for being limited to physical realism" ("Outside the Frame" 124). In her study of photography in Hardy's oeuvre, Arlene M. Jackson agrees, writing, "Hardy disparages the kind of literary realism based on mere photographic detail, and dismisses the photograph as incapable of the selectivity that is the basis of art" ("Photography as Style and Metaphor" 93). This dismissal is not absolute, Jackson and Green admit in different contexts in their separate arguments: Hardy does feature photography repeatedly in his literary works, treating it in more metaphoric ways than we might anticipate, given the connection he made between photography and the realism he criticized.[2] In his analysis of photography across Hardy's works, Mark Durden suggests that Hardy alternates between two Victorian approaches to photography. In the first instance, photography tells inner truths; in the second, it reveals deception. He observes that "much has been made of the relationship between Hardy's fiction and painting," but there is also an "influence of photography on his writing," and we may see his texts "marked by a visual sensibility that is *photographic*" (57–58).[3] My own argument draws on but departs from these analyses of the complex ways Hardy uses photography in his works. Rather than seeing photography as an agent of the real, I suggest that Hardy uses it to document absence, particularly the absence of real people or places. Photography signals affective attachment, but only to negate the realization of that attachment. Viewing Hardy's photographic sensibility in this way, through absence and separation, provides a new reading of both his relationship to realism and the cultural work that photography performs.

Hardy's works feature a negotiation with photography on a continuum of skepticism of the technology and desire for its mimetic promise. Throughout his literary treatments of photography, Hardy toys with the literal and figurative connotations of the photographic negative, as though aware that the negative's chief characteristics of reproduction and verisimilitude also render the technology suspect. Playing with the concept of the negative directly in *A Laodicean* through his description of the corrupt photographer Dare, Hardy figures the negative more metaphorically in "An Imaginative Woman" as the negation of the photographic subject altogether. Throughout these tales, photography operates as powerfully captivating but ultimately deceitful—a lie that cannot be avoided in an era of modernization and nostalgia. A challenge to verisimilitude as well as a more profound challenge to presence and certainty, this lie evokes a quality of the photographic negative I have traced throughout this project.

Photography most obviously functions as a lie in *A Laodicean*. Helping his father woo the wealthy heiress Paula Power and triumph over his rival, George Somerset, photographer William Dare uses technology to trick Paula and his own aunt Charlotte into believing that Somerset has fallen into a state of drunken depravity. Dare sends a telegram to Paula under the guise of Somerset, begging for money. While "the esteem in which she had held Somerset up to that hour suffered a tremendous blow by his apparent scrape," the telegram does not quite have the desired effect, and Dare must create a fictional photograph to help seal the deal and sever Paula from Somerset more conclusively (256). He contrives to let a photograph fall out of his pocket during a meeting with Paula and Charlotte, and the ladies are given an opportunity to take in this image at length, both "drawn as by fascination towards the photograph on the floor, which, contrary to his first impulse, Dare, as has been said, now seemed in no hurry to regain" (281). This image "was a portrait of Somerset; but by a device known in photography the operator, though contriving to produce what seemed to be a perfect likeness, had given it the distorted features and wild attitude of a man advanced in intoxication" (281). Hardy lets his readers know right away that the photograph is a fake, but to help explain how Paula and Charlotte fail to detect the ruse, he puts things in gendered terms: "No woman, unless specially cognisant of such possibilities, could have looked upon it and doubted that the photograph was a genuine illustration of a customary phase in the young man's private life" (281). Indeed, Hardy suggests this is perhaps because the gentler sex is so less accustomed to the mysteries of science:

> Of all the thoughts which filled the minds of Paula and Charlotte De Stancy, the thought that the photograph might have been a fabrication was probably the last. To them that picture of Somerset had all the cogency of direct vision. Paula's experience, much less Charlotte's, had never lain in the fields of heliographic science, and they would as soon have thought that the sun could again stand still upon Gibeon, as that it could be made to falsify men's characters in delineating their features. (283)

The efficacy of the photographic lie depends on Paula and Charlotte's absolute trust in photographic objectivity—to Charlotte it "seemed so improbable to her that God's sun should bear false witness"—yet Hardy shows us consistently throughout the novel that photography and the photographer are not to be trusted (335).[4]

Dare's introduction to De Stancy Castle and the plot is accompanied by hints of his unscrupulousness and suggestions that his lies extend beyond his art to his very being. "Mr. Dare *says* he is a photographic amateur," says Charlotte, introducing Dare to Somerset with a hint of doubt (44, emphasis added). Somerset's first encounter with the man is tainted by his desire to see Paula instead. Dare's coming is "a sort of counterfeit of Miss Power" and compels Somerset "to judge him with as much severity as justice would allow" (45). Somerset thinks he is going to be seeing Paula, so the photographer is an unwelcome "counterfeit" of that encounter. This unexpected substitution causes Somerset to behave in a way that is out of proportion—he is living a lie of sorts through his reaction. Nevertheless, if Dare compels this reaction, it is in part a result of his strange presence. There is something of a lie to the photographer as well as the photographs, as we see in Hardy's first description of the man. Somerset's first impression of Dare is that:

> His age it was impossible to say. There was not a hair upon his face which could serve to hang a guess upon. In repose he

> appeared a boy; but his actions were so completely those of a man that the beholder's first estimate of sixteen as his age was hastily corrected to six-and-twenty, and afterwards shifted hither and thither along intervening years as the tenor of his sentences sent him up or down. (45)

Somerset does not know how to place Dare age-wise, which has a disorienting effect on the observer. His incongruous appearance extends to his gender, his class, and his attitude toward others. He wore his hair "in the fashion sometimes affected by the other sex," and while he has a fancy ring, it is of dubious quality for "the gold seemed good, the diamond questionable, and the taste indifferent" (45). Somerset has the distinct impression that Dare does not like him. Like a photograph before it is developed, Dare the "man, or boy" has a "latent power" that makes Somerset particularly attuned to him as an unlikable individual (45). In other words, Somerset detects something latent and unsavory in Dare. This introduction foreshadows the novel's marriage plot crisis at Dare's machinating hands.

Dare's counterfeit, latent qualities of character are tied repeatedly to his role as a photographer and specifically pivot around the image of the negative, which Hardy evokes as a material object or process and deploys more metaphorically. Somerset is not the only one to notice that something about Dare is a lie. Conversing with his rival, Havill, and Mrs. Goodman, Somerset remarks that Dare appears to be "a being of no age, no nationality, and no behavior" (63). "A complete negative," concludes Havill: "That is, he would be, if he were not a maker of negatives well known in Markton" (63). Dare circumvents accurate description of age, nationality, and character—becoming, like Hyde, a "complete negative," or the negation of those descriptors. Playing with multiple senses of "negative," Hardy indicates that insofar as he is well known as a photographer, Dare cannot be a truly negative figure, a negation of all that makes an individual distinct—he is too well known. Of course, although he is recognized, we learn through the novel that there is nothing about him that is actually well known. Characters notice his curious negative-like qualities, but no one—not even his aunt—suspects he is De Stancy's son. Furthermore, no one realizes he has such dark designs on Somerset and such a compulsion to advance De Stancy's cause "by such unscrupulous blackening of Somerset's character," as Charlotte thinks of it, reinforcing the image of Dare as a photographer who seeks to obscure rather than illuminate—to deal with negatives rather than positives (337). Dare seems aware of his connection to photographic inversion, responding to Mr. Power's suggestion that he go to Peru: "And if I meet your proposal with a negative?" (324). In "ironic contrast," Arlene Jackson writes of the parallel photographic lies in both *Desperate Remedies*[5] and *A Laodicean*, "to Hardy's own comment on photographic record, on copies of reality, the picture is of course not the reality it is purported to be" ("Photography as Style and Metaphor" 98). If we lend weight to Hardy's depiction of Dare as a negative, the lie of his photograph is not so much ironic as it is fitting.

The connection between photographer and photographic lie extends beyond Dare to the broader photographic community. Feeling that there is something inauthentic about Dare's photograph of the drunken Somerset, Charlotte "inquired of herself whether after all it might not be possible for photographs to represent people as they had never been" (336). To resolve this question, she goes to the photographic studio of Mr. Ray, "an obscure photographic artist" (336). Ray allows that although he finds "such misrepresentations" to be "libellous," they are nonetheless "quite possible, and that they embodied a form of humour which was getting more and more into vogue among certain facetious classes of society" (336). He disavows ever dabbling in this duplicitous form of photography—in fact, initially he does not want to answer her directly and does so only when he realizes "she meant no harm to him"—but Ray clearly lives a double life himself, perhaps sharing more with the "specimens of such work" than he allows:

> Ray's establishment consisted of two divisions, the respectable and the shabby. If, on entering the door, the visitor turned to the left, he found himself in a magazine of old clothes, old furniture, china, umbrellas, guns, fishing-rods, dirty fiddles, and split flutes. Entering the right-hand room, which had originally been that of an independent house, he was in an ordinary photographer's and print-collector's depository, to which a certain artistic solidity was imparted by a few oil paintings in the background. (336)

The photographer is depicted as internally divided between shabby home life and the semblance of respectable work, the image "imparted" by the "artistic solidity" of oil paintings. Ray's fragile respectability hinges not on his profession but on the oil paintings adorning his walls.

Indeed, photography occupies an uneasy space vis-à-vis painting in the novel. Durden argues that "photography like painting is in fact part of Hardy's way of bringing into his fiction a more intensified relationship with things," but in *A Laodicean* the two more frequently appear in tension (58). Paula's romantic sensibilities make her want to return the portraits of the dead De Stancys adorning the walls of her castle to the living De Stancys, and she meets a contrast in Sir William, who asks: "What is the utility of such accumulations? . . . Their originals are but clay now . . . Nothing can retain the spirit, and why should we preserve the shadow of the form?" (39). Captain De Stancy seems to detect a reason, capitalizing on Paula's romantic notions and using the preservation of portraits through photographic reproduction as an excuse to visit the castle every day. De Stancy and Dare photograph the portraits, and De Stancy goes so far as to ask to photograph Paula's portrait. While her portrait hangs alongside the others in the castle, she sees photographing it as a manifestation of "a dreadfuly encroaching sex" (174). His photographic project "seemed" to be "a perfect mania with him"—though we realize that Paula is his true mania and the preservation of the family portraits through photography is but a means to this end (174).

A Laodicean thematizes photography as a lie, dangerous because it is wielded by a duplicitous man[6] whose only motivation is a share of the inheritance he hopes to gain and who has no discernible affective attachments to family or friends. "An Imaginative Woman" explores a more emotional side of the photographic lie. Ella Marchmill, Hardy's titular imaginative woman, finds herself bored with her husband and her life and falls in love with a poet, Robert Trewe, who lived in the rooms she and her family rent for a summer holiday. She falls in love with him as a rival poet first, but after living in his rooms finds herself drawn to his things—including his photograph. She learns that Trewe's photograph sits behind an image of the duke and duchess and defers disclosing his image much like a striptease: "Ella idled about the shore with the children till dusk, thinking of the yet uncovered photograph in her room, with a serene sense of something ecstatic to come. . . . To gratify her passionate curiosity she now made her preparations, first getting rid of superfluous garments and putting on her dressing-gown" (67–68). She reads some of his poetry and then looks at the image for the first time. She kisses the photograph and brings it to bed with her, thinking "how wicked she was, a woman having a husband and three children, to let her mind stray to a stranger in this unconscionable manner" (68). The poet kills himself because he has no female companion with whom to share his life, and Ella later dies in childbirth. After her death, Marchmill discovers what by an "inexplicable trick of Nature" seems to him to be proof of Ella's marital infidelity: a photograph of Trewe along with a lock of hair, which he compares to his infant son (78). He thinks he sees "strong traces of resemblance" between the man in the photograph and his son, and the story ends with him disavowing his child (78). The tragic pivot of the story is that the image of Trewe does not offer Marchmill or Ella the truth—and this lie ends up ruining several lives. Whereas Hardy critiqued photography for its relationship to realism, in this story he seems to question its connection to the real.

While photography is a cold and calculated lie in *A Laodicean*, it is a mystical force in Hardy's later story.[7] However, photography lies in "An Imaginative Woman" as well, suggesting a proof of presence that cannot be. In this story, characteristics of the negative appear more metaphorically and metaphysically than in the earlier novel: the photograph duplicates the image of the poet, but this process lies to Ella by giving her a false presence—thus a false sense of verisimilitude—of the poet and lies to Marchmill by suggesting that his son is not his own. In fact, Marchmill's conclusion is the inverse of reality: the photograph has shown him the exact opposite of the truth. In both tales the photograph lies, but it also possesses power by demanding or questioning affective attachment. In each, Hardy suggests the photograph is not to be trusted and that there is an emptiness or negative at the center of the truth photography intends to represent. It is not just Dare's photograph that is suspect in *A Laodicean*, but photography more generally—even as practiced by the innocuous Ray. Although the photograph lies to Marchmill about his son's parentage, in a more abstract sense it does not lie after all—for his wife was surely in love with Trewe. Photography lies, but just enough to keep its viewer unsure where presence ends and image begins. Photography's lie of presence, as we will see, is developed further in *Jude the Obscure* and infused throughout Wessex.

Missing Mementos in *Jude*

Technological developments encroach on rural Wessex across Hardy's canon, often signaling a grim, automated modernization. In *Tess of the d'Urbervilles*, for instance, the "threshing-machine" is characterized as a "red tyrant" that maintains "a despotic demand upon the endurance" of the field workers (404). As signs of modernity encroaching on Wessex, photographs in *Jude the Obscure* have taken a critical backseat to the train, the novel's more ominously present technology. Photographs nevertheless pepper the text, and in doing so they signify affective attachment between characters, introduce friction, and generally help propel the narrative forward the eight times they are mentioned. Yet Sue and Jude have no portraits of their own children. Sue goes so far as to dig at the graves of her dead children to look at their faces. At a time when postmortem photographs were so prevalent and in a text that features modern technologies and photography more specifically, why don't Jude and Sue retain images of their dead children through photography? In this section I consider the history of postmortem photography in the later nineteenth century alongside the disappearance of the photographic record from *Jude* and argue that Hardy's work highlights a contradiction about photography both in the novel and beyond. In *Jude*, photographs initially appear to signal affective attachment through their presence and their absence. Photography's affective power, however, proves unstable, and its presence itself proves to signal absence. This calls into question the assumption that photography can provide a faithful record and the emotional attachments supposedly signified by the photographic object. Photography represents the messiness of the novel's interpersonal attachments and lends emotional valence—if in absentia—to the novel's most graphic tragedy.

Postmortem photographs aren't negatives in the material sense of the term, but they more abstractly feature inversion by suggesting a presence that is already gone. Hardy denies us these images altogether. Through absent postmortem photographs, Hardy's focus shifts from the material negative-as-inversion/lie in *A Laodicean* and "An Imaginative Woman" to a more theoretical sense of the negative as absent presence in *Jude*. In Dickens inversion evokes a dialectic whereby light equates to truth and dark to its opposite; in Hardy it also signifies the play between the truth and its missing opposite. In *Jude* this play of inversion is most poignantly expressed through the deaths of the children and their missing portraits.

The first description of photography comes at the end of the first part of novel, after Jude has separated from Arabella. He is in Alfredston, when he notices "a little framed photograph" in a pawnbroker's shop "which turned out to be his own portrait . . . It was one which he had specially taken and framed by a local man in bird's-eye maple, as a present for Arabella, and had duly given her on their wedding-day. On the back was still to be read, '*Jude to Arabella*,' with the date" (72). The pawnbroker, who does not recognize that the person in the photograph is Jude, advises him, like the mother in "The Son's Portrait," that the frame "is a very useful one, if you take out the likeness." The repetition of this scene in novel and poem reinforces its poignancy—the worthlessness of the photograph to the shop owner stands in sharp relief against its value to the mother or husband. Seeing the photograph discarded in this way affects Jude greatly, and he purchases it and burns it, frame and all. Susan Sontag interprets this as a sign of primitivistic magic (161), and indeed, Jude's discovery of the photograph holds symbolic weight in the novel. As Hardy puts it, "the utter death of every tender sentiment in his wife, as brought home to him by this mute and undesigned evidence of her sale of his portrait and gift, was the conclusive little stroke required to demolish all sentiment in him" (72). The photograph here wields significant affective power—it was a wedding gift and its rejection hardens Jude's heart against Arabella. We do learn Arabella has retained some images of Jude, for near the end of the novel she asks Cartlett if he recognizes Jude "from the photos I have showed you" (290). This moment belies what we think we know about Arabella's feelings toward Jude—indeed, it belies what Jude thinks he knows about Arabella's feelings—by signaling some residual emotional connection. By way of this reference to kept photographs, we discover that perhaps Jude's photograph in the pawn shop lied to him by allowing him to misread Arabella's emotions. Placed together, these two scenes suggest that photography is an index of emotional attachment, but one that may easily be misinterpreted.

Even without the added significance of a wedding, photographs matter greatly in the novel; they are, as Jackson puts it, "an essential part of the novel's iconography," displaying the central conflict "between reality and idealism" ("Photography as Style and Metaphor" 104). Jude's relationship with Sue is introduced by his glimpse of her in a photograph at his aunt's house. He "observed between the brass candlesticks on her mantelpiece the photograph of a pretty girlish face, in a broad hat, with radiating folds under the brim like the rays of a halo," and asks his great-aunt who she is. She replies "that she was his cousin Sue Bridehead, of the inimical branch of the family" (77–78). He remembers this image of a cousin he has never met later on in Christminster: "how he wished he had that pretty portrait of her!," he thinks, and he writes to his aunt and asks her to send it, which she does. Jude, "a ridiculously affectionate fellow . . . put the photograph on the mantelpiece, kissed it—he did not know why—and felt more at home. She seemed to look down and preside over his tea. It was cheering—the one thing uniting him to the emotions of the living city" (85). Before Jude even meets Sue, he finds himself attached to her through her image—or, perhaps more accurately, he finds himself attached to her image.[8] The absent Sue is present as an object for Jude—a "thing" that looks down at him, a thing he kisses and that comforts him.

Once they meet, Sue gives Jude another photograph of herself:

> "O, I bought something for you, which I had nearly forgotten," she said quickly, searching her pocket. "It is a new little photograph of me. Would you like it?" "*Would* I!" He took it gladly, and the porter came. There seemed to be an ominous glance on his face when he opened the gate. (139, emphasis in original)

The porter's ominous glance reinforces the impression that Sue and Jude's relationship is clandestine and that the photographic gift is a sign of their deepening affection for one another. This idea of the photographic gift as a sign of attachment is reinforced in a scene at Sue's lodging house. One of the mistresses of the house notices that Sue has on her dressing table, like many other girls, framed photographs: "two men in their filigree and velvet frames standing together beside her looking-glass." "Who are these men," asks the mistress, "Strictly speaking, relations' portraits only are allowed on these tables, you know" (141). Photographs are powerful: they can lead young women astray.

Indeed, photographs stand as a proxy for Sue's liberal affections. Thinking about Sue, Phillotson looks in an envelope where he keeps photographs. He takes out several photos of Sue, the first "as a child, long before he had known her," the next "as a young woman, her dark eyes and hair making a very distinct and attractive picture of her, which just disclosed, too, the thoughtfulness that lay behind her lighter moods." This second image is "a duplicate of the one she had given Jude, and would have given to any man. Phillotson brought it half-way to his lips, but withdrew it in doubt at her perplexing phrases: ultimately kissing the dead pasteboard with all the passionateness, and more than all the devotion, of a young man of eighteen" (161). Echoing Ella's photographic kiss in "An Imaginative Woman," this kiss confirms the auratic value of the photograph, which by itself is mere "dead pasteboard." Like Jude and the boarding house mistress, Phillotson acknowledges a power in photography that goes beyond mere record—in these instances, the photograph holds power over the viewer and creates and sustains an emotional attachment predicated on an assumed proximity to the photographic subject her- or himself. Sue echoes this emotional attachment to the photograph. As Jude stands outside the window, he sees her look at a photograph: "Having contemplated it a little while she pressed it against her bosom, and put it again in its place . . . 'Whose photograph was she looking at?' he said. He had once given her his; but she had others, he knew" (206). Here photographs are placeholders for the individuals they represent, and Sue's collection of multiple images speaks to the dangerous liberality of her affections.

These references indicate the pervasive power of photographs in the novel. Photographs of people appear throughout the text—they are promiscuously given, jealously coveted, and they seem to exist in abundance. Characters don't just have one precious image of each other; they have several. There are at least three images of the relatively impoverished Jude—the one Arabella discards and the two or more "photos" she has kept and shows Cartlett. There are also at least three of Sue—the image owned by Jude's aunt, the one Sue gives Jude and Phillotson, and the photograph of herself as a child that Phillotson also has. There are mysterious images of multiple men—Jude and Phillotson, perhaps—on Sue's dressing table. For as many photographs as there seem to be in circulation in this novel, they are nonetheless treated as precious, singular objects and imbued with an excess of attachment as though they are the individuals they represent. Photographs act on the emotions in a variety of ways—they signify attachment intentionally or unintentionally, truly or falsely,[9] and expectedly or unexpectedly. The prevalence and range of emotional significance of photography in *Jude*, coupled with the implication that photographs seem to exist in abundance in the Wessex of the novel, make their notable disappearance from the final part even more striking.

One of the most grotesquely memorable scenes in *Jude* is, of course, the murder-suicide of Jude's son, Little Father Time, and the other children in the sixth part of the novel. Following these deaths, the surgeon comes to the house, a jury comes to view the bodies, an inquest is held, and the funeral takes place. This all takes an undisclosed amount of time, culminating in the burial Sue attempts to stop: "A man with a shovel in his hands was attempting to earth in the common grave of the three children, but his arm was held back by an expostulating woman who stood in the half-filled hole" (340). Ranting, Sue protests to Jude:

> "I want to see them once more. O Jude—please Jude—I want to see them! . . . You said perhaps I should see them once more before they were screwed down; and then you didn't, but took them away! . . . Can't I see them once more—just once! Can't I? Only just one little minute, Jude? It would not take long! . . . I would go home quietly afterwards, and not want to see them any more! Can't I?. . . . Why can't I?" (340–41)

Sue repeats her desire to "see them" five times in this passage, indicating not so much a hysterical wish that the deaths be undone as a desire to simply see the bodies of her children one last time. While her plea is represented as a repetitious rant, what she asks for is quite reasonable. Why can't Sue see her children one more time, we might ask?

This is an era in which postmortem photography, a form of memento mori portraiture, was common and culturally acceptable.[10] Indeed, in a novel in which characters have and give away multiple images of one another, it would make sense for Sue to have postmortem photographs of the children—to seek to reproduce her children through the photographic image in order to remember them. Speaking to the power of photography generally, Jesse Hoffman writes that the technology "makes it possible to invest all objects with indexical significance and create a traceable relationship with the subject who will inevitably disappear" (615).[11] This function is even more poignant in the case of the postmortem photograph. Death photography was practiced from the early days of photography in the 1840s to the end of the century, but Geoffrey Batchen notes that it was particularly common in the last two decades of the nineteenth century for people to produce cabinet cards as memorials for people who had recently died. This was an international phenomenon with specific national and regional distinctions. In the American Midwest, for instance, "A professional photographer would be hired as part of the funeral ceremonies to shoot a collodion glass negative of a still life . . . comprised of the various flower arrangements displayed at the funeral itself. The resulting photograph would then be reproduced many times" for those who had attended the funeral or had sent flowers (*Suspending Time* 109–10). More common than these photographs of floral arrangements were images taken of dead individuals. While some scholars have suggested that postmortem photography was an American practice, it was in vogue all over Europe throughout the century.[12] It would have been available to Sue and Jude, therefore, living in England sometime in the late nineteenth century. Furthermore, it was a mainstream practice: as Jay Ruby notes, "During the first 40 years of photography (ca. 1840–1880), professional photographers regularly advertised" that they would photograph the dead, and this practice "was sufficiently common that black mats, often decorated with floral patterns, were sold by photographic supply houses" (*Secure the Shadow* 52–53). This type of photography was practiced frequently enough that photographers advertised they would come to the house with as little as an hour's notice (52).

Several archives focus on postmortem and funerary photography, illustrating the popularity of this photographic trend throughout the nineteenth century on both sides of the Atlantic. Among them, the Stanley Burns Archive in New York, the Jay Ruby Collection at Penn State, and the Walter A. Johnson Postmortem Collection at the George Eastman Museum, have notable collections.[13] The volume—and, increasingly toward the end of the century, the duplication—of these materials suggests the extent to which death was memorialized. Postmortem photographs assumed different forms: the body might be photographed inside the coffin, outside the coffin but clearly shown to be dead, posed as though asleep, or posed as though awake, with or without other family members.[14] Occasionally these photographs are touched up with rouge or other coloring to give the illusion of life. In the Johnson Collection, children are by far the most popular subjects of postmortem photography,[15] appearing in most of these images throughout the nineteenth century and particularly common in those photographs posing the dead subject as though alive.[16] The most common pose throughout the collection is that of the "last sleep," which Sobieszek and Appel note "dominates from 1840 to 1880" (65).

Toward the end of the century, postmortem photographs increasingly featured bodies in coffins. When taken of children—or nearly anyone in the earlier years of photographic practice—postmortem photographs were often the only photographic record of an individual, making them extremely desirable. By 1850 daguerreotypes were a shilling each in England or twenty-five cents in the United States—a not insignificant amount to pay for all but the wealthy, but still affordable for most. High-end Boston studio Southworth and Hawes advertised $12 postmortem daguerreotype sittings at midcentury (Guynn).[17] Because comparable Boston daguerreotypes could be purchased for $1 around this time, the practice was "a middle- and lower-middle-class activity" (Ruby, *Secure the Shadow* 164). These images were therefore accessible, affordable, and widespread. It is furthermore important to note, as does Stanley B. Burns, that although North American and European postmortem photography differed in aim—in America the subjects were almost always for private, domestic circulation, whereas in Europe private images existed along with more public and mass-produced images of "royalty, nobility, the wealthy and other notables"—this was a popular tradition in both regions.

By the 1890s, when *Jude* was written, the dry-plate process would have driven down prices further, making such images affordable to most.[18] Given Sue and Jude's dire financial circumstances—circumstances that led Little Father Time to his desperate act—expense might have inhibited them from procuring a postmortem photograph. The fact that the deaths were murder-suicides might have constituted a taboo, making it difficult for them to find a photographer willing to photograph the children.[19] Leaving these unstated objections aside, it would have made sense to have such a photograph taken at this moment in history, given a culture in which such photographs were prevalent, and in a novel in which even lower class characters had multiple photographs of themselves and others. Sue's insistence that she be allowed to see her children one more time seems to draw even more attention to the photograph's absence.[20]

Reproducible through negative technology, postmortem photographs are negations of the living—a hyperbolic version of all reproducible photography. Although Victorian photography, as Jennifer Green-Lewis argues, expresses an "acute" desire to "fix shadows,"[21] such fixity often proves unobtainable ("Not Fading Away" 563). When we focus on the role of the negative and negativity in photography, we see such fixity is only ever realized through its absence, each photograph a permanent reminder of its own failure. As Batchen, Susan Sontag, Roland Barthes, and others theorize, in many ways photographs are about loss itself, and thus the loss of the photograph is a kind of double negative in Hardy. Sontag writes, "photographs actively promote nostalgia. . . . All photographs are *memento mori*. To take a photograph is to participate in another person's (or thing's) mortality, vulnerability, mutability" (15). This is because, as Barthes puts it, the photograph is not a representation of a memory itself but a "counter-memory"; it is "reality in a past state: at once the past and the real" (91, 82). Echoing Barthes, Batchen notes that photography is haunted by "a specter of its own making, the specter of death . . . photographs can't help but draw attention to our own imminent passing" (*Suspending Time* 108). There is a poetic loss present in every photograph—not just postmortem photographs. Rather than giving us the moment or person pictured, photographs remind us of their loss. Indeed, as Barthes writes, they block memory and fill the space instead with sight (91).

Postmortem photographs are a melancholic lie in this way, a reminder of absence rather than an affirmation of presence. Snapshot photographs, Batchen writes, "remind us . . . that we primarily take photographs in order to deny the possibility of death. . . . But that very same photograph, by placing us indisputably in the past, is a kind of mini–death sentence, a prediction of our ultimate demise at some future time" (126). This reminder of absence becomes a double negative in *Jude*, where postmortem photographs are subtly missing—notably missing, if we consider the larger context of photography in this novel and Hardy's works more broadly. If photographs present absence, their absence presents us with the absence of

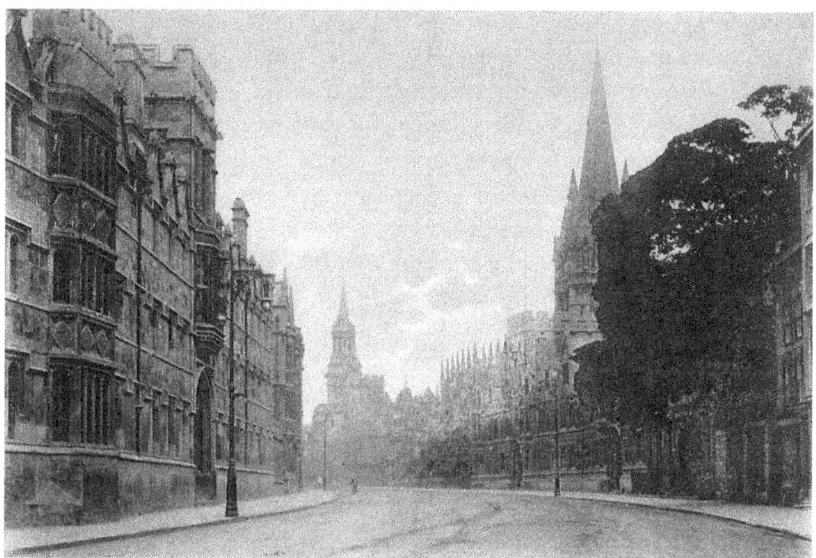

Figure 5.1. Hermann Lea, "Christminster," frontispiece for the Thomas Hardy *Jude the Obscure* Wessex edition (London: Macmillan, 1912).

an absence. This is a philosophical negation of the representative work of photography—a circumventing of the photographic negative's qualities of reproduction and inversion through the denial of a more intrinsic quality of photography: representation.

Seeing Wessex

To some degree, nearly all photography promises representation, and this extends beyond the characters in Hardy's novel to Wessex more broadly. Herman Lea's Wessex edition frontispiece photograph represents "Christminster" through an iconic view of Oxford. This image asks us to see a representation of a factual locale assuming the role of a fictional place. By way of conclusion, I would like to speculate just a bit about what photographic absence might mean within the larger context of photography across Hardy's works. While photography as an absent presence is cast in personal terms in *Jude*, this apparent contradiction takes on a wider cultural valence through nostalgia. The Wessex photographs in the 1912 Wessex edition reproduce nostalgia and even bereavement for a rural England that no longer is and paradoxically (for Wessex) never was.[22] They do this by giving us a glimpse of that rural past, but on some level we know in looking at the photographs that they represent a lie: the rural past of Hardy's novels is not captured by those photographs, for the photographs exist in another time and place. Their proximity to that other time and place makes the disconnect even more poignant. Like postmortem photographs, the Wessex edition photographs offer a false sense of presence—they negate the thing they purportedly represent—and thus the subject of these images is absence itself.

The nostalgia Sontag describes as common to all photographs is particularly apparent in the Wessex edition photographs, which Hardy commissioned from Hermann Lea in 1912. Lea's frontispiece photographs generally depict locales similar to the Wessex novels editions etchings. Despite Hardy's protestation that his Wessex places should be read as "only *suggested* by those real ones given—as they are not literally portraits of such," the photographs introducing each novel in the Wessex edition belies this point (qtd. in O'Sullivan 71, emphasis in original). Hardy gave Lea "considerable assistance in selecting camera position and otherwise commenting on perspective as well as subject matter for the many photographs" of Wessex in the Wessex edition and Lea's *Thomas Hardy's Wessex* of 1913 (A. Jackson, "Photography as Style and Metaphor" 91). In the Wessex edition, each photograph stands in for the fictional region, implying that Wessex is an actual place rather than a fictional locale.

As I have argued elsewhere,[23] Wessex is far from a transparent fictional locale. Named for the Anglo-Saxon kingdom that today comprises Dorset County and environs, Wessex is a historic region with a persistent cultural afterlife. Through his novels and poems, Hardy gradually superimposed an entire world of new names (and some old) on top of actual southwestern England. Wessex names overlie Dorset ones, but Hardy's descriptions remain as traces identifying their Dorset referents.[24] The verisimilitude of Hardy's Wessex locations has helped produce and sustain an entire tourist industry. This industry was alive and well in Hardy's era, and letters to Lea in 1904 "reveal Hardy's somewhat humorous irritation about becoming a subject for the snapshooter-tourist" (91). Wessex, however, was the main celebrity figure in this instance. "Hardy Country" participates, according to Joss Marsh, in a "celebrification of landscape that dates back to Wordsworth's *Guide to the Lakes* of 1820" ("Rise of Celebrity Culture" 101).[25] It also participates, as Elizabeth Edwards indicates, in the photographic survey movement in England (1885–1918). This movement, she writes, illustrates a "vacillation between providing a visualised national narrative and a local one," and its concerns were not always documentary: the Dorset photographs, Edwards notes, were "closely entangled" with Hardy's imagined Wessex (13, 203).

This conflation of Dorset and Wessex has continued to the present day. For example, the West Dorset District Council has produced a visitor's guide, available online, for people who would like to "explore the area that inspired Thomas Hardy," including the Hardy Trail, specialist tours, and Hardy events ("Exploring Thomas Hardy's Rural Dorset"). The Thomas Hardy Society links to several other regional tourism sites linking Wessex and Hardy, and the web is replete with smaller sites dedicated to describing the author's connection to the region. Hardy claimed that his novels were located in a fictional space, loosely connected to the real world, but this claim seems to have fallen on largely deaf ears. Wessex is painstakingly constructed such that each fictional locale is identifiable as a factual town or landscape in late nineteenth-century England. This layering of invention on top of reality gives Wessex a sense of reality recognized by the scores of tourists who flock to "Wessex country" every year. Clearly Hardy based his fictional settings on actual locations and intended his readers to be able to crack his code.

The Wessex edition photographs of 1912 contribute to Wessex's reality and undermine the realism they seem to evoke. The Wessex novels edition of 1895–96 and the later Wessex edition were, according to Claire Tomalin, a "marketing strategy of presenting his fiction as a unified series" (279). In addition to firmly establishing a Wessex tourist industry comprised of visitors who came to see "where Bathsheba and Tess had lived," the collected editions helped solidify the world of the novels as a single world (280). Hardy's friend Lea contributed to this project greatly by producing, in addition to the frontispiece photographs for the 1912 edition, a *Handbook to the Wessex Country of Thomas Hardy* and another guide still in print, *Thomas Hardy's Wessex*. In all but one instance (*Tess of the D'Urbervilles*), Lea's photographs re-create H. Macbeth-Raeburn's etchings from the earlier Wessex novels edition. These re-creations reinforce the visualizations of Wessex rendered in the etchings, but with a difference: the photographs suggest that rather than being fictional, these locations exist in the real world. Many of the photographic frontispieces in the Wessex edition are structural or otherwise easily identifiable: the frontispiece to *Jude*, for instance (figure 5.1), is clearly an image of Oxford, or "Christminster" in Hardy's nomenclature. At the same time, identifying a photograph of Oxford by the name Christminster destabilizes the realism Lea's photograph seems to offer. The photographs are fictions of verisimilitude—lies of presence.

Hardy lent Wessex a visual precision long before the Wessex edition photographs were published in 1912, namely, through the extensive maps that accompanied earlier editions. Hardy created or commissioned numerous maps of Wessex from the earliest editions of his novels, and fans have produced others. The first full map of the Wessex region, for instance, was an anonymous map accompanying a description of "Thomas Hardy's Wessex" in the London monthly magazine the *Bookman* in 1891. The accompanying piece reads like a tour guide directed at "wanderers through our south and south-western counties" (26). The writer notes that those visiting the region "will find few better guides than Mr. Hardy . . . for though Mr. Hardy, as an artist, works with a free hand, and is not a mere photographer, yet in many instances his indications of localities, partially veiled by fictitious names, are clear enough to leave little room for doubt in their identification." Although Hardy is no "mere photographer," the writer notes that the fictionalized Dorset is described with an accuracy that leaves "little room for doubt" (26).[26] Hardy's own map of Wessex (figure 5.2), again appearing in the 1912 Wessex edition, likewise reinforces the link between fictional Wessex place names and factual referents.

The maps share with the photographs a promise of geographic precision—a promise that the tale that follows is clearly locatable in a real place. The photographs do something more through their promised proximity to the real: they promise presence. As Sontag puts it, "As photographs give people an imaginary possession of a past that is unreal, they also help people to take possession of space in which they are insecure" (9). People cannot "possess reality," but "can possess (and be possessed by) images" (163). Photographic images stand in for the reality one cannot contain by promising—but then denying—that presence.

Photography thus operates on multiple levels across Hardy's works, but provocatively it repeatedly highlights its own failure. The absent postmortem photograph may be read as the ultimate failure of photography, and its absence contributes affective weight to the novel's most unbearable scene. What is most ironic is that the presence of a postmortem photograph and its absence amount to the same thing: loss. Rather than a distinct treatment of photography, the missing postmortem photograph stands on a continuum with the rest of photography in the novel and beyond to the nostalgic solidification of Wessex. All photographs in *Jude* fail to give the characters what they seek, just as the Wessex photographs fail to give readers of the Wessex edition the Wessex we seek; Hardy's photographs deceive by representing absence in the guise of presence. In *Jude*, this culminates in the deaths of

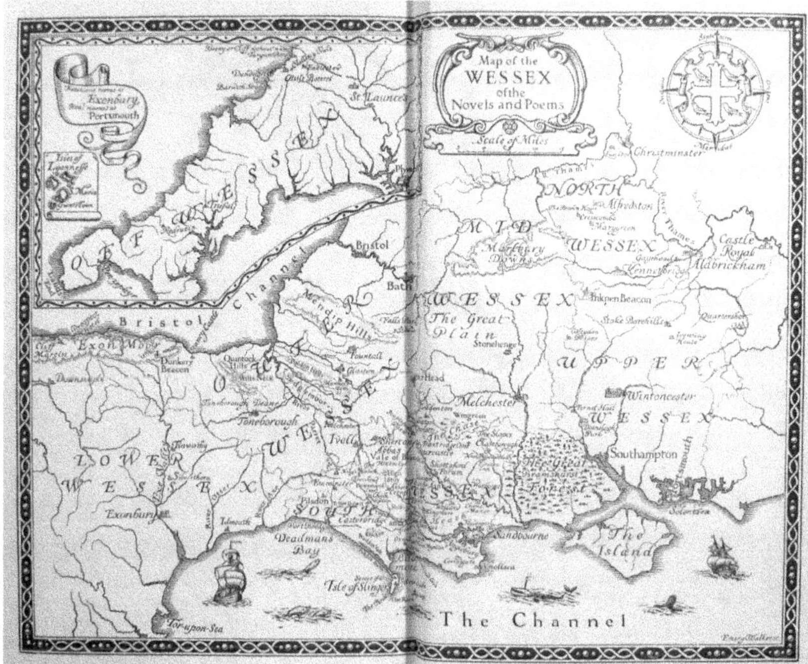

Figure 5.2. Thomas Hardy, "Map of the Wessex of the Novels and Poems," *Jude the Obscure* Wessex edition (London: Macmillan, 1912).

the children, children who are not photographed. The refusal of the photographic record here highlights the horror—the unrepresentability—of these deaths. Photographic absence in the novel is ultimately displaced, articulated through the absence of photography—but then reintroduced paratextually through the photographic "record" of Wessex, as though the novel just can't help wanting us to see, even as it negates the reality of the image.

Conclusion

Photographic Absence and the Vampire's Modern Celebrity

I began this project by claiming that the photographic negative's qualities of inversion and reproducibility became subjects of interest to a Victorian culture engaging with ideas of individuality and celebrity. Furthermore, I argued that this interest was explored in fiction of the period both directly and indirectly. Inversion and reproducibility affected the literary realist project and the celebrity authors of many of those works. The photographic negative did not create inversion or reproducibility, but the popularity of negative-based photography highlighted these qualities and certainly influenced the distinctly Victorian literary response. Photography and the photographic image, as Nancy Armstrong puts it, grounds Victorian fiction: "the kind of visual description we associate with literary realism refers not to things, but to visual representations of things" (3). I extended this argument by noting that photography also substantiates, legitimizes, and reinforces literary culture beyond textual description and into the very lives of authors and worlds of the texts beyond their narrative limits. The literary marketplace was increasingly tied to notions of celebrity authorship, and photography affected the development of that authorship. Also essential to my claims is the fact that photography was not a monolithic entity, operating on the culture in the same way in all its manifestations. Indeed, I claim it is photography's different processes and material forms that led it to affect culture differently. In this book, I addressed how the daguerreotype, solarization, forensic photography, common cabinet cards, double exposures, and postmortem portraiture affected literary culture in distinct ways, each relative to their association with the photographic negative. The negative assumed multiple forms, which evoked distinct literary responses; nevertheless, the negative as a unifying, at times figurative category lends these distinct responses coherence and marks through-lines running between and among the texts and examples collected herein.

The negative was increasingly an essential part of photographic processes as the nineteenth century went on, yet it puts pressure on photography's ostensible truth claims: itself an inversion of the image and one that facilitates potentially endless reproduction of that image, the negative poses an existential challenge to realism understood as verisimilitude. It challenges how we have grown to think about photography's relationship to literature across the century, and more broadly our understanding of photography. Photography is not singular but a series of technological processes, and the specifics of those processes matter for the history of photography and a fuller understanding of literary culture. The authors I have examined grapple with the negative directly or indirectly in their lives or works, registering in various ways an uneasiness with reproducibility as well as fidelity to originality. This uneasiness is manifested as a loss of control over the image amid reproduction, plus a discomfort with a representation that is at least formally grounded in its opposite. The authors I considered here also engage with the negative in different ways, demonstrating strategies that function at the level of form and plot to either illuminate the negative's effects (as in Conan Doyle, Hornung, Bennett, Stevenson, and Wilde) or to limit and repurpose those effects (as in Dickens). Hardy repurposes photography as well, but in the process begins to refuse the photographic record, drawing our attention to what lies outside—the presence that is absent from the photograph—and the lies inside the frame.

This move beyond the image continues in another late Victorian text, and it is with this text that I conclude my study. Bram Stoker's *Dracula* absorbs metatextual concern with the celebrity image into its own narrative, extending the logic of the celebrity image to its extreme conclusion by denying us the image altogether. The novel represents the specter of photography as an absence, represented through its negation. It features photography metaphorically as a negative and as a celebrity image, thereby bringing the two strands of this study into one. Reading *Dracula*'s absent photographic trace alongside late nineteenth-century celebrity culture, I suggest that the vampire's absent reflection mirrors the experience of the fan. Hovering at the brink of the nineteenth century, *Dracula* presents a new view of photography, an extension of Hardy's displacement of the photographic record: Stoker's novel presciently represents the negation of negative-based photography.

Dracula is poised to comment on cutting-edge technologies such as photography; indeed, its narrative is constructed of technologies that are, in Jonathan Harker's words, "up-to-date with a vengeance" (40). The novel opens with Harker's journal, which we are informed is kept in shorthand. From this journal, we move to Mina's typewritten letter, to Dr. Seward's diary (kept in phonograph), to a letter from Quincey Morris, to a telegram—all within the novel's first five chapters. Subsequent communications include newspaper cuttings, a ship's log, more telegrams, phonographs, letters, journals, a memorandum, a doctor's report, a tabloid, an undelivered note, and typed transcripts of additional journal entries. The novel draws our attention repeatedly to new and modernized modes of communication, yet the novel's form is not notably modified through these technologies—the novel does little to represent formal differences between shorthand, photograph, letter, and diary, for example. We do not see Jonathan's journal in shorthand; rather, we are told it is and then asked to suspend our disbelief—or assume the journal has been transcribed—for the narrative that follows is not actually rendered in shorthand. We have no reproductions of letters or newspaper clippings, no handwritten memos to highlight the typewritten documents. In other words, the novel claims to be composed of a range of modern communication technologies that we, the readers, must all take on faith.

These technologies have attracted much critical attention. Glennis Byron, for instance, writes that the technologies in the novel show the extent to which "*Dracula* flaunts its modernity" (12), and David Punter observes that technology "stands in stark contrast to the figure of Dracula himself, who signifies a clinging to older roots of power. Seen in this light, the novel ends by demonstrating the superiority of modern technology over older ways of life" (36). Some critics consider science more broadly, and others focus on a single communication technology, such as the typewriter.[1] All agree that technology affects the plot of the novel, its form, and our understanding of its historical position vis-à-vis modernity.

However, the actual absence of any outward signs of these technologies is significant. Although *Dracula* ostensibly revels in communication novelty—to the point where critics have named it a "textual *bricolage*" (Anita Levy 141, emphasis in original)—that novelty is not extended to the level of the narrative. The novel explains its own textual homogenization as a function of the plot. Mina, the dutiful group secretary, compiles the narratives into a single typescript. Dracula destroys the originals, and Harker notes at the end of the novel that

> We were struck with the fact, that in all the mass of material of which the record is composed, there is hardly one authentic document; nothing but a mass of type-writing, except the later notebooks of Mina and Seward and myself, and Van Helsing's memorandum. We could hardly ask anyone, even did we wish to, to accept these as proofs of so wild a story. (326–27)

Narrative homogenization is thus presented as a flaw in an otherwise painstakingly objective and comprehensive account. In addition, the absent original records operate like absent negatives. All that remain, as in the case of the reproducible cabinet card in "A Scandal in Bohemia," are reproductions. These reproductions cannot ultimately prove the truth of the story.

This novel, which is so frequently discussed in terms of its communication technologies, negates many of the distinguishing characteristics and purposes of those technologies. It also notably negates photography. Leanne Page has written that *Dracula* is actually a story of "failed techno-performances," a narrative about botched technology rather than an account of modernity's triumph over the old guard (110). In a similar vein, I read the novel's treatment of photography as a sign of discomfort with the new technology the novel purports to valorize. Photography is a type of modern communication technology like those featured in the novel, silently informing us about its subject. But photography is coy, ultimately holding its subject at arm's length. In the case of the celebrity photograph in particular—a form of photography that particularly illustrates this particular push and pull—the image communicates presence but then withholds that presence. In *Dracula*, photographic technology adheres to the logic of the celebrity photograph in that it is foregrounded but then hidden, rendered invisible. Rather than a direct mark of modernity, this formal investment in the logic of celebrity registers an engagement with the new by way of negation. Celebrity culture, as we have seen, is a vital component of literary culture, and one in which Stoker participated. Thus although it may appear strange that photography is all but missing in this novel, the structure of celebrity helps explain its absence. Rather than ignoring the photographic image, Dracula is a representation of the photographic negative in celebrity culture. A reading of Dracula as a celebrity affords us an interpretation of photography's absence in this novel and complicates the argument that *Dracula* is simply a novel reveling in its modernity by glorifying the new and rejecting the old. Dracula's missing reflection—the first literary example of this now infamous vampire characteristic—stands in as a reminder of the absent photographic image.

The missing reflection reminds us that Dracula—corrupt old world order incarnate—cannot be visually contained or reproduced through photography, a technology that relies on mirrors to capture image. While modern communication technologies assist the vampire hunters, the vampire easily nullifies the nineteenth century's most famous visual technology.

Photography is only mentioned once in *Dracula*, in an early and fleeting reference: during Jonathan's second conversation with Dracula, the two discuss the property the count would like to purchase in England. Jonathan notes that the property contains an old chapel, which he could not enter but has "taken with my Kodak views of it from various points" (29). Aside from this reference, photography is absent from the text, an absence Daniel Martin interprets as "an explicit effacement of the visual from the novel's repertoire of technologies" (527). As photography is a technology reliant on mirrors and mirrored surfaces, we may surmise that Dracula could not be captured on film any more than his reflection can be seen in Harker's shaving glass. Stoker's working notes describing the vampire indicate that he intended this implication: "no looking glasses in Count's house," reads the notes; "never can see him reflected in one—no shadow? . . . painters cannot paint him—their likenesses always like some one else . . . Could not codak [*sic*] him—come out black or like skeleton corpse" (Eighteen-Bisang and Miller 19–21). In other words, Dracula resists representation. He cannot be captured visually, leaving critics to simply "ponder," as Martin puts it, the outcome "had Stoker developed further his mention of Harker's Kodak camera" (528). Indeed, most critical discussions of photography in the novel are couched in speculative language, noting what might have been.

Why is photography all but missing in a novel so ostensibly fond of the technologically up-to-date? *Dracula*'s absent photograph may be read beyond the mythology of the vampire to celebrity culture more broadly, and thus as a paradoxical facet of modern culture. The absent photograph echoes the experience of the fan in late nineteenth-century celebrity culture. To a large degree, celebrity culture works, as noted in chapter 1, through the celebrity image. The image cultivates desire, but the desire is never fulfilled. *Dracula* extends the logic of the celebrity image to its extreme conclusion by suggesting but then denying us the image altogether. The vampire's absent image is not an instance of old (prephotographic vampire) besting new (photographic technology). Rather, it is an illustration of how the modern celebrity image destroys itself through its own logic. This novel is not so much about new overcoming old but about the internal contradictions found at the heart of the new.

As also discussed in chapter 1, Victorian England sustained a celebrity culture in which the rich, famous, and notorious circulated in popular media. The literary world, central to the development of this culture, continued to sustain it throughout the century. As integral subjects in this culture, celebrity authors were repeatedly and sometimes excessively photographed. Bram Stoker was not unduly concerned with the circulation of his own image, but he participated in celebrity culture in other ways. Meredith Hindley chronicles in her article "When Bram Met Walt" that Stoker encountered Walt Whitman's poetry as a young student and, "like many fans," contacted the American writer. Whitman, who was also famously photographed throughout his career, was accustomed to letters filling his mailbox, but he took special interest in Stoker and the two struck up a literary friendship. Stoker also worked with actor and Lyceum Theatre owner Henry Irving, a much-photographed celebrity and the reported inspiration for *Dracula* (West 206). Irving was the subject of dozens of photographs at the Lyceum, the "sheer number of photographs" a testament to "the importance photography must have had" for his public image (195).

Dracula thematizes this negotiation with the celebrity photograph. To begin, Dracula himself is described as looking like a photograph. Seeing the count for the first time, Harker describes "a tall old man, clean shaven save for a long white moustache, and clad in black from head to foot, without a single speck of colour about him anywhere" (21). Here Dracula appears as though a black-and-white image. Furthermore, "He held in his hand an antique silver lamp, in which the flame burned without chimney or globe of any kind, throwing long quivering shadows as it flickered in the draught of the open door" (21–22). Throughout the novel Dracula is surrounded by shadows, as critics have often noted, but also by light. He loves "the shade and the shadow," as he admits to Harker, and "throws no shadow" himself (29, 211).

In the 1931 film adaptation, the play between light and dark is dramatically emphasized through the chiaroscuro effect across Dracula's body and face. In figure C.1 the strip of light across actor Bela Lugosi's eyes draw the viewer's own eyes to this part of the screen, emphasizing Dracula's hypnotic powers and reinforcing the conceit of him as a creature of the dark—and light. Dracula is, of course, confined by the light: "His power ceases, as does that of all evil things, at the coming of the day," Van Helsing notes (211). Dracula, a being who appears as black and white, who is visible through a play of light and dark, and yet for whom the light ultimately means destruction, is described as being like an undeveloped photographic

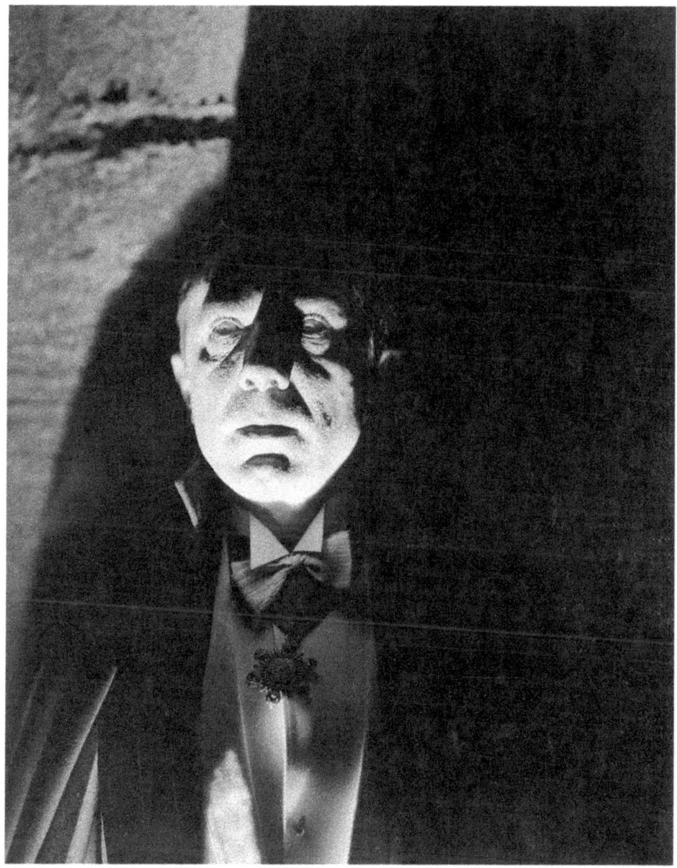

Figure C.1. Bela Lugosi as Dracula in *Dracula* (1931). Publicity image film still. Courtesy of Universal Studios Licensing LLC. Photo © Universal Pictures Corporation.

negative. Indeed, writes Martin, "As various nineteenth-century theories of photography attested, the taking of a photograph was often understood as the equivalent of a vampiric act—an emptying out of the vitality that constitutes a life, but also the process of storing eternal celluloid bodies" (527). The negative-vampire is dangerous and potentially reproducible everywhere, yet sensitive to the light.

Rather than any photographic image, the vampire is more specifically like the negative photographic image of a celebrity. Lucy and Mina repeatedly use terms like *horror*, *terrible*, *dread*, and *fear* to describe their interactions with the count, yet they find themselves involuntarily attracted to him, as though in a trance. Lucy repeatedly attempts to leave the house to meet Dracula, seeming "even in her sleep, to be a little impatient at finding the door shut" (90), and Mina finds herself unable to resist Dracula in his mist or embodied forms. Also captivated and motivated by revenge, the vampire hunters pursue Dracula. And so do we: the vampire is a celebrity figure in the sense that he enthralls his victims, the vampire hunters, and us, the readers of this novel. As Nina Auerbach notes, the vampire is a transhistorical figure onto which we encode our desires and fears. We do this time and time again as we construct and reconstruct, tell and retell, and consume and seek new narratives about this figure—a figure like that of the celebrity. We invent the vampire, as Jeffrey Cohen has succinctly written of monsters at large, because "fear of the monster is really a kind of desire" (16). We interpret the vampire to contain it and to contain and understand our fear and desire. What makes the vampire truly terrifying is its resistance to such containment.

The search for Dracula—our search and the search of the vampire hunters—is about desire as much as a need to destroy a threat. Killed by simultaneous knife wounds to the throat and heart, Dracula's body turns to dust: "It was like a miracle," Mina narrates, "before our very eyes, and almost in the drawing of a breath, the whole body crumbled into dust and passed from our sight" (325). The vampire vanishes, forever uncontainable even in death. The photography that is notably missing in the novel is subsumed into the figure of Dracula himself as the celebrity image one can never truly possess, and we are ultimately placed in the position of the fan, seeking the celebrity we can never truly have. Dracula's missing photograph registers an inability to arrest a single photographic subject. As a symbol of the modern celebrity, Dracula is an unobtainable image, a desirable but also a deeply disturbing figure—a negative representation and critique of the new.

The concept of a negative image so central to the circulation of the positive image—and one that facilitates the unregulated circulation of the image—extends beyond *Dracula* and into its multimedia afterlife. While Tod Browning's 1931 film adaptation featuring Bela Lugosi in all his chiaroscuro glory is certainly the most famous direct adaptation, an earlier version remains more infamous. F. W. Murnau's 1922 *Nosferatu: A Symphony of Horror* was an unauthorized adaptation of Stoker's original, a film that, as David Skal puts it, "mined *Dracula*'s metaphors and focused its meanings into visual poetry" (143). When Stoker's widow, Florence Stoker, learned of the film, she sued the film's German production company, Prana Films. Florence Stoker was backed by the British Incorporated Society of Authors in her suit, and the court ultimately found in favor of the Stoker estate. Prana Films was forced to file bankruptcy and ordered to destroy the film's negative and all copies. A handful of copies survived this purge, making their way to the United States, where they could be released: Stoker had not secured proper US copyright protections for *Dracula*.[2] Today *Nosferatu* enjoys cult status, its popularity tied partly to its near destruction and the way it was able, like a vampire itself, to come back from its own court-ordered death to circulate and multiply. Although the film's negative was destroyed, technological advancements made it possible for copies to be made from a copy of the film, negating the need for a negative altogether.

If it grew easier to reproduce images without a negative in the twentieth century, that ease increased dramatically in the 1990s with the shift to digital photography. Negatives are no longer a part of the process; a digital image may be reproduced ad infinitum without a photographer ever referencing the inverse of that image. This may be seen as liberating, for as Roger Bruce puts it, digital images "never acquire the burden of being originals because they do not pass through a material phase" (17). An original may be read as a "burden" because with that original comes the responsibility to protect it—it is the single source, the core of the record, even the fetish. The original—the negative—is the possibly irritating reminder that no matter how many copies are made, they are derivative. The Victorians' interest in the photographic negative shows us that they thought intently about originality and duplication, and the inversion supporting it, to the point that these concerns influenced the narratives they wrote about themselves and their worlds. Rather than a burden, the idea of the original was for the Victorians a concept worth returning to even as it was threatening to disappear.

This book has focused on the history of specific photographic technologies, most of which use negatives and all of which may be read to affect different spheres of Victorian literary culture. In our own culture, digital photography has profoundly changed how the image circulates and is reproduced. Indeed, it has become somewhat of a critical commonplace to end discussions of Victorian or earlier twentieth-century photography with a gesture toward the way digital photography changes—or does not change—this discourse. For instance, in *Techniques of the Observer*, Jonathan Crary suggests that digital imaging is "radically different" from film (1). Joanna Sassoon similarly writes that the digital "obscures the subtleties of visual clues that originate from the materiality of the photograph and have become an automatic part of the lexicon of reading an original photographic object" (201). Daniel Novak concludes his book by surveying additional claims that the digital is wholly different before suggesting ways that it is instead a return to a "Victorian theory of the photographic" as "a process that evacuated identity rather than fixed it" (147). Like Novak, I believe the digital shares a Victorian wariness about identity and objectivity. Yet like other scholars, I also believe that the digital heralds something new. It is not only that "photography has never been any one technology," as Geoffrey Batchen puts it; more specifically, negative-based photography and photography without negatives occupy different relationships to the origin of the image (*Burning with Desire* 213). The negative is a material object, a demand for a historicization not just of the image but also of the photographic object. The digital, conversely, obfuscates its own point of origin.[3] Thus, while Christopher Rovee suggests "virtual photographs" still contain "a certain *idea* of paper" in the form of "tinting options, trash-can icons, 'camera rolls,' etc.," I would note that the idea omits, ever more, the negative foundation of photography's early reproducible form (389, emphasis in original). The negative is now relegated to a filter, an effect superimposed on the "original," positive digital image.

It has been a central argument of this book that negative-based photography was, throughout the Victorian era, in implicit and explicit conversation with literary culture—and that this conversation was rooted in the materiality of the photographic technology. If Victorian realism and other narrative genres refer to concurrent developments in negative-based photography in an effort to reference, create, and challenge the notion of the real, our contemporary narratives are concomitant with a different style of realism and a different literary culture. They reveal a different relationship between text and image. As images without negatives, digital photographs herald new narrative forms, altering our ideas of representation, literary culture, and celebrity.

We are still in the midst of the shift to this new relationship. Digital cameras were first sold commercially in 1990 and started to overtake film in the early 2000s.[4] My own early coursework in photography took place in a darkroom: I learned to develop rolls of black-and-white film in utter darkness. I practiced reading negatives by interpreting the way the inverse image would appear as a print. I created regular black-and-white photographs, solarized prints, and other experimental images in the red glow of darkroom lights amid the unmistakable smell of developer, stop, and fix.

At the center of the process stood the negative—that essential inversion that made each print possible. As I created these images, I participated in a process, updated but still recognizable, shared by the Victorians. Those of us who have been in a darkroom still have a material connection to negatives, to this increasingly outmoded photographic process. Soon our relationship to the negative will become more detached as we view it with increasing historical remove. We will be called on to read it differently. Our connection to the origin of the image will change, and our understanding of original and reproduction will adapt. Our narratives will be refracted from these originals, illuminating something new. The Victorians may have presaged the disjunction between representation and context with their uneasiness about photographic reproducibility, but we are the ones who now inhabit the simulacrum, unhinged as we are from the negative.

Notes

Introduction

1. This view was generally accepted. For instance, in 1851 in the *Art Journal*, Robert Hunt laments that the British have not advanced photography "in the way in which the French and Americans have done. . . . We believe one reason for this to be the check which has been put upon progress by the clogs of two patents" ("On the Application of Science" 106).

2. Although the *Journal of the Photographic Society of London* inaugurated its first issue in March 1853 with the declaration that "under the more general title of 'Photography' are included, of course, 'Daguerreotypes,' 'Talbotypes,' and all processes whereby images are developed by the agency of light," nineteenth-century photographers frequently distinguished daguerreotypy from negative processes ("Introductory Address" 1).

3. See, for instance, John Frederick William Herschel's letter to William Henry Fox Talbot dated February 10, 1839 (Talbot, *Correspondence*).

4. This distinction between the more artistic or beautiful daguerreotypes and the more useful calotypes or wet collodion prints was common from the earliest days of photography. In a letter to Henry Fox Talbot on May 27, 1839, for instance, Jean-Baptiste Biot writes, "I remain convinced that if drawings on paper cannot be as perfect as M. Daguerre's pictures *as works of art*, they can be of infinite service to physicists and travellers, and there is an infinite variety of applications" (Talbot, *Correspondence*, emphasis in original). The value of these "drawings on paper" is in their "infinite" number of applications as well as the infinite number of reproductions possible.

5. Similarly, in an 1871 article on "Negative Preservers" for the *British Journal of Photography*, the writer explains, "Much of the real profit, in most communities, of the photographic gallery is derived from the sale of duplicates" (315).

6. As Catherine Waters notes, "The supposed resemblance" between Sweetwort and Tippets "is particularly unflattering for a literary lion like Sweetwort, given that the heads of pugilists were typically used to exemplify the phrenological and physiognomic expression of animal propensities or passions, in contrast to the

higher moral and intellectual faculties expressed by a straight profile and refined features" (36).

7. For a helpful overview of the critical terrain through 1995, see Carol T. Christ and John O. Jordan, eds., *Victorian Literature and the Victorian Visual Imagination.* Christ and Jordan argue that two accounts of Victorian visual culture dominate: "One has stressed the predominance of realist modes of representation, culminating in photography and, in the twentieth century, the cinema. The other has emphasized a break with realism, an increasingly subjective organization of vision leading to modernism" (xxi). This interdisciplinary field has remained active in the years since the publication of Christ and Jordan's book. See, for instance, Jennifer Green-Lewis's *Framing the Victorians*, Nancy Armstrong's *Fiction in the Age of Photography*, Kate Flint's *The Victorians and the Visual Imagination*, Isobel Armstrong's *Glassworks: Glass Culture and the Imagination 1830–1880*, Daniel A. Novak's *Realism, Photography, and Nineteenth-Century Fiction*, Linda M. Shires's *Perspectives: Modes of Viewing and Knowing in Nineteenth-Century England*, and Owen Clayton's *Literature and Photography in Transition, 1850–1915.*

8. Linda Shires, for instance, articulates the typical construct I am seeking to revise when she writes, "*The* central technology of photography has been credited with shaping novel form" (2–3, emphasis added).

9. For another, foundational argument about the diversity of photographic processes, see John Tagg, *The Burden of Representation.* Writing of amateur photography, for instance, Tagg notes, "There can be no totalizing definitions of originality or imagination spanning the complexly demarcated spheres of modern cultural practice" (18).

10. In *From a Photograph: Authenticity, Science, and the Periodical Press, 1870–1890*, Geoffrey Belknap similarly notes that "in both scientific and popular periodicals, labeling an image as being 'from a photograph' . . . elevated the photographic image for its veracity and verisimilitude" (10).

11. Notably, however, in writing for the *Art Journal*, Robert Hunt oscillates between describing photography as a science and as an art. Hunt's exhibition catalog entry describes "Hyalotypes, or photographs on glass, both positive and negative" as "a very pleasing application of the art. On the whole," the description continues, "we may regard the examples of sun-drawing exhibited as a very complete exemplification of the state of the art up to the present time" ("The Science of the Exhibition" XII). Steve Edwards notes in *The Making of English Photography: Allegories* that by midcentury "some writers would argue that photography belonged among the fine arts, while others insisted that it should properly be understood as an objective scientific practice untouched by human hands. Still others believed that photography was all of these things at once" (11). In their "Introductory Address" of the *Journal of the Photographic Society of London* in 1853, editors attempted to resolve the art/science question by explaining the society's objective as "the promo-

tion of the Art and Science of Photography," but the debate nevertheless continued throughout the century (1).

12. In "The Wont of Photography," Lindsay Smith argues that photography is antimimetic. She writes that the view of photography as strictly mimetic forms photography's "founding story," and that "it remains common to assume that the invention of photography in the nineteenth century represented the epitome of imitation, a perfect culmination of the age-old debate on mimesis" (65). Indeed, "Few technologies attracted such contrasting attitudes in the nineteenth century as photography," writes Jennifer Tucker. "On the one hand, it was widely believed to be a technique that would create a new and more objective basis for empirical knowledge. . . . On the other hand, photography was hardly welcomed with uniform praise and awe. It was not only a new way of seeing; it was also a tool for being seen in novel, unaccustomed, and at times very unwelcome ways. Someone with a camera was 'behind every window curtain,' complained one person in the 1880s, around the time of the popularization of photographic methods" ("The Social Photographic Eye" 38). While photography's objective potential was often emphasized, this objective potential also figured as a threat.

13. Photography's status as art versus science was controversial throughout the nineteenth century, and this controversy reached a fevered pitch following the first display of photography at an art exhibition, the Parisian Salon of 1859. In "The Salon of 1859," Charles Baudelaire excoriates photography as a corruption of art, a diminishment of art's "self-respect," and an agent that will weaken the "faculties of judging and of feeling what are among the most ethereal and immaterial aspects of creation" (68). Although this argument was forcefully made, it did not have lasting influence—in the Great Britain and Northern Ireland Fine Art Copyright Act of 1862, for instance, Parliament linked photography to other works of art, grouping "painting, drawing, or photograph, or negative of a photograph" together.

14. As Jennifer M. Green succinctly puts it, "From its beginnings, photography had figured in the debate between what we may loosely term the schools of realism and romanticism. Indeed, the power of a photograph as a test lay precisely in its potential to be identified either as proof of the *nature* of the world's existence, which is nothing beyond what we see, or as proof that the world *cannot be so represented*—that its true nature must somehow be absent from any representation" ("The Right Thing" 100, emphasis in original).

15. This issue remains vexed. As Susan Sontag writes, "something about photography still keeps the first-rate professionals defensive and hortatory: virtually every important photographer right up to the present has written manifestoes and credos expounding photography's moral and aesthetic mission" (115).

16. Daston and Galison remind us that truth, objectivity, certainty, precision, and replicability have their "own historical trajectory and scientific practices" (33). "Seeking truth," they write, "is the ur-epistemic virtue, with its own long and

variegated history" containing "a metaphysical dimension, and aspiration to reveal a reality accessible only with difficulty" (58). For Enlightenment naturalists, they write, "sharp and sustained observation was a necessary prerequisite for discerning the true genera of plants and other organisms. The eyes of both body and mind converged to discover a reality otherwise hidden to each alone" (58). While these authors see a general progression from truth-to-nature to objectivity to trained judgment, they note that "the new did not always edge out the old . . . In some cases it is possible to pursue several simultaneously" (28). Tucker makes a similar qualification when she notes, "Although nineteenth-century faith in photography was powerful, the idea that people over a hundred years ago accepted photographs at face value is exaggerated and misleading. Indeed, nineteenth-century viewers frequently asked many of the same questions that are asked today" (*Nature Exposed* 4). See also W. J. T. Mitchell, who argues in *Picture Theory* that "it is getting increasingly hard to find anyone who will defend the view . . . that photographs have a special causal and structural relationship with the reality that they represent" (282).

17. For a helpful gloss of scholarly discussions of realism, see Daniel Brown, *Representing Realists in Victorian Literature and Criticism.*

18. Most studies of realism begin with such a declaration: "Yes," writes Levine in his introduction to the collection *Realism and Representation*, "once again, realism rears its hydra head" (3). Realist and realism are "slippery" terms, writes Pam Morris in her *Realism*, and discussions of them are filled with "difficulties defining them in any precise and unambiguous way" (2). "Most critics nowadays are willing to admit that the term 'realism,' or any of its near relations, represents a presumptuous, ambiguous, and philosophically loaded designation," writes Alan Harvey Spiegel before he rejects the term in favor of "reified form" (2). "A basic cause of the confusion bedeviling the notion of Realism," explains Linda Nochlin in *Realism*, "is its ambiguous relationship to the highly problematical concept of reality" (13). Brown historicizes the indeterminacy of the concept, writing that "perhaps realism was always a fundamentally pessimistic movement waiting to find its culmination at the end of the century, when writers would become sick of it at the same time that they decided that they had finally figured out what it was" (179).

19. For examples, see Carol T. Christ, *The Finer Optic: The Aesthetic of Particularity in Victorian Poetry*; Lindsay Smith, *Victorian Photography, Painting, and Poetry: The Enigma of Visibility in Ruskin, Morris and the Pre-Raphaelites*; Ana Parejo Vadillo, *Woman Poets and Urban Aestheticism: Passengers of Modernity*; Helen Groth's *Victorian Photography and Literary Nostalgia*; Susan Shelangoskie, "Domesticity in the Darkroom: Photographic Process and Victorian Romantic Narratives"; and Amelia Scholtz, "Photographs before Photography: Marking Time in Tennyson's and Cameron's *Idylls of the King.*"

20. Photography, notes Jennifer Green-Lewis, "provided a locus of debate for issues having to do with realism, especially literary realism . . . What realism ought to do and what it was actually capable of were topics for which photography was able

to provide confirmation" (*Framing the Victorians* 19–20). "In order to be realistic," Nancy Armstrong writes, "literary realism referenced a world of objects that either had been or could be photographed." Both literary realism and photography evolved in response to a public "hungry for certain kinds of visual information" (7–8).

21. Thus, writes Stuart Burrows of American fiction and the camera, realism's visibility "is actually the sign of a loss of faith in fiction's ability to represent the world" (5). In her book on women's writing and photography, Katherine Henninger makes a similar argument, suggesting that photographs featured in fiction make visible the extent to which the photographic image is an act of representation (9).

22. Making a similar claim in *The Real Thing: Imitation and Authenticity in American Culture, 1880–1940*, Miles Orvell writes that "the impact of the camera in the nineteenth century was based on its powers of description and generalization: it summed up experience, presenting a normative vision of the world that could enter the common memory as a facsimile of reality, and imitation founded on typological representation" (198).

23. Rather than understanding either photographic or literary realism as unmediated "truth," Novak argues that manipulation was not seen as "anomalous or incidental to the project of realism but as absolutely *essential* to it" (4, emphasis in original).

24. Many critics writing about realism note this apparent paradox: "Fictions have to lie in order to tell the truth," Peter Brooks writes (6). "Realism itself grew out of the impulse to contradict," notes Alison Byerly in *Realism, Representation, and the Arts in Nineteenth-Century Literature* (4). "Realism recognizes both the need for factual detail and the delusion of completeness that facts can come to represent, for the material world is exactly that place that is both too imperatively real in its effect on character and not 'real' enough," Katherine Kearns argues in *Nineteenth-Century Realism: Through the Looking Glass* (11).

25. Indeed, Baudrillard notes, theorizations of original and double are not new to the late twentieth century: "Of all the prostheses that mark the history of the body, the double is doubtless the oldest. But the double is precisely not a prosthesis: it is an imaginary figure, which, just like the soul, the shadow, the mirror image, haunts the subject like his other, which makes it so that the subject is simultaneously itself and never resembles itself again, which haunts the subject like a subtle and always averted death" (*Simulacra and Simulation* 95).

26. Although this concept is ubiquitous in most photographic theory, for my own understanding of it I am indebted to my first photography professor, Roy W. Traver.

27. According to Reichardt, light imagery shifts in connotation from religious truth to rational truth and finally to punitive truth. I would add photographic representation to this catalog of shifting light/dark metaphors. A technological development, photography uses light in its attempt to convey a kind of empirical truth. As Kate Flint notes, metaphors of vision were used not least of all by scientists

themselves (*The Victorians and the Visual Imagination* 33)—that is, nineteenth-century scientists frequently used visual metaphors to communicate their discoveries. See also Eduardo Cadava, *Words of Light: Theses on the Photography of History.*

Chapter 1

1. This is not an abnormal reaction. As Susan Sontag notes, "Many people are anxious when they're about to be photographed: not because they fear, as primitives do, being violated but because they fear the camera's disapproval. People want the idealized image: a photograph of themselves looking their best" (85).

2. This sentiment is echoed in an 1857 article, "Your Life or Your Likeness," by James White in *Household Words*. According to Catherine Waters, the "photography mania" depicted in the article "has given birth to the first paparazzi" (35).

3. Joseph Roach argues for the duality of that celebrity power of apparently effortless embodiment of contradictory qualities simultaneously: strength *and* vulnerability, innocence *and* experience, and singularity *and* typicality among them. . . . Theatrical performance and the social performances that resemble it consist of struggle, the simultaneous experience of mutually exclusive possibilities—truth and illusion, presence and absence, face and mask" (8–9, emphasis in original).

4. Rovee's article "Secrets of Paper" reads *In Memoriam* unconventionally, as part of the history of photography: "Whether Tennyson knew about photographic experimentation prior to 1839 or had it specifically in mind after 1839 is not my point . . . it is precisely the absence in the poem of any specific reference to the new medium that draws *In Memoriam* into a history of photography . . . at photography's source is the kind of desire we find impressed across the surface of Tennyson's page" (388).

5. Daguerreotypes can be reproduced through a process of redaguerreotyping the original daguerreotype—see, for instance, the instructions for this process as set forth by M. P. Simons in his 1858 *Photography in a Nutshell.* See also Beaumont Newhall's more recent *The History of Photography*: "The daguerreotype . . . could be duplicated only by making a copy of it with a camera or by hand" (19). Perhaps one of the most famous daguerreotypes, Daguerre's "Boulevard du Temple," was given to the king of Bavaria. A copy of the daguerreotype was made prior to World War II, and the original was accidentally destroyed during a cleaning mishap after the war. The image that circulates of "Boulevard" today is thus a double copy: a digitization of a copy of a daguerreotype. Notwithstanding these exceptions, daguerreotypy is not inherently reproducible like negative-based photography.

6. In referring to the "photographic imagination" or "Daguerrean imagination" in this chapter, I aim to highlight the extent to which photography, for all its apparent claims to objective realism, is a cultural product, a mode of representation that intersects in creative ways with the imaginations of its viewers. The rise of

photography in the nineteenth century amounted to a cultural phenomenon, and it altered the way we picture images in our minds. Yet photography is not immune to creative reimaginings, and here I want to signal the way photography arrested the interest of an entire culture and note the destabilization of photography's objectivity through that imaginative process. For more on the photographic imagination, see Martha Langford. For the visual imagination more broadly, see Kate Flint's *The Victorians and the Visual Imagination* and Carol T. Christ and John O. Jordan, eds., *Victorian Literature and the Victorian Visual Imagination.*

7. For a discussion of *A Christmas Carol*'s disappointing first edition profit margin, see Philo Calhoun and Howell J. Heaney, "Dickens' *Christmas Carol* After a Hundred Years: A Study in Bibliographical Evidence."

8. These cartes and cabinet cards often ended up in family photo albums. A survey of nineteenth-century albums at the Victoria and Albert Museum in London and the George Eastman Museum in Rochester, New York, reveals that families would frequently compile cartes of friends, family, acquaintances, and celebrities in a single album. An album in the Eastman Sipley Collection, for instance, includes images of the British royal family and family photographs; another in the same collection includes people known to the collector in addition to an image of John Wilkes Booth. For more on nineteenth-century photographic albums, see Beaumont Newhall's *The History of Photography.*

9. For more on cartomania, see Rachel Teukolsky, "Cartomania: Sensation, Celebrity, and the Democratized Portrait."

10. This attitude was not exclusively held toward photography: compare his distaste for the proof of Daniel Maclise's portrait (1839) and Ary Scheffer's portrait (1855). He also disliked Frith's painting, writing, "It is a little too much . . . as if my next door neighbour were my deadly foe, uninsured, and I had just received tidings of his house being a-fire; otherwise, very good" (Dickens, *Letters* 9:71). In *Becoming Dickens: The Invention of a Novelist*, Robert Douglas-Fairhurst writes that this reaction to the Frith painting is indicative of his general reaction to his likeness, "which he tended to regard with a kind of amused detachment, as when he wrote to W. P. Frith in 1859 about his painting of 'the gifted Individual whom you will transmit to posterity,' almost as if it depicted someone else" (298). Kate Flint remarks that Dickens often "recognised a likeness, but nonetheless usually felt something was missing" ("Visual Culture" 155).

11. Janet Browne remarks in her study of "Charles Darwin as a Celebrity" that "two elements, public appearances and pictures, are key features of any modern analysis of celebrity culture" (178).

12. M. H. Abrams's distinction between the mirror and the lamp as metaphors for the mind and poetry is useful to consider and complicate in this context. Abrams argues that beginning with Romanticism, the older metaphor of mind-as-mirror is replaced with the image of mind-as-lamp. The figure of the lamp implies a greater degree of participation on the part of the poet, for rather than merely reflecting the

world, the poet actually projects a new element outward—illuminating and thus creating. As a technology designed to reflect and illuminate, photography stands at the crux of these metaphors.

13. In "Image Analysis and Documentation of the Condition of Daguerreotypes," J. S. Arney and J. Michael Maurer explain that "a daguerreotype can present to the viewer either a positive or a negative image, depending on the geometries of illumination and viewing. This occurs because the daguerreotype is fundamentally a polished silver mirror. . . . If one views an illuminated white card through the daguerreotype mirror . . . shadow areas of polished mirror now appear white and the exposed, scattering areas appear dark. This produces the negative-appearing image" (145).

14. Citing Victorian self-censorship and censorship practices in *Household Words*, Peter Brooks suggests that "so much of Dickens appears as the avoidance or suppression of realism . . . Isn't there an incompatibility in the realist's claim to name the harshest realities and the context of self-censorship generally accepted by the Victorian novel, and surely by *Household Words*?" (40). Alexander Bove focuses on the writer's "affinity for comic distortion" in *David Copperfield*, arguing that such distortions challenge bourgeois aspirations of realistic totality (659). Oost argues that Dickens aligns painted portraits and photographs in *Bleak House* to challenge the veracity of both (155). For Emily Walker Heady, the Victorian photograph "was fraught with deep contradictions: it could tell half-truths—or lie altogether—and yet, paradoxically, still be real" (3). According to Heady, Dickens collapses "the realms of the ghostly phantasmagoria and the reliable photograph" in two of his Christmas books, teaching us "to think beyond binaristic questions of images' reliability" (10, 4).

15. This appeal to truth is important, Natalie Bell Cole argues in "'Prowling About' London: Dickens and the Photographic Lens," to make the case that the novel "needs to come before the public's eye and heart" (23).

16. In Dickens's novels, there are only, as Daniel Novak puts it, "a handful" of references—in *Great Expectations* and *Our Mutual Friend*, and obliquely in *Oliver Twist* (64).

17. See Ronald Thomas, for example, who writes that the development of photography and the detective story are not simply "analogous or continuous occurrences but . . . dynamically interrelated events" ("Arresting Images" 91). *Bleak House* is, like *A Tale of Two Cities*, similarly set back in time, in this case to the 1830s, during the early years of photographic experimentation and development. Given Dickens's references to photography in several novels and his engagement with debates surrounding the technology, it is not far-fetched to read a photographic subtext in his meditations on detection and light and dark.

18. Paul Virilio notes that nineteenth-century science uses photography's own light metaphors: "physicists themselves promoted their work on electricity and electromagnetism using Nièpce's very metaphors as provisional expedients." Photography in this sense heralds a kind of "latter-day sun worship" (20).

19. For more readings of the relation between historical past and compositional present in the historical novel, see, Harry E. Shaw, *The Forms of Historical Fiction: Sir Walter Scott and His Successors*, and Elliot Gilbert, "'To Awake from History': Carlyle, Thackeray, and *A Tale of Two Cities*."

20. This condensation has long been the subject of analyses and judgments about the novel: in a letter that does not survive, Edward Bulwer-Lytton complains directly to Dickens that the feudalism in the novel was anachronistic. Dickens's reply, as quoted in Maxwell, is that abridgment is necessary to his more picturesque, expressive intention: "Surely, when the new philosophy was the talk of the salons and the slang of the hour, it is not unreasonable or unallowable to suppose a nobleman wedded to the old cruel ideas, and representing the time going out, as his nephew represents the time going in" (xix).

21. *A Tale of Two Cities* does not simply use the past to comment on the present or emphasize the distinction between precisely documented and expressively fluid time; the novel also positions this historical movement spatially, featuring two cities, London and Paris. The choice of these cities—the more properly representative of the French Revolution and the other of Dickens's own Victorian reading public—emphasizes, through place, the slippage of time from past into present. The novel incorporates past into present, specific time into what Maxwell calls a "half-imaginary cultural moment," and the ahistorical London with the revolutionary Paris (xix).

22. Daguerre was originally a panorama and diorama painter and is cited as the father of the diorama, or "drama of light."

23. Richard L. Stein points to two "early examples" of Dickens's interaction with visual representation: the full title of *Sketches by Boz and Cuts by Cruikshank*, which draws a direct parallel between author and illustrator; and the illustration of Dickens in *Nicholas Nickleby* (167).

24. Sarah Solberg describes the practical motivations underlying this reversion to line drawings in her "A Note on Phiz's Dark Plates."

25. For more on the *A Tale of Two Cities* illustrations, see Michael Steig, *Dickens and Phiz* (311–12).

Chapter 2

1. See, for instance, J. Hillis Miller, *Charles Dickens: The World of His Novels*; Elaine Showalter, "Guilt, Authority, and the Shadows of *Little Dorrit*"; Henry N. Rogers, "Shadows of Irony: The Comic Structure of *Little Dorrit*"; and Brian Rosenberg, *Little Dorrit's Shadows: Character and Contradiction in Dickens*.

2. Miller reads *Little Dorrit*'s shadows as a metaphor for the novel's theme of secrecy, specifically the theme of personal secrecy: "one has a diffused consciousness of the opacity of other people. This opacity is present as a kind of heavy thickness in the air, an impenetrable 'shadow' of secrecy" (243). Miller claims "shadow" as

the novel's dominant key term, a position Showalter shares when she describes it as the "darkest of Dickens's novels" (Showalter 21).

3. For morning light, see 74; morning sun, 377; moonlight, 150, 284, and 545; watch-light, 151; magic lantern light, 151; flaring gaslight, 188, 196, and 662; candlelight, 292; twilight, 361, 656, and 661; and sunset, 390.

4. See also Jerome Beaty, "The 'Soothing Songs' of *Little Dorrit*: New Light on Dickens's Darkness."

5. Hardinge argues that we must account for light and dark in the novel and aligns the novel's shadows with identity and its light with the exposing and impersonal gaze of society.

6. The phrase "natural picture" was increasingly considered synonymous with photography as the nineteenth century progressed.

7. "There is an influence other than the *quantity* of light, and that is, without dispute, the *quality* of light" (*L'Art du Photographe* 132, translation mine) ("il existe un autre influence que celle de la *quantité* de lumière il y a, sans contredit, la *qualité* de la lumière").

8. William Jolly, however, argues that the Sabatier after whom the technique is named is a different doctor. According to Jolly, we do not know much about the Sabatier of the Sabatier effect—not even his first name. Even the spelling of his last name is questionable: though it is spelled "Sabatier" in his first *Cosmos* article and *Bulletin* correspondence, it is spelled "Sabattier" in a subsequent *Bulletin* letter dated November 14, 1862. Jolly writes in his first chapter that Armand Sabattier lived in Cette and was a marine zoologist who was not yet a doctor when "Dr. Sabatier" wrote about his photographic findings in 1860. Jean-Baptiste Sabatier was another contemporaneous Sabatier and a daguerreotypist, although he is not the Sabatier effect's namesake.

9. The authors of *Life Library of Photography: The Print* agree: "True solarization takes place when film, not printing paper, is greatly overexposed" (168).

10. See Jolly, chapter 3. Although there are at least two accounts of Man Ray's and Lee Miller's rediscovery, they share an element of contingency: the rediscovery was accidental and not the result of deliberate experimentation. Miles writes that Miller's discovery narrative curiously blends accident with subsequent mastery. In a 1975 interview, Miller claims she was frightened by a mouse and turned the light on during development. This accident then "became grist for Man Ray's creative mill" (Miles 345).

Chapter 3

1. Traditionally, critical readings of the Holmes canon support this view. As Elizabeth Miller notes, critical attention "has focused on the stories' innovative faith in the power of vision and detection, their empiricism, their panopticism,

their modern certainty about identity's location in the body, and their revolutionary merging of the science of crime and the science of physiology" (26).

2. Along these same lines, in 1871 *Punch* describes"A Photographic Thief-Trap," asking, "Is it not possible to construct a photographic trap so contrived that, when a spring connected with it is trodden on, a screen shall be raised and lowered after an interval long enough to admit the formation of an image on the camera?. . . . That image might be the image of a thief, who, coming to steal where the trap had been set, had unconsciously trodden on the spring, and so got photographed" (264).

3. Perhaps the most famous crime scene photographs of the nineteenth century are those of the Jack the Ripper murders, still circulating online on several sensational Jack the Ripper sites.

4. Much of the critical work on forensic science, photography, and literature tends to be Foucauldian, following the paradigms established by Michel Foucault in *Discipline and Punish* (1975). Foucault's argument that visual apparatuses of surveillance constitute the modern subject through discipline is echoed in Crary's work on the observer but has come under some fire more recently. Chris Otter argues in *The Victorian Eye* that "visual practices, and the technologies securing them, have a political history that cannot be captured with the limited range of concepts provided by cultural theory" (10). Our "reductive visual paradigms should be replaced by a multiplicity of overlapping, intersecting, and contrasting perceptual 'patterns' that recur throughout the nineteenth century and capture visual experience in all its everyday richness and complexity far better than monolithic abstracts like the panopticon ever could" (21). For different accounts of the interaction between literature and true crime, see Andrew Maunder and Grace Moore's edited collection, *Victorian Crime, Madness and Sensation.*

5. Booth surmises that Conan Doyle's subsequent advocacy of spiritualism and more specifically spirit photography may have made him ashamed of this early caustic critique of psychic photography. Booth's argument echoes the one put forth by John Michael Gibson and Richard Lancelyn Green in *The Unknown Conan Doyle: Essays on Photography*: "Doyle never mentioned the articles after he had left Southsea. It was not that he had forgotten about them . . . but rather that he wished to suppress some details of the hardship and poverty of his early years. . . . He might also have felt that as one of the early contributions made unflattering references to psychic phenomena, it would be inadvisable to draw attention to it" (ix).

6. Conan Doyle also appeals to logic in *The Case for Spirit Photography*: "Every reader with an open mind will agree that the evidence for the reality of psychic photography is overwhelming. It is only necessary to repeat that these reports form but a part of a tremendous mass of accumulated evidence, which is available for any serious student to investigate . . . these photographic effects are being accumulated and preserved so as to form a permanent record of the truth of psychic photography" (132).

7. Although he observed that the Cottingley fairy photograph episode had "nothing to do with the larger and far more vital question of spiritualism," Conan Doyle also wrote in defense of the fairy photographs (*The Coming of the Fairies* 3). Highly critical of "*truth*, which is obsessed by the idea that the whole spiritualistic movement and everything connected with it is one huge, senseless conspiracy to deceive, concocted by knaves and accepted by fools," he responds that it is a "stale and rotten argument by which the world has been befooled so long, that because a conjurer under his own conditions can imitate certain effects, therefore the effects themselves never existed" (33, 41–42).

8. As Jon Lellenberg puts it, "many who look to Sherlock Holmes as the supreme literary spokesman for rationalism feel dismay and bewilderment about his creator having become a leading champion of a doctrine that seems at odds with his education and literary ideals" (11).

9. Gibson and Green note that "Sherlock Holmes never used a camera, despite the development of the miniature 'detective' cameras concealed in binoculars, watches, and hats which were popular at the time" (xvii).

10. According to Janice Hart, "the larger idea that Conan Doyle develops is that photography's indexicality is so incontrovertible that it can literally assume the status of evidence" (115).

11. Perhaps by complete coincidence, a photographic studio named "Adler," run by several brothers, operated in Romania in the late nineteenth century and sold cabinet cards. Several of the brothers moved to Bohemia in the 1870s ("Attractive Romanian Wedding Couple").

12. Similarly, the photographer J. P. Proctor of Rochdale Road, Manchester, advertised on the back of his cards "Negatives kept, copies can always be had" (Sipley Collection).

13. According to Michael and Barbara Foster in *Dangerous Woman*, "Dumas owed Liebert [*sic*] money. To cancel the debt, he brought Adah to the studio, and afterward he looked the other way while Liebert sold to boulevard stationary shops multiple copies of the intimate photos" (269).

14. The powerful potential of the cabinet card extends beyond this story. As Gil Pasternak explains, "nineteenth-century conventional studio formats, such as cabinet photographs, constituted a politically subversive platform for those who were looking to perform a distinct identity within nineteenth-century European or American society" (229).

15. The Holmes illustrations deny us visual certainty on a metafictional level as well: before Paget became the go-to illustrator of the Holmes stories, six others tried the job. The Paget illustrations are not consistent, either: "at least six different engravers are known to have been employed in reproducing Paget's illustrations for *The Adventures* and *The Memoirs*," documents Walter Klinefelter (18). "Under the circumstances," Klinefelter writes, "a noticeable lack of uniformity in the Holmseian portraiture was inevitable" (18).

16. Maxwell also used photography to illustrate his theories of color vision and created the first color photograph in 1861 as part of this work.

17. "It has been estimated," writes Mussell, "that pure science represented about 5–6 per cent of books published between 1840 and 1870"—a "substantial proportion" (329). See also Graeme Gooday, " 'I Never Will Have the Electric Light in My House': Alice Gordon and the Gendered Periodical Representation of a Contentious New Technology."

Chapter 4

1. "I can't get no satisfaction" is, by one reading, a deliberate deployment of the double negative's uneducated connotation, wielded to critique media and consumerism. Yet insofar as the speaker in the song may be interpreted as a member of the band and thus not necessarily an uneducated character, it is also possible the line uses the double negative to arrive at the right number of syllables for the melody.

2. See also *Hamlet* III.i.156–57 and *The Tempest* III.ii.17 (for example).

3. For a thorough analysis of the connection between Victorian art photography and composition photography techniques, see Novak.

4. Writing in 1856, Sir David Brewster observes, "It is generally supposed that photographic pictures, whether in Daguerreotype or Talbotype, are accurate representations of the human face and form, when the sitter sits steadily, and the artist knows the resources of his art. . . . The sun never errs in the part which he has to perform" (135). Echoing other writers addressed in previous chapters of this study, Brewster notes, "When the processes of the Daguerreotype and Talbotype, the sister arts of Photography, were first given to the world, it was the expectation of some, and the dread of others, that the excellence and correctness of their delineations would cast into shade the less truthful representations of the portrait and the landscape painter" (166).

5. Such general enthusiasm is also registered through the 810 inventions and twenty-two designs issued photographic patents by the US government alone, according to Schimmelman.

6. For more on this democratization, see Teukolsky.

7. According to Brewster, the stereoscope "is now in general use over the whole world, and it has been estimated that upwards of half a million of these instruments have been sold" (36).

8. See also Crary's challenge to traditional conceptions of realism in photography: "some of the most pervasive means of producing 'realistic' effects in mass visual culture, such as the stereoscope, were in fact based on a radical abstraction and reconstruction of optical experience, thus demanding a reconsideration of what 'realism' means in the nineteenth century" (9).

9. See Christopher Rovee, "Secrets of Paper," and Jesse Hoffman, "Arthur Hallam's Spirit Photograph and Tennyson's Elegaic Trace."

10. See Judith R. Walkowitz, *City of Dreadful Delight*; Walter Houghton, *The Victorian Frame of Mind*; and Jerrold E. Hogle, "The Struggle for a Dichotomy: Abjection in Jekyll and His Interpreters," for examples of these readings.

11. Jekyll, Stevenson writes at one point, "was composite" (55) and indeed, writes Owen Clayton, this description is not coincidental: influenced by Muybridge and Galton, Stevenson used composite photography "as a metaphor to examine mankind's paradoxical aspects further, leading him to a reappraisal of the supposed unity of self" (74).

12. For more on Stevenson's relationship to photography, see Sara Stevenson, "Robert Louis Stevenson and the Portrait Photographers." As Stevenson concludes, the author "was pictured in photography from an early age," and his "curiosity about photography was often balanced by his disappointment or amusement when seeing the results" (239). Throughout his life, he was interested in photography but "distinctly critical" (240).

13. Also reading Dorian as photographic, Novak writes, "Making both portrait and body the creation of another artist, Wilde makes Dorian's sexuality and subjectivity, body and soul, person and personality, both already a reproduction and eminently reproducible. In other words, Wilde makes Dorian's identity and body at one and the same time a work of fiction and a photographic reproduction"—he is "a *negative* body and a photographic body" (123, emphasis in original).

14. For another example of Wilde's complicated presentation of morality, see "Phrases and Philosophies for the Use of the Young," published in *The Chameleon* in 1894.

15. See Rolf Breuer, "Paradox in Oscar Wilde." Wilde's aphorisms are frequently used as examples of paradox in literary handbooks; see "Paradox Definition," for instance.

16. Dollimore historicizes this fusion of sexuality and personality, noting that "the homosexual had become a species of being whereas before sodomy had been an aberration of behavior . . . by the time of Wilde, homosexuality could be regarded as rooted in a person's identity" (67). The discourse surrounding sexual inversion dates to Richard von Krafft-Ebing's *Psychopathia Sexualis* in 1886 and Havelock Ellis's *Studies in the Psychology of Sex* in 1897. Whereas these theorists conflate homosexual practices and inversion in their discussions, in today's parlance inversion is closer to transgenderism: "In inverted women a certain subtle masculinity or boyishness is equally prevalent . . . Even in inversion the imperative need for a certain sexual opposition—the longing for something which the lover himself does not possess—still rules in full force" (Ellis 236). For modern discussions of inversion and homosexuality at the fin de siècle, see Joseph Bristow, "Symonds's History, Ellis's Heredity: Sexual Inversion," and Jay Prosser, "Transsexuals and Transsexologists: Inversion and the Invention of Transsexual Subjectivity."

17. For more on the differences between the *Lippincott's* edition of the novel and the first single volume edition—the original version and the "purged" version, as Carson puts it (Hyde 111)—see Stuart Mason, ed., *Oscar Wilde: Art and Morality*.

18. In *Modernism Is the Literature of Celebrity*, Jonathan Goldman similarly argues that Wilde gives twentieth-century celebrity its "originary moment" (20). Furthermore, "the signature styles of modernism and celebrity produce similar forms of cultural value and together strive to reaffirm the centrality of the individual within mass society" (2).

Chapter 5

1. On the literal level, each poem features a photograph as subject that is lost, either by fire or sale. Of course, each photograph represents another subject—a person—who is also lost.

2. As Arlene Jackson puts it, although Hardy "disliked the current craze of filling out one's fiction with 'photographic,' literal detail, his was not a closed mind. As the photograph became more and more an accepted part of nineteenth-century popular culture, Hardy responded to that assimilation in his own art" ("Photography as Style and Metaphor" 107).

3. Analyzing the poems "The Photograph" and "The Son's Portrait," as well as the short story "An Imaginative Woman" and the novel *A Laodicean*, Durden suggests that Hardy alternates between two approaches to photography: the first resonates with "earlier discourses around photography, discourses in which the medium was linked to magic and superstition," and the second with later discourses that "tended to view it as a cultural artefact within human agency and subsequently open to manipulation and distortion" (62). In the first case, photography tells inner truths; in the second, it reveals deception. In these uses in Hardy's work, Durden writes, "The photograph never functions as mere document. . . . Caught up in deception and ritual, photography never serves realism in Hardy's writing" (68). He thus argues that Hardy's uses of photography are more in line with painting than technological modernization—more of a critique of a technically precise realism than a reference to it.

4. Arlene Jackson observes that a photograph is also used "to deceive" in the earlier *Desperate Remedies*: "Photography here is part of the plot machinery, but it is also a part of the novel's treatment of deception, and in its time was a rather fresh way of handling that old chestnut of literary themes, appearance and reality" (98).

5. In Hardy's 1871 novel, a photograph is placed inside a sewing box so as to convince people that Mrs. Manston is still alive when she is actually dead.

6. Indeed, and a modern man: as Jennifer M. Green writes, "Representative of the new forces that will raze the old establishments, the photographer slips away unapprehended to practice his evil elsewhere" (*Framing the Victorians* 85).

7. As Green notes, Hardy "suggests that photography has the potential" to offer "spiritual insight" ("Outside the Frame" 124–25).

8. As Penelope Vigar puts it, "Jude falls in love with his cousin's photograph" (191).

9. Arlene Jackson suggests that photographs in the novel represent "an essential step removed from the reality they may record" ("Photography as Style and Metaphor" 107).

10. It is notably not as common today: Jay Ruby writes that "some people are so uncomfortable with the idea of a photograph of a corpse or funeral that they destroy any images of death should they discover them in their family photo collection" (*Secure the Shadow* 52). Indeed, perhaps evidence of this more modern discomfort extends to the critical record. John Morley's 1971 book *Death, Heaven and the Victorians* documents death practices in Victorian culture but does not mention postmortem photography.

11. Theorizations of photography are often bound up with death. For instance, as Christopher Rovee writes of the photographic sensibility of Tennyson's *In Memoriam*, photography may be best thought of as a "*desire* spelled out in words and lines that summon into presence a dead man's touch" (388). Describing Julia Margaret Cameron's postmortem photographs of Adeline Grace Clougstoun, Jordan Bear observes that one of the "central aspirations" of photography is the "achievement of posthumous agency" (101).

12. See Ruby, *Secure the Shadow* and Dan Meinwald, "Memento Mori: Death and Photography in Nineteenth Century America." Ruby explains that "the practice of portraying the dead did not originate with photography nor was it ever exclusively American. It was and is found throughout Europe and many other parts of the world" (51). Robert A. Sobieszek and Odette M. Appel note that memento mori photographs were tremendously popular (70).

13. The Johnson collection, for instance, comprises a range of photographic objects related to death. It contains 1,108 postmortem and memento mori daguerreotypes, ambrotypes, tintypes, collodion cartes de visite, cabinet cards, stereoviews, and other photographic objects spanning the 1840s into the twentieth century.

14. All these poses and conventions are represented in the Johnson collection and indeed via any Google image search of Victorian postmortem photography. It is worth noting that the Johnson collection indicates a greater incidence of dead people posed as though asleep or in a coffin.

15. In her study of childhood, desire, memory, and photography, Carol Mavor observes that childhood shares with photography a desire to "keep time still, innocent, untouched" (3).

16. An interesting subgenre related to the postmortem photograph is the "hidden mother" photograph. These images feature (or attempt to obscure) a figure shrouded in the background holding the child or children in the image either to keep them from moving or to prop them up and preserve the illusion of life. See Linda Fregni Nagler, *The Hidden Mother*.

17. "The cost of a deceased 'sitting' ranged from $10 to $15 with $12 being the most frequent charge" (Ruby, *Secure the Shadow* 165).

18. It is difficult to know for certain how much a postmortem cabinet card would have cost in the 1890s because, Ruby notes, trade journals no longer carried articles about death photography after the 1880s and photographers no longer advertised the service. This does not indicate a decline in the practice, however: "the activity continued in a seemingly undiminished manner," so "the editors of these journals must have decided that a public discussion of the task was either unnecessary or no longer in the best interests of the profession. Apparently, the knowledge that photographers offered this service was sufficiently widespread as to make the public announcement of the fact unnecessary" (*Secure the Shadow* 59).

19. However, as evidenced by the nineteenth-century photographic images of violent deaths in Barbara P. Norfleet's *Looking at Death*, such photographic subjects were not out of the question.

20. It is possible to read the scene of Sue digging at the graves as a replacement for another common memento mori: a family portrait taken at a gravesite or around a casket: these images "first appear in the 1880s when the funeral became more elaborate. The emphasis is placed on those gathered, their grief, and on the funeral as a social gathering—an approach that continues up to the present" (Ruby, *Secure the Shadow* 97).

21. Helen Groth makes a similar claim in *Victorian Photography and Literary Nostalgia*, arguing that Victorian literary culture and particularly poetry intersected with photography in the "desire to arrest time" (2).

22. It is worth mentioning that the tradition of photographing "Wessex" continues to this day. A fairly typical example, the website "An Introduction to Hardy's Wessex," for example, off the South Coast Central regional tourism site, features eleven unidentified photographs of "Wessex" alongside a description of Hardy's life, works, and "partly real, partly dream country" of Wessex.

23. See Cook, "Mapping Hardy and Brontë."

24. Hardy's attention to place settings is underscored by his critical reception as a writer of place. Scholars have long associated Hardy with regionalism, the local, or the rural. In her comparative analysis of Hardy and Scott, Jane Millgate argues that Scott provides Hardy with a "romance paradigm," but in "specifically regional terms" (730). In this same tradition, J. Hillis Miller writes that Hardy is "always a local writer" (*Thomas Hardy* 53), and W. J. Keith argues Wessex allows us to establish "more precisely what constitutes a region" (37). For more on Hardy's regionalism, see J. I. M. Stewart, *Thomas Hardy: A Critical Biography*, and George Wing's essay "Hardy and Regionalism."

25. Marsh argues that Hardy " 'betrayed' the British public, in *Jude the Obscure* (1895), not only by advancing radical views about marriage and religious belief, but also by abandoning the lush landscapes, rich descriptions and serial pleasure they had come to expect of 'our greatest living novelist' " ("Rise of Celebrity Culture" 101).

26. Hardy did not think very highly of this particular map, as indicated by his letters to John Lane in 1892: on January 22, he requests that if Lane publishes "a map of Wessex it would, I presume, be rather more distinct than that which appeared in The Bookman," and on June 22 he clarifies that "the Map of Wessex in the *Bookman* was not made by me. It seems to have been suggested by an observation of mine that I had begun one—I do not intend to finish mine at present; & hardly think it advisable for you to repeat what the Bookman has done" (*Collected Letters* 256, 275).

Conclusion

1. Carol A. Senf, for instance, expands her analysis to consider science more broadly in the novel, while Jennifer Wicke focuses in on a single communication technology, the typewriter. See also Herbert Sussman, "Machine Dreams: The Culture of Technology"; Christopher Keep, "Blinded by the Type: Gender and Information Technology at the Turn of the Century"; and Seth Jacobowitz, "Photography and Automatic Writing as *Idee Fixe* in Oaki Koyo's *The Gold Demon*."

2. See Jonathan Bailey, "Dracula vs. Nosferatu: A True Copyright Horror Story," and David J. Skal, *Hollywood Gothic*.

3. Sassoon reminds us, "The concept of 'the original' functions differently for photography and for other forms of documents or art works," because while the negative is the original, "the document that conveys the message is the print made from the negative" (201). Furthermore, "multiple photographic originals with similar or identical image content cannot be assumed to be duplicates, as each may contain subtle material differences affecting the image, owing to variations in printing styles and papers, be enlarged or cropped, be in different physical conditions and survive in a range of contexts of equal importance" (201). By this logic, no duplication of a material object is ever possible.

4. The Dycam Model 1 and the Fotoman were the first digital consumer cameras sold in the United States; both were released in 1990 ("1990").

Works Cited

"1990." *Digital Camera History*. Digicamhistory.com/1990.html, accessed 16 June 2018.

A B C of Photography. 2nd ed., London Stereoscopic, 1857.

Abrams, M. H. *The Mirror and the Lamp: Romantic Theory and the Critical Tradition*. Oxford UP, 1953.

Adams, James Eli. *A History of Victorian Literature*. Wiley-Blackwell, 2009.

Altick, Richard D. *The Shows of London*. Harvard/Belknap, 1978.

Andrews, Malcolm. "Mathew Brady's Portrait of Dickens: 'a fraud and imposition on the public'?" *History of Photography*, vol. 28, no. 4, 2004, pp. 375–79.

"Anonymous Letter to City of London Police about Jack the Ripper." British Library, London Metropolitan Archives, 5 October 1888, https://www.bl.uk/collection-items/anonymous-letter-to-city-of-london-police-about-jack-the-ripper, accessed 16 June 2018.

Armstrong, Isobel. *Victorian Glassworks: Glass Culture and the Imagination 1830–1880*. Oxford UP, 2008.

Armstrong, Nancy. *Fiction in the Age of Photography: The Legacy of British Realism*. Harvard UP, 1999.

Arney, J. S., and J. Michael Maurer. "Image Analysis and the Documentation of the Condition of Daguerreotypes." *Journal of Imaging Science and Technology*, vol. 38, no. 2, March/April 1994, pp. 145–53.

"Attractive Romanian Wedding Couple." *The Cabinet Card Gallery: Viewing History, Culture and Personalities through Cabinet Card Images*, http://cabinetcardgallery.com, accessed 16 June 2018.

Auerbach, Nina. *Our Vampires, Ourselves*. U of Chicago P, 1995.

Bailey, Jonathan. "Dracula vs. Nosferatu: A True Copyright Horror Story." *Plagiarism Today*, 17 October 2011, https://www.plagiarismtoday.com/2011/10/17/dracula-vs-nosferatu-a-true-copyright-horror-story/, accessed 16 June 2018.

Baillargeon, Claude. *Dickensian London and the Photographic Imagination*. Exhibition catalog, Johnston Lithograph, 2003.

Barthes, Roland. *Camera Lucida: Reflections on Photography*. Translated by Richard Howard, Hill and Wang, 1981.

Batchen, Geoffrey. *Burning with Desire: The Conception of Photography*. MIT P, 1997.

———. *Suspending Time: Life, Photography, Death*. Izu Photo Museum, 2010.

Baudelaire, Charles. "The Salon of 1859." *Literature and Photography: Interactions 1840–1990*, edited by Jane M. Rabb, U of New Mexico P, 1995, pp. 65–68.

Baudrillard, Jean. "Aesthetic Illusion and Virtual Reality." *Jean Baudrillard, Art and Artefact*, edited by Nicholas Zurbrugg, Sage, 1997, pp. 19–31.

———. *Simulacra and Simulation*. 1981. Translated by Sheila Faria Glaser, U of Michigan P, 1994.

Bean, Andrew D., and Catherine Griffey. "The Samuel Drummond Portrait of Charles Dickens." *Dickensian*, vol. 92, no. 438, 1996, pp. 25–30.

Bear, Jordan. *Disillusioned: Victorian Photography and the Discerning Subject*. Penn State UP, 2015.

Beaty, Jerome. "The 'Soothing Songs' of *Little Dorrit*: New Light on Dickens's Darkness." *Nineteenth-Century Literary Perspectives: Essays in Honor of Lionel Stevenson*, Duke UP, 1974, pp. 219–36.

Belknap, Geoffrey. *From a Photograph: Authenticity, Science, and the Periodical Press, 1870–1890*. Bloomsbury, 2016.

Benjamin, Walter. "The Work of Art in the Age of Mechanical Reproduction." *Illuminations*, edited by Hannah Arendt, translated by Harry Zohn, Schocken, 1968, pp. 217–51.

Bennett, Cyril. "The Spirit Photograph." *Murray's Magazine: A Home and Colonial Periodical for the General Reader*, vol. 3, 1888, pp. 361–72.

Berger, Shelia. *Thomas Hardy and Visual Structures*. New York UP, 1990.

Blanchere, H. de la. *L'Art du Photographie*. Amyot, 1859.

———. "Proceedings of the Société Française de Photographie." Reprinted in *Photographic News*, 17 February 1860, p. 291.

Booth, Martin. *The Doctor and the Detective: A Biography of Sir Arthur Conan Doyle*. Thomas Dunne, 1997.

Bove, Alexander. "The 'Unbearable Realism of a Dream': On the Subject of Portraits in Austen and Dickens." *ELH*, vol. 74, no. 3, 2007, pp. 655–79.

Breuer, Rolf. "Paradox in Oscar Wilde." *Irish University Review*, vol. 23, no. 2, 1993, pp. 224–35.

Brewster, Sir David. *The Stereoscope: Its History, Theory, and Construction*. John Murray, 1856.

Bristow, Joseph. "Symonds's History, Ellis's Heredity: Sexual Inversion." *Sexology in Culture: Labeling Bodies and Desires*, edited by Lucy Bland and Laura Doan, Polity, 1998, pp. 77–99.

———. "Wilde, *Dorian Gray*, and Gross Indecency." *Sexual Sameness: Textual Differences in Lesbian and Gay Writing*, edited by Joseph Bristow, Routledge, 1992, pp. 44–63.

Brooks, Peter. *Realist Vision*. Yale UP, 2005.

Brown, Daniel. *Representing Realists in Victorian Literature and Criticism*. Palgrave, 2016.

Browne, Janet. "Charles Darwin as a Celebrity." *Science in Context*, vol. 16, nos. 1/2, 2003, pp. 175–94.

Bruce, Roger. "Will the Digital Image Change Curatorial Practice?" *Image*, vol. 37, nos. 1/2, pp. 17–25.

Buffaloe, Edwin. "Controlling the Sabatier Effect." *Unblinking Eye*, Unblinkingeye.com/Articles/Solarization/solarization.html, accessed 16 June 2018.

Burns, Stanley B. *Sleeping Beauty II: Memorial Photography: The Children*. Burns Archive P, 2011.

Burrows, Stuart. *A Familiar Strangeness: American Fiction and the Language of Photography, 1839–1945*. U of Georgia P, 2008.

Butler, Allen H. "A Speculation: Did Holmes Have Photo-Processing Capability at the Villa?" *Baker Street Journal*, vol. 40, no. 3, 1990, pp. 159–60.

Byerly, Alison. *Realism, Representation, and the Arts in Nineteenth-Century Literature*. Cambridge UP, 1997.

Byrne, Georgina. *Modern Spiritualism and the Church of England, 1850–1939*. Boydell & Brewer, 2010.

Byron, Glennis, editor. *Dracula*. Broadview, 1997.

Cadava, Eduardo. *Words of Light: Theses on the Photography of History*. Princeton UP, 1997.

Calhoun, Philo, and Howell J. Heaney. "Dickens' *Christmas Carol* after a Hundred Years: A Study in Bibliographical Evidence." *Papers of the Bibliographical Society of America*, vol. 39, no. 4, 1945, pp. 271–317.

Cantor, Geoffrey et al., editors. Introduction. *Culture and Science in the Nineteenth-Century Media*, Ashgate, 2004, pp. xvii–xxv.

Carr, John Dickson. *The Life of Sir Arthur Conan Doyle*. Harper & Row, 1949.

Christ, Carol. T. *The Finer Optic: The Aesthetic of Particularity in Victorian Poetry*. Yale UP, 1975.

Christ, Carol T., and John O. Jordan, editors. *Victorian Literature and the Victorian Visual Imagination*. U of California P, 1995.

Clayton, Jay. *Charles Dickens in Cyberspace: The Afterlife of the Nineteenth Century in Postmodern Culture*. Oxford UP, 2003.

Clayton, Owen. *Literature and Photography in Transition, 1850–1915*. Palgrave, 2015.

Cohen, Jeffrey Jerome. "Monster Culture (Seven Theses)." *Monster Theory: Reading Culture*, edited by Jeffrey Jerome Cohen, U of Minnesota P, 1996, pp. 3–25.

Cole, Natalie Bell. " 'Prowling About' London: Dickens and the Photographic Lens." Claude Baillargeon, *Dickensian London and the Photographic Imagination*, exhibition catalog, Johnston Lithograph, 2003, pp. 21–28.

"Commercial Photography." *British Journal of Photography*, vol. 14, no. 352, 1 February 1867, pp. 47–48.

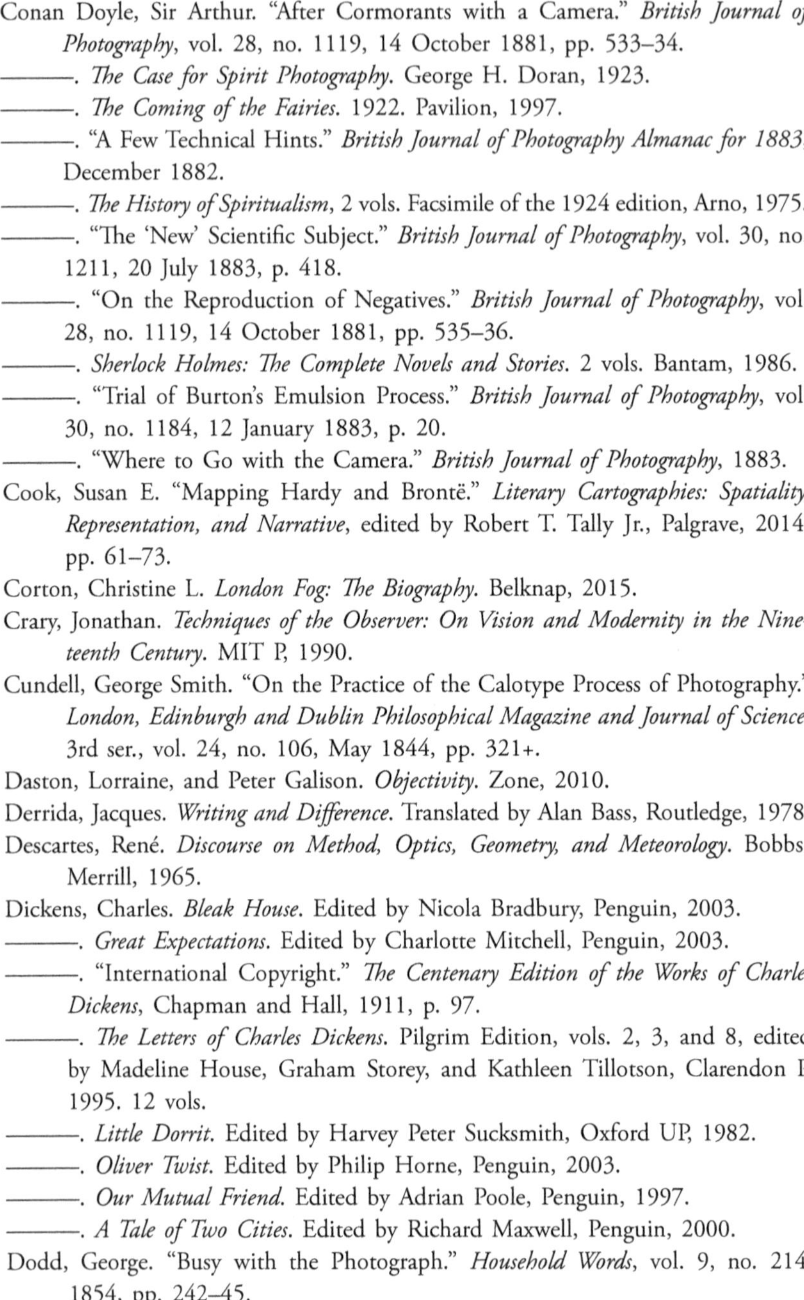

Conan Doyle, Sir Arthur. "After Cormorants with a Camera." *British Journal of Photography*, vol. 28, no. 1119, 14 October 1881, pp. 533–34.

———. *The Case for Spirit Photography*. George H. Doran, 1923.

———. *The Coming of the Fairies*. 1922. Pavilion, 1997.

———. "A Few Technical Hints." *British Journal of Photography Almanac for 1883*, December 1882.

———. *The History of Spiritualism*, 2 vols. Facsimile of the 1924 edition, Arno, 1975.

———. "The 'New' Scientific Subject." *British Journal of Photography*, vol. 30, no. 1211, 20 July 1883, p. 418.

———. "On the Reproduction of Negatives." *British Journal of Photography*, vol. 28, no. 1119, 14 October 1881, pp. 535–36.

———. *Sherlock Holmes: The Complete Novels and Stories*. 2 vols. Bantam, 1986.

———. "Trial of Burton's Emulsion Process." *British Journal of Photography*, vol. 30, no. 1184, 12 January 1883, p. 20.

———. "Where to Go with the Camera." *British Journal of Photography*, 1883.

Cook, Susan E. "Mapping Hardy and Brontë." *Literary Cartographies: Spatiality, Representation, and Narrative*, edited by Robert T. Tally Jr., Palgrave, 2014, pp. 61–73.

Corton, Christine L. *London Fog: The Biography*. Belknap, 2015.

Crary, Jonathan. *Techniques of the Observer: On Vision and Modernity in the Nineteenth Century*. MIT P, 1990.

Cundell, George Smith. "On the Practice of the Calotype Process of Photography." *London, Edinburgh and Dublin Philosophical Magazine and Journal of Science*, 3rd ser., vol. 24, no. 106, May 1844, pp. 321+.

Daston, Lorraine, and Peter Galison. *Objectivity*. Zone, 2010.

Derrida, Jacques. *Writing and Difference*. Translated by Alan Bass, Routledge, 1978.

Descartes, René. *Discourse on Method, Optics, Geometry, and Meteorology*. Bobbs-Merrill, 1965.

Dickens, Charles. *Bleak House*. Edited by Nicola Bradbury, Penguin, 2003.

———. *Great Expectations*. Edited by Charlotte Mitchell, Penguin, 2003.

———. "International Copyright." *The Centenary Edition of the Works of Charles Dickens*, Chapman and Hall, 1911, p. 97.

———. *The Letters of Charles Dickens*. Pilgrim Edition, vols. 2, 3, and 8, edited by Madeline House, Graham Storey, and Kathleen Tillotson, Clarendon P, 1995. 12 vols.

———. *Little Dorrit*. Edited by Harvey Peter Sucksmith, Oxford UP, 1982.

———. *Oliver Twist*. Edited by Philip Horne, Penguin, 2003.

———. *Our Mutual Friend*. Edited by Adrian Poole, Penguin, 1997.

———. *A Tale of Two Cities*. Edited by Richard Maxwell, Penguin, 2000.

Dodd, George. "Busy with the Photograph." *Household Words*, vol. 9, no. 214, 1854, pp. 242–45.

Dollimore, Jonathan. *Sexual Dissidence: Augustine to Wilde, Freud to Foucault.* Clarendon, 1991.

Douglas-Fairhurst, Robert. *Becoming Dickens: The Invention of a Novelist.* Belknap P, 2011.

Dracula. Directed by Tod Browning. Universal Pictures, 1931.

Draper, John William. "On the Process of Daguerreotype, and Its Application to Taking Portraits from the Life." *London and Edinburgh Philosophical Magazine and Journal of Science*, vol. 17, no. 109, September 1840, 217–25.

Dumas, Alexandre *père*. "Across Hungary." 1866. *Literature and Photography: Interactions 1840–1990*, U of New Mexico P, 1995, pp. 74–79.

Durden, Mark. "Ritual and Deception: Photography and Thomas Hardy." *Journal of European Studies*, vol. 30, no. 117, March 2000, pp. 57–69.

Easley, Alexis. *Literary Celebrity, Gender, and Victorian Authorship, 1850–1914.* U of Delaware P, 2011.

Eastlake, Lady Elizabeth. "Photography." 1857. *Photographic Theory: An Historical Anthology*, edited by Andrew E. Hershberger, Blackwell, 2014, pp. 62–65.

Edwards, Elizabeth. *The Camera as Historian: Amateur Photographers and the Historical Imagination, 1885–1918.* Duke UP, 2012.

Edwards, Steve. *The Making of English Photography: Allegories.* Penn State UP, 2006.

Eighteen-Bisang, Robert, and Elizabeth Miller. *Bram Stoker's Notes for* Dracula*: A Facsimile Edition.* McFarland, 2008.

Eliot, George. *The Letters of George Eliot*, vol. 5. Edited by Gordon S. Haight, Yale UP, 1955. 9 vols.

Ellis, Havelock. *Studies in the Psychology of Sex*, vol. 1: *Sexual Inversion.* Wilson and Macmillan, 1897.

English, James F., and John Frow. "Literary Authorship and Celebrity Culture." *A Concise Companion to Contemporary British Fiction*, edited by James F. English, Blackwell, 2006, pp. 39–57.

Evans, Frederick H. "On Pure Photography." 1900. *Photography: Essays and Images*, edited by Beaumont Newhall, New York Museum of Modern Art, 1980, pp. 177–84.

Ex-collection of Louis Walton Sipley. George Eastman Museum, accessed 17 July 2015.

Ex-collection of Walter A. Johnson. George Eastman Museum, accessed 16 July 2015.

"Exploring Thomas Hardy's Rural Dorset." West Dorset District Council, http://www.visit-dorset.com, accessed 16 June 2018.

Fine Art Copyright Act, 1862. Great Britain and Northern Ireland, 1862, p. 68.

Flint, Kate. *The Victorians and the Visual Imagination.* Cambridge UP, 2000.

———. "Visual Culture." *Charles Dickens in Context*, edited by Sally Ledger, Cambridge UP, 2011, pp. 148–57.

Foster, Michael, and Barbara Foster. *Dangerous Woman: The Lives, Loves, and Scandals of Adah Isaacs Menken, 1835–1868, America's Original Superstar*. Rowman and Littlefield, 2011.

Foucault, Michel. *Discipline and Punish: The Birth of the Prison*. 1975. Translated by Alan Sheridan, Vintage, 1977.

Fox, Paul, and Gil Pasternak. *Visual Conflicts: On the Formation of Political Memory in the History of Art and Visual Culture*. Cambridge Scholars, 2011.

Freedgood, Elaine. "Fictional Settlements: Footnotes, Metalepsis, the Colonial Effect." *New Literary History*, vol. 41, no. 2, 2010, pp. 391–411.

Friedman, David M. *Wilde in America: Oscar Wilde and the Invention of Modern Celebrity*. Norton, 2014.

Frith, Francis. "The Art of Photography." *Photography: Essays and Images*, edited by Beaumont Newhall, New York Museum of Modern Art, 1980, pp. 115–19.

Gaines, Jane. *Contested Culture: The Image, the Voice, and the Law*. U of North Carolina P, 1991.

Gibson, John Michael, and Richard Lancelyn Green. *The Unknown Conan Doyle: Essays on Photography*. Secker & Warburg, 1982.

Gilbert, Elliot. " 'To Awake from History': Carlyle, Thackeray, and *A Tale of Two Cities*." *Dickens Studies Annual*, vol. 12, 1983, pp. 247–65.

Goldman, Jonathan. *Modernism Is the Literature of Celebrity*. U of Texas P, 2011.

Gooday, Graeme J. N. " 'I Never Will Have the Electric Light in My House': Alice Gordon and the Gendered Periodical Representation of a Contentious New Technology." *Culture and Science in the Nineteenth-Century Media*, edited by Louise Henson et al., Ashgate, 2004, pp. 173–85.

Green, Jennifer M. "Outside the Frame: The Photographer in Victorian Fiction." *Victorians Institute Journal*, vol. 19, 1991, pp. 111–40.

———. " 'The Right Thing in the Right Place': P. H. Emerson and the Picturesque Photograph." *Victorian Literature and the Victorian Visual Imagination*, edited by Carol T. Christ and John O. Jordan, U of California P, 1995, pp. 88–110.

Green-Lewis, Jennifer. *Framing the Victorians: Photography and the Culture of Realism*. Cornell UP, 1996.

———. "Not Fading Away: Photography in the Age of Oblivion." *Nineteenth-Century Contexts*, vol. 22, 2001, pp. 559–85.

Groth, Helen. *Victorian Photography and Literary Nostalgia*. Oxford UP, 2003.

Gunning, Tom. "Invisible Worlds, Visible Media." *Brought to Light: Photography and the Invisible 1840–1900*, edited by Corey Keller, San Francisco Museum of Modern Art in Association with Yale UP, 2008, pp. 51–63.

Guynn, Beth Ann. "Postmortem Photography." *Encyclopedia of Nineteenth-Century Photography*, edited by John Hannavy, Routledge, 2008, pp. 1164–67.

Hannavy, John. "Beard, Richard (1801–1885)." *Encyclopedia of Nineteenth-Century Photography*, edited by John Hannavy, Routledge, 2008, pp. 126–27.

Hardinge, Emma. "Identity, Self, and Shadow in *Little Dorrit*." *Sydney Studies*, vol. 18, 1992, pp. 111–28.

Hardy, Thomas. *The Collected Letters of Thomas Hardy*, vol. 1. Edited by Richard Little Purdy and Michael Millgate, Clarendon P, 1978.

———. "An Imaginative Woman." *The Short Story and Photography 1880's–1980's: A Critical Anthology*, edited by Jane M. Rabb, U of New Mexico P, 1998, pp. 57–79.

———. *Jude the Obscure*. Edited by Dennis Taylor, Penguin, 1998.

———. *A Laodicean*. Edited by John Schad, Penguin, 1997.

———. "The Photograph." *Literature and Photography: Interactions 1840–1990*, edited by Jane M. Rabb, U of New Mexico P, 1995, pp. 206–7.

———. "The Science of Fiction." *Thomas Hardy's Personal Writings*, edited by Harold Orel, Macmillan, 1966, pp. 134–38.

———. "The Son's Portrait." *Poetry Nook*, http://www.poetrynook.com/poem/sons-portrait, accessed 16 June 2018.

———. *Tess of the d'Urbervilles*. Edited by David Skilton, Penguin, 1985.

Harrison, William H. "The Invisible Photograph Image Considered as Motion." *British Journal of Photography*, vol. 14, no. 383, 6 Sepember 1867, pp. 424–25.

Hart, Janice. "The Girl No One Knew: Photographs, Narratives, and Secrets in Modern Fiction." *Mosaic: A Journal for the Interdisciplinary Study of Literature*, vol. 37, no. 4, December 2004, pp. 111–26.

Heady, Emily Walker. "The Negative's Capability: Real Images and the Allegory of the Unseen in Dickens's Christmas Books." *Dickens Studies Annual*, vol. 31, 2002, pp. 1–21.

Henninger, Katherine. *Ordering the Façade: Photography and Contemporary Southern Women's Writing*. U of North Carolina P, 2007.

Herschel, John. *Herschel Memoranda*. Harry Ransom Center, U of Texas, Austin.

Hindley, Meredith. "When Bram Met Walt." *Humanities*, vol. 33, no. 6, November/December 2012, http://www.neh.gov/humanities/2012/novemberdecember/feature/when-bram-met-walt, accessed 16 June 2018.

Hoffman, Jesse. "Arthur Hallam's Spirit Photograph and Tennyson's Elegaic Trace." *Victorian Literature and Culture*, vol. 41, 2014, pp. 611–36.

Hogle, Jerrold E. "The Struggle for a Dichotomy: Abjection in Jekyll and His Interpreters." *Dr. Jekyll and Mr. Hyde after One Hundred Years*, edited by William Veeder and Gordon Hirsch, U of Chicago P, 1988, pp. 161–207.

Hollingshead, John. "A Counterfeit Presentment." *Household Words*, vol. 18, no. 432, 3 July 1858, pp. 71–72.

Holmes, Oliver Wendell. "The Stereoscope and the Stereograph." Beaumont Newhall, *The History of Photography*, New York Museum of Modern Art, 1964, pp. 23–31.

Hornung, E. W. "A Spoilt Negative." *The Short Story and Photography 1880's–1980's: A Critical Anthology*, edited by Jane M. Rabb, U of New Mexico P, 1998, pp. 1–15.

Houghton, Walter. *The Victorian Frame of Mind*. Yale UP, 1957.

Hubbard, William John. "On Photographic Pictures." *Photographic Journal*, vol. 15, 16 May 1872, pp. 141–50.

Hunt, Robert. "On the Application of Science to the Fine and Useful Arts." *Art Journal*, vol. 1, 1 April 1851, pp. 106–7.

———. "The Science of the Exhibition." *Art Journal Illustrated Catalogue: The Industry of all Nations 1851*, Bradbury and Evans, 1851, pp. I–XVI.

Hyde, H. Montgomery. *The Trials of Oscar Wilde*. Dover, 1962.

"Introductory Address." *Journal of the Photographic Society of London*, vol. 1, no. 1, 3 March 1853, pp. 1–2.

"An Introduction to Hardy's Wessex." http://south-coast-central.co.uk/hardy.htm, accessed 16 June 2018.

Jackson, Arlene M. "Dickens and Photography in *Household Words*." *History of Photography*, vol. 7, no. 2, 1983, pp. 147–49.

———. "Photography as Style and Metaphor in the Art of Thomas Hardy." *Thomas Hardy Annual*, vol. 2, 1984, pp. 91–109.

Jackson, William Esq. "On a Method of Reversing the Action of Light on the Collodion Film, and Thereby Producing Transparent Positives, at One Operation, in the Camera." *Journal of the Photographic Society of London*, vol. 4, no. 60, 21 November 1857, pp. 76–78.

Jacobowitz, Seth. "Photography and Automatic Writing as *Idee Fixe* in Oaki Koyo's *The Gold Demon*." *Proceedings of the Association for Japanese Literary Studies*, vol. 7, 2006, pp. 107–18.

Jay, Martin. *Downcast Eyes: The Denigration of Vision in Twentieth-Century French Thought*. U of California P, 1993.

Jenkins, William D. "We Were Both in the Photographs: I. Adler and Adah I." *Baker Street Journal*, vol. 36, no. 1, March 1986, pp. 6–16.

Jespersen, Otto. *Negation in English and Other Languages*. Høst, 1917.

Jolly, William L. *Solarization Demystified: Historical, Artistic and Technical Aspects of the Sabatier Effect*. http://web.archive.org/web/20070517093239/http://www.cchem.berkeley.edu:80/~wljemw/, accessed 16 June 2018.

Kappel, Andrew J. "The Gurney Photograph Controversy." *Dickensian*, vol. 74, no. 386, 1978, pp. 167–72.

Kearns, Katherine. *Nineteenth-Century Literary Realism: Through the Looking Glass*. Cambridge UP, 1996.

Keep, Christopher. "Blinded by the Type: Gender and Information Technology at the Turn of the Century." *Nineteenth-Century Contexts*, vol. 23, 2001, 149–73.

Keith, W. J. "A Regional Approach to Hardy's Fiction." *Critical Approaches to the Fiction of Thomas Hardy*, edited by Dale Kramer, Macmillan, 1979, pp. 36–49.

Keller, Corey. "Sight Unseen: Picturing the Invisible." *Brought to Light: Photography and the Invisible 1840–1900*, edited by Corey Keller, San Francisco Museum of Modern Art, 2008, pp. 19–35.

Kelsey, Robin. *Photography and the Art of Chance*. Belknap P, 2015.

Klinefelter, Walter. *Sherlock Holmes in Portrait and Profile*. Syracuse UP, 1963.

Kincaid, James R. *Dickens and the Rhetoric of Laughter*. Clarendon P, 1971.

Krafft-Ebing, Richard von. *Psychopathia Sexualis, with Especial Reference to Contrary Sexual Instinct: A Medico-Legal Study*. Davis, 1918.

Langford, Martha. *Image and Imagination*. McGill-Queen's UP, 2005.

Langford, Michael. *The Darkroom Handbook*. Knopf, 1989.

Lea, Hermann. *Handbook to the Wessex Country of Thomas Hardy*. Macmillan, 1905.

———. *Thomas Hardy's Wessex*. Macmillan, 1913.

Lellenberg, Jon L., editor. *The Quest for Sir Arthur Conan Doyle*. Southern Illinois UP, 1987.

Leonardi, Nicoletta, and Simone Natale, editors. *Photography and Other Media in the Nineteenth Century*. Penn State UP, 2018.

Levine, George. "Looking for the Real: Epistemology in Science and Culture." *Realism and Representation: Essays on the Problem of Realism in Relation to Science, Literature, and Culture*, U of Wisconsin P, 1993, pp. 3–23.

Levy, Amy. *The Romance of a Shop*. Edited by Susan David Bernstein, Broadview, 2006.

Levy, Anita. *Reproductive Urges: Popular Novel-Reading, Sexuality, and the English Nation*. U of Pennsylvania P, 1999.

Life Library of Photography: The Print. New Time-Life Books, 1970.

Linehan, Katherine. "A Checklist of Major Performance Adaptations." Robert Louis Stevenson, *Strange Case of Dr. Jekyll and Mr. Hyde*, Norton, 2003, pp. 170–80.

Litvack, Leon. "Dickens Posing for Posterity: The Photographs of Herbert Watkins." *Dickens Quarterly*, vol. 34, no. 2, June 2017, pp. 96–158.

Lowth, Robert. *A Short Introduction to English Grammar with Critical Notes*. J. Dodsley and T. Cadell, 1775.

Lukács, Georg. *The Historical Novel. Theory of the Novel: A Historical Approach*. Edited by Michael McKeon, Johns Hopkins UP, 2000, pp. 219–64.

Marcus, Sharon. "Salome!! Sarah Bernhardt, Oscar Wilde, and the Drama of Celebrity." *PMLA*, vol. 126, no. 4, October 2011, pp. 999–1021.

Marsh, Joss Lutz. "Inimitable Double Vision: Dickens, *Little Dorrit*, Photography, Film." *Dickens Studies Annual*, vol. 22, 1993, pp. 239–82.

———. "The Rise of Celebrity Culture." *Charles Dickens in Context*, edited by Sally Ledger, Cambridge UP, 2011, pp. 98–108.

Martin, Daniel. " 'Some Trick of the Moonlight': Seduction and the Moving Image in Bram Stoker's *Dracula*." *Victorian Literature and Culture*, vol. 40, no. 2, September 2012, pp. 523–47.

Mason, Stuart, editor. *Oscar Wilde: Art and Morality, A Defence of* The Picture of Dorian Gray. J. Jacobs, 1908.

Matsuoka, Mitsu. "A Hyper Concordance of the Works of Charles Dickens." *Victorian Literary Studies Archive Hyper-Concordance*, http://Victorian-studies.net/concordance/dickens/, accessed 16 June 2018.

Maunder, Andrew, and Grace Moore, editors. *Victorian Crime, Madness and Sensation*. Ashgate, 2004.

Mavor, Carol. *Pleasures Taken: Performances of Sexuality and Loss in Victorian Photographs*. Duke UP, 1995.

Maxwell, Richard. Introduction. Charles Dickens, *Tale of Two Cities*, Penguin, 2000, pp. ix–xxxiii.

Mees, C. E. Kenneth. "The Photography of Coloured Objects in Principle and Practice." *British Journal of Photography*, vol. 55, no. 2525, 25 September 1908, pp. 735–37.

Meinwald, Dan. "Memento Mori: Death and Photography in Nineteenth Century America." California Museum of Photography, 1990, http://vv.arts.ucla.edu/terminals/meinwald/meinwald1.html, accessed 16 June 2018.

Mencken, Henry Louis. "The Double Negative." *The American Language: An Inquiry into the Development of English in the United States*, 2nd edition, Knopf, 1921.

Miles, Melissa. "The Burning Mirror: Photography in an Ambivalent Light." *Journal of Visual Culture*, vol. 4, no. 3, 2005, pp. 329–49.

Millgate, Jane. "Two Versions of Regional Romance: Scott's *The Bride of Lammermoor* and Hardy's *Tess of the d'Urbervilles*." *Studies in English Literature, 1500–1900*, vol. 17, no. 4, 1977, pp. 729–38.

Miller, Elizabeth. *Framed: The New Woman Criminal in British Culture at the Fin de Siècle*. U of Michigan P, 2008.

Miller, J. Hillis. *Charles Dickens: The World of His Novels*. Harvard UP, 1958.

———. *Thomas Hardy: Distance and Desire*. Harvard UP, 1970.

Miller, Karl. *Doubles: Studies in Literary History*. Oxford UP, 1985.

Mitchell, W. J. T. *Picture Theory: Essays on Verbal and Visual Representation*. U of Chicago P, 1994.

Monteiro, Stephen. "Crime, Forensic, and Police Photography." *Encyclopedia of Nineteenth-Century Photography*, edited by John Hannavy, Routledge, 2008, pp. 344–45.

Moore, Tara. "Charles Dickens." *Edgar Allan Poe in Context*, edited by Kevin J. Hayes, Cambridge UP, 2012, pp. 279–87.

Morley, Christopher J. *Jack the Ripper: A Suspect Guide*, 2005, http://www.casebook.org/ripper_media/book_reviews/non-fiction/cjmorley/index.html, accessed 16 June 2018.

Morley, Henry, and William Henry Wills. "Photography." *Household Words*, vol. 7, no. 156, 19 March 1853, pp. 54–61.

———. "The Stereoscope." *Household Words*, vol. 8, no. 181, 10 September 1853, pp. 37–42.

Morley, John. *Death, Heaven and the Victorians*. Studio Vista, 1971.

Morris, Pam. *Realism*. Routledge, 2003.

Moss, Sidney P. "A New-Found Mathew Brady Photograph of Dickens." *Dickensian*, vol. 79, no. 400, 1983, pp. 105–7.

Mussell, James. "Science." *Charles Dickens in Context*, edited by Sally Ledger and Holly Furneaux, Cambridge UP, 2011, pp. 326–33.

Nagler, Linda Fregni. *The Hidden Mother*. Mack, 2013.
"Negative Preservers." *British Journal of Photography*, 7 July 1871, p. 315.
Newhall, Beaumont. *The History of Photography*. New York Museum of Modern Art, 1964.
Nochlin, Linda. *Realism*. Penguin, 1971.
Norfleet, Barbara P. *Looking at Death*. David R. Godine, 1993.
North, Michael. *Camera Works: Photography and the Twentieth-Century Word*. Oxford UP, 2005.
———. "The Picture of Oscar Wilde." *PMLA*, vol. 125, no. 1, January 2010, pp. 185–91.
Nosferatu. Directed by F. W. Murnau. Jofa-Atelier Berlin-Johannisthal, Prana-Film, 1922.
Novak, Daniel A. *Realism, Photography, and Nineteenth-Century Fiction*. Cambridge UP, 2008.
O'Connor, John. "Helmholtz, Hermann Ludwig Ferdinand von (1821–1894)." *Encyclopedia of Nineteenth-Century Photography*, edited by John Hannavy, Routledge, 2008, pp. 646–67.
Oost, Regina B. " 'More Like Than Life': Painting, Photography, and Dickens's *Bleak House*." *Dickens Studies Annual*, vol. 30, 2001, pp. 141–58.
Ortoleva, Peppino. "In the Time of Balzac: The Daguerreotype and the Discovery/Invention of Society." *Photography and Other Media in the Nineteenth Century*, edited by Nicoletta Leonardi and Simone Natale, Penn State UP, 2018, pp. 149–61.
Orvell, Miles. *The Real Thing: Imitation and Authenticity in American Culture, 1880–1940*. U of North Carolina P, 1989.
Osterman, Mark. Discussion on 18 Nov. 2008. George Eastman Gannett Foundation Photographic Study Center.
———. "How to *See* a Daguerreotype." *Image*, vol. 43, no. 2, 2005, pp. 12–15.
O'Sullivan, Timothy. *Thomas Hardy: An Illustrated Biography*. Macmillan, 1975.
Otter, Chris. *The Victorian Eye: A Political History of Light and Vision in Britain, 1800–1910*. U of Chicago P, 2008.
Oxford English Dictionary. 2nd ed. Oxford UP, 1989, OED Online.
Page, Leanne. "Phonograph, Shorthand, Typewriter: High Performance Technologies in Bram Stoker's *Dracula*." *Victorian Network*, vol. 3, no. 2, 2011, pp. 95–113.
Page, Norman. Introduction. Oscar Wilde, *The Picture of Dorian Gray*, Broadview, 1998, pp. 7–35.
"Paradox Definition." *Literary Devices: Definition and Examples of Literary Terms*, http://Literarydevices.net/paradox, accessed 16 June 2018.
Pasternak, Gil. "Intimate Conflicts: Foregrounding the Radical Politics of Family Photographs." *Photography, History, Difference*, 2014, pp. 217–40.
Pater, Walter. "A Novel by Mr. Oscar Wilde." *Sketches and Reviews*, Boni and Liveright, 1919, pp. 126–33.

Petersen, Stephen. "Frauds and Fakes." *Encyclopedia of Nineteenth-Century Photography*, edited by John Hannavy, Routledge, 2008, pp. 552–53.

"Photographic Print." *All the Year Round*, vol. 1, no. 7, 11 June 1859, pp. 162–64.

"A Photographic Thief-Trap." *Punch, or the London Charivari*, 24 June 1871, p. 264.

Plunkett, John. "Celebrity and Royalty." *Encyclopedia of Nineteenth-Century Photography*, edited by John Hannavy, Routledge, 2008, pp. 279–83.

Poe, Edgar Allan. "The Daguerreotype." *Literature and Photography: Interactions 1840–1990*, edited by Jane M. Rabb, U of New Mexico P, 1995, pp. 3–5.

Prosser, Jay. "Transsexuals and Transsexologists: Inversion and the Emergence of Transsexual Subjectivity." *Sexology in Culture: Labeling Bodies and Desires*, edited by Lucy Bland and Laura Doan, Polity, 1998, pp. 116–32.

Punter, David. "Bram Stoker's *Dracula*: Tradition, Technology, Modernity." *Post/modern Dracula: From Victorian Themes to Postmodern Praxis*, edited by John S. Bak, Cambridge Scholars, 2007, pp. 31–41.

Rabb, Jane M. "Introduction: Notes Toward a History of Literature and Photography." *Literature and Photography: Interactions 1840–1990*, U of New Mexico P, 1995, pp. xxxv–lx.

———, editor. *The Short Story and Photography 1880's–1980's: A Critical Anthology*. U of New Mexico P, 1998.

Reichardt, Rolf. "Light against Darkness: The Visual Representation of a Central Enlightenment Concept." Translated by Deborah Louise Cohen, *Representations*, vol. 61, 1998, pp. 95–148.

Reid, Thomas. *The Works of Thomas Reid, D. D.* Vol. 1, 8th ed., Longmans, 1895.

Richter, David, reviewer. *The Historical Novel from Scott to Sabatini: Changing Attitudes toward a Literary Genre 1814–1920* by Harold Orel. *YES*, vol. 27, 1996, pp. 264–65.

Roach, Joseph. *It*. U of Michigan P, 2007.

Rogers, Henry N. "Shadows of Irony: The Comic Structure of *Little Dorrit*." *Publications of the Arkansas Philological Association*, vol. 5, nos. 2–3, 1979, pp. 58–63.

Romer, Grant B. "Introduction to the Biographies of Selected Innovators of Photographic Technology." *The Focal Encyclopedia of Photography: Digital Imaging, Theory and Applications, History, and Science*, edited by Michael R. Peres, 4th ed., Focal P, 2007, pp. 123–48.

Rosenberg, Brian. *Little Dorrit's Shadows: Character and Contradiction in Dickens*. U of Missouri P, 1996.

Rosenfeld, Paul. "Stieglitz." *Photography: Essays and Images*, edited by Beaumont Newhall, Museum of Modern Art, New York, 1980, pp. 209–18.

Rovee, Christopher. "Secrets of Paper." *Word and Image*, vol. 30, no. 4, 2014, pp. 388–400.

Ruby, Jay. *Secure the Shadow: Death and Photography in America*. MIT Press, 1995.

Sabatier, M. "Adresse à la Société." *Bulletin de la Société Française de Photographie*, 4 July 1862, pp. 175–78.

———. "Photographie: Positifs directs sur Collodion." *Cosmos*, vol. 17, 1860, pp. 407–11.

Sabattier, M. "Address la letter suivante sur l'obtention des epreuves positives directes." *Bulletin de la Société Française de Photographie*, 14 November 1862, pp. 289–90.

Sassoon, Joanna. "Photographic Materiality in the Age of Digital Reproduction." *Photographs Objects Histories: On the Materiality of Images*, edited by Elizabeth Edwards and Janice Hart, Routledge eBook, 2005, pp. 196–213.

Schimmelman, Janice G. *American Photographic Patents 1840–1880: The Daguerreotype and Wet Plate Era.* Carl Mautz, 2002.

Scholtz, Amelia. "Photographs before Photography: Marking Time in Tennyson's and Cameron's *Idylls of the King*." *LIT: Literature Interpretation Theory*, vol. 24, no. 2, 2013, pp. 112–37.

Schor, Hilary. *Dickens and the Daughter of the House.* Cambridge UP, 1999.

Schulz, David. "Redressing Oscar: Performance and the Trials of Oscar Wilde." *Drama Review*, vol. 40, no. 2, 1996, pp. 37–59.

"Seeing Double." *American Museum of Photography*, 2003, http://www.photography-museum.com/seeingdouble.html, accessed 16 June 2018.

Seiberling, Grace. *Amateurs, Photography, and the Mid-Victorian Imagination.* U of Chicago P, 1986.

Seltzer, Mark. *Bodies and Machines.* Routledge Revivals, 1992.

Sen, Sambudha. *London, Radical Culture, and the Making of the Dickensian Aesthetic.* Ohio State UP, 2012.

Senf, Carol A. "*Dracula* and *The Lair of the White Worm:* Bram Stoker's Commentary on Victorian Science." *Gothic Studies*, vol. 2, no. 2, 2000, pp. 218–31.

Shadbolt, George. "Valedictory and Introductory." *British Journal of Photography*, vol. 11, 15 June 1864, p. 199.

Shakespeare, William. *As You Like It.* Edited by Michael Hattaway, Cambridge UP, 2009.

———. *Hamlet.* Edited by Philip Edwards, Cambridge UP, 2003.

———. *The Tempest.* Edited by David Lindley, Cambridge UP, 2013.

Shaw, Harry E. *The Forms of Historical Fiction: Sir Walter Scott and His Successors.* Cornell UP, 1983.

Shelangoskie, Susan. "Domesticity in the Darkroom: Photographic Process and Victorian Romantic Narratives." *LIT: Literature Interpretation Theory*, vol. 24, no. 2, 2013, pp. 93–111.

Shires, Linda M. *Perspectives: Modes of Viewing and Knowing in Nineteenth-Century England.* Ohio State UP, 2009.

Showalter, Elaine. "Guilt, Authority, and the Shadows of *Little Dorrit*." *Nineteenth-Century Fiction*, vol. 43, no. 1, June 1979, pp. 20–40.

Simons, M. P. *Photography in a Nutshell; or The Experience of an Artist in Photography of Paper, Glass, and Silver, with Illustrations.* King and Baird, 1858.

Skal, David J. *Hollywood Gothic: The Tangled Web of* Dracula *from Novel to Stage to Screen*. Revised ed., Norton, 2004.

Smajić, Srdjan. *Ghost-Seers, Detectives, and Spiritualists*. Cambridge UP, 2010.

Smith, Grahame. *Dickens and the Dream of Cinema*. Manchester UP, 2003.

———. "The Life and Times of Charles Dickens." *The Cambridge Companion to Charles Dickens*, edited by John O. Jordan, Cambridge UP, 2001, pp. 1–15.

Smith, Lindsay. *Victorian Photography, Painting and Poetry: The Enigma of Visibility in Ruskin, Morris and the Pre-Raphaelites*. Cambridge UP, 1995.

———. "The Wont of Photography, or the Pleasure of Mimesis." *Illustrations, Optics and Objects in Nineteenth-Century Literary and Visual Cultures*, edited by Luisa Cale and Patrizia Di Bello, Palgrave, 2010, pp. 65–86.

Sobieszek, Robert A., and Odette M. Appel. *The Spirit of Fact: The Daguerreotypes of Southworth & Hawes, 1843–1862*. David R. Godine, 1976.

Solberg, Sarah. "A Note on Phiz's Dark Plates." *Dickensian*, vol. 76, no. 390, 1980, pp. 40–44.

Sontag, Susan. *On Photography*. Farrar, Straus and Giroux, 1977.

Spiegel, Alan Harvey. *Fiction and the Camera Eye: A Study of Visual Form in the Modern Novel*. Ph.D. dissertation, University of Virginia, 1973.

Stead, W. T. "Another Murder—and More to Follow?" *Pall Mall Gazette*, 8 September 1888, p. 1.

Steichen, Eduard J. "Ye Fakers." *Camera Work*, vol. 1, January 1903, p. 107.

Steig, Michael. *Dickens and Phiz*. Indiana UP, 1978.

Stein, Richard L. "Dickens and Illustration." *The Cambridge Companion to Charles Dickens*, edited by John O. Jordan, Cambridge UP, 2001, pp. 167–88.

Stevenson, Robert Louis. "Letter to A. Trevor Hadden." 5 July 1883. *The Biographical Edition of the Works of Robert Louis Stevenson*, vol. 2, edited by Sidney Colvin, Charles Scribner's Sons, 1912, pp. 147–49.

———. *Strange Case of Dr. Jekyll and Mr. Hyde*. Norton, 2003.

Stevenson, Sara. "Robert Louis Stevenson and the Portrait Photographers." *History of Photography*, vol. 37, no. 2, 2013, pp. 235–42.

Stewart, J. I. M. *Thomas Hardy: A Critical Biography*. Dodd Mead, 1971.

Stoker, Bram. *Dracula*. 1897. Edited by Nina Auerbach and David Skal, Norton, 1997.

Sussman, Herbert. "Machine Dreams: The Culture of Technology." *Victorian Literature and Culture*, vol. 28, no. 1, 2000, pp. 197–204.

Tagg, John. *The Burden of Representation: Essays on Photographies and Histories*. U of Massachusetts P, 1988.

Talbot, William Henry Fox. *The Correspondence of William Henry Fox Talbot*. Edited by Larry Schaaf, Knowledge Media Design, De Montfort University, http://foxtalbot.dmu.ac.uk, accessed 16 June 2018.

———. *The Pencil of Nature*. http://www.thepencilofnature.com, accessed 16 June 2018.

———. "Some Account of the Art of Photogenic Drawing." 1839. *Photography in Print: Writings from 1816 to the Present*, edited by Vicki Goldberg, U of New Mexico P, 1988, pp. 36–48.

Taylor, Roger. *Impressed by Light: British Photographs from Paper Negatives, 1840–1860.* Yale UP, 2007.

Teukolsky, Rachel. "Cartomania: Sensation, Celebrity, and the Democratized Portrait." *Victorian Studies*, vol. 57, no. 3, 2015, pp. 462–75.

"The Theatre: Mr. Richard Mansfield at the Lyceum." *Daily News*, 6 August 1888.

"Thomas Hardy's Wessex." *Bookman*, vol. 1, no. 1, October 1891, pp. 26–28.

Thomas, Jane. "Thomas Hardy and the Visual Arts." *Thomas Hardy in Context*, Cambridge UP, 2013. 436–45.

Thomas, Ronald R. *Detective Fiction and the Rise of Forensic Science.* Cambridge UP, 1999.

———. "Double Exposures: Arresting Images in *Bleak House* and *The House of the Seven Gables*." *Novel*, vol. 31, no. 1, 1997, pp. 87–113.

———. "Making Darkness Visible: Capturing the Criminal and Observing the Law in Victorian Photography and Detective Fiction." *Victorian Literature and the Victorian Visual Imagination*, edited by Carol T. Christ and John O. Jordan, U of California P, 1995, pp. 134–56.

Timmons, Christine, and Frank Gibney. *The Britannica Book of English Usage.* U Michigan P, 1980.

Tomalin, Claire. *Thomas Hardy*. Penguin, 2007.

"To-Night's Entertainments." *Pall Mall Gazette*, 8 September 1888, p. 12.

Towler, John. *The Silver Sunbeam*. Joseph H. Ladd, 1864.

Trollope, Anthony. A.l.s. dated 1 March 1876. *The Prime Minister*, Chapman and Hall, 1875.

Tucker, Jennifer. *Nature Exposed: Photography as Eyewitness in Victorian Science.* Johns Hopkins UP, 2005.

———. "The Social Photographic Eye." *Brought to Light: Photography and the Invisible 1840–1900*, edited by Corey Keller, San Francisco Museum of Modern Art in Association with Yale UP, 2008, pp. 37–49.

Vadillo, Ana Parejo. *Women Poets and Urban Aestheticism: Passengers of Modernity.* Palgrave, 2005.

Vigar, Penelope. *The Novels of Thomas Hardy: Illusion and Reality.* Bloomsbury Academic, 2014.

Virilio, Paul. *The Vision Machine*. Translated by Julie Rose, Indiana UP, 1994.

Walkowitz, Judith. *City of Dreadful Delight.* U of Chicago P, 1992.

Waters, Catherine. *Commodity Culture in Dickens's* Household Words*: The Social Life of Goods.* Ashgate, 2008.

Webster, Chris. "Spirit, Ghost, and Psychic Photography." *Encyclopedia of Nineteenth-Century Photography*, edited by John Hannavy, Routledge, 2008, pp. 1331–34.

Webster, Roger. "From Painting to Cinema: Visual Elements in Hardy's Fiction." *Thomas Hardy on Screen*, Cambridge UP, 2005, pp. 20–36.

West, Shearer. "The Photographic Portraiture of Henry Irving and Ellen Terry." *Ruskin, the Theatre and Victorian Visual Culture*, edited by Anselm Heinrich, Katherine Newey, and Jeffrey Richards, Palgrave, 2009, pp. 187–215.

White, James. "Your Life or Your Likeness." *Household Words*, vol. 8, 15 October 1853, pp. 156–62.

White, Stan. "A Blue Bosom Boy: In the Footsteps of Daguerre." *Photographic Society of America Journal*, vol. 62, December 1996, pp. 30–32.

Wicke, Jennifer. "Vampiric Typewriting: *Dracula* and its Media." *English Literary History*, vol. 59, 1992, pp. 467–93.

Wilde, Oscar. "The Decay of Lying." 1891. *The Artist as Critic: Critical Writings of Oscar Wilde*, edited by Richard Ellmann, Random House, 1969, pp. 290–320.

———. "To the Editor of the 'St. James's Gazette.'" 1890. Oscar Wilde, *Artist as Critic: Critical Writings of Oscar Wilde*, edited by Richard Ellmann, Random House, 1969, pp. 238–40.

———. "The Fisherman and His Soul." *Oscar Wilde: The Complete Short Stories by Oscar Wilde*, edited by John Sloan, Oxford UP, 2010, pp. 171–201.

———. "Phrases and Philosophies for the Use of the Young." *Chameleon*, vol. 1, no. 1, 1894, pp. 1–3.

———. *The Picture of Dorian Gray*. Broadview, 1998.

Wilkins, William Glyde, and B. W. Matz. *Charles Dickens in Caricature and Cartoon*. Bibliophile Society, 1924.

Willis, Nathaniel Parker, and Timothy O. Porter, editors. "The Pencil of Nature: A New Discovery." 1839. *Photographic Theory: An Historical Anthology*, edited by Andrew E. Hershberger, Blackwell, 2014, pp. 44–47.

Wing, George. "Hardy and Regionalism." *Thomas Hardy*, edited by Norman Page, Bell and Hyman, 1980, pp. 76–101.

Woodbury, Walter E. *The Encyclopaedic Dictionary of Photography*. Scovill and Adams, 1896.

Xavier, Andrew. "Charles and Catherine Dickens: Two Fine Portraits by Samuel Laurence." *Dickensian*, vol. 92, no. 439, 1996, pp. 85–90.

Zillman, Linda Goforth. *Sir William Newton: Miniature Painter and Photographer, 1785–1869*. Arizona State UP, 1986.

Zimmerman, James R. "Sun and Shadow in *Little Dorrit*." *Dickensian*, vol. 83, no. 412, 1987, pp. 93–105.

Index

www.ingramcontent.com/pod-product-compliance
Lightning Source LLC
LaVergne TN
LVHW020432080826
844660LV00034B/1410
9781438475363